The Boy Behind the China Cabinet

—

A Memoir about Addiction, Hollywood, Mother Teresa and Me

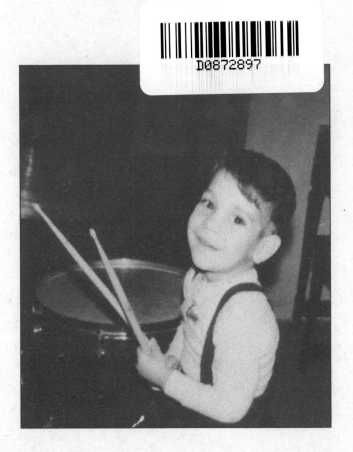

Paul LaGreca

For Mom and Dad

The Boy Behind the China Cabinet
Copyright © 2020 Paul LaGreca

Book cover and interior designed by Jess LaGreca.

I have changed names, locations and certain circumstances to protect the identity of many people in this book. These are my experiences as I remember them. The dialogue has been recorded to the best of my recollection.

Ruckmond Pond, Closter, New Jersey.

Prologue

I left Ruckmond Pond. I had to. I was freezing and literally could not feel my hands or feet. For once I felt like I fit in—a young boy of nine ice-skating on a cold day in the dead of winter where other kids from my school were also skating. I thought, *isn't this what other boys do? Isn't this what I am supposed to do?*

It was an especially exciting day for me after receiving new ice-skates for Christmas. I was wearing them for the first time, but the fact remained that I did not know how to ice-skate. My feet kept slipping and I kept leaning to the left and the right. I had trouble staying on top of the blades so I started to walk on the ice with my skates, rather than skate. Everyone was shouting at me, "Skate, Paulie, you can do it." I was embarrassed and starting to strain my feet. I tried to be aggressive to appear not to struggle, but every time I tried, I fell. On one fall, I hurt my wrist but kept pretending to have fun.

The sky was cloudy, and the afternoon sun was quickly descending. The wind began to pick up, and the temperature was in the low twenties. I could no longer bear the cold and the struggle for fun. While I watched classmates playing ice hockey, young girls making figure eights, and parents holding the hands of their children and laughing, a panic fell upon me. I felt deep loneliness. It was a deep well; a well of not fitting in, of knowing that I did not belong there, and an inner knowledge that no matter how hard I tried, this thing was not meant for me.

No one else appeared cold. Children who fell just laughed and picked themselves up. For me, it was painful, and each fall frightened me. *Who was I, and why wasn't I like these other kids?*

I gave up the effort of pretending and knew I had to escape as quickly as possible. I did not have the stamina, the willingness, or the strength to remain. All sensation was gone from my hands and feet. I pulled off my skates, which I now hated, and pulled on my sneakers. I flung my skates over my shoulder and walked as quickly as I could back to my house on High Street. I was so panicked that I started to cry but tried not to let others see me. I could not run because I could not feel my feet, and when I removed my gloves to look at my hands, they were as white as snow. I didn't know it at the time, but I lost all circulation in my hands and feet.

It was now dark and, even though I only had a half a mile to walk, it felt like ten miles. I was alone. But then I remembered God, and through my panic, I prayed. I prayed out loud. I prayed that He would get me to my warm home and my Mom. I no longer cared if anyone saw me. I hoped someone who knew me would drive by, but there was no one. Something in my heart said, just keep taking one step at a time. I began to rock to the left and the right in order to take steps forward. I felt God with me, and my spirit felt like it plugged into the warmth of LOVE—a love that cannot come from people but only the

Divine. He helped me, embraced me, and got me home safely on that blustery winter night in 1972.

I had never felt so alone and frightened in my young life, but God showed me that He was there for me. All I had to do was ask. I learned what it meant to be carried by God. My experience was only a preview of what was to come.

In deep contemplation. Marina del Rey, California, 1985.

Chapter One

Leaving the World

I walked through the iron gates of the front garden of Sacred Heart Convent. The black rusted latch lifted with a snap, and the gate squeaked loudly as I opened it. I turned around to face the street and wave goodbye to my father. I could tell he was crying as he pulled away in his truck, his head down. I tried to choke back my tears, and a part of me wanted to chase his work truck down the street. But, as Mother Teresa would say, "For love to be real, it has to hurt," and this hurt. I watched his truck drive down 168th street in the Bronx. I tried to pull myself together and be brave. I was all for Jesus now. This was the sacrifice of *my* life to Him.

I handed Jesus my pain as I shut the gate and turned towards the concrete stairway of Mother Teresa's newly established branch for priests, my new home, the Motherhouse of the Missionaries of Charity

Fathers in the High Bridge section of the Bronx. It was August 15th, 1986, the feast of the Assumption of Mary—the date of my official entrance into religious life. The time it took me to walk to the front door seemed endless as I second-guessed my choice to enter the priesthood, and a million thoughts ran through my mind. *Lord*, I thought, *please let this fear go away.*

I climbed the steps of the convent and rang the doorbell. I waited with my one suitcase in hand containing everything I'd been instructed to bring: my Bible, one change of clothes, underwear, and pajamas. Brother Andre, whom I knew from my "Come and See" visit experience a few months earlier, opened the door. He was also new, having arrived a few days earlier, and would be a classmate of mine. He escorted me in silence to my new room and whispered that I should wait until Father Eugene arrived to let me know what would be happening. I was nervous and paced the room but decided to at least unzip my suitcase and start unpacking—although it wasn't like I was at the Beverly Hills Hotel with trunks of clothes to unpack.

Nestled in between a few shirts, I noticed a white envelope which I did not remember packing. The envelope was old and yellowed and looked like the unused envelopes Dad piled in his desk drawer. "To My Darling Paulie" was written on it. I said to myself, *what the heck is this?* I opened it quickly recognizing my mother's handwriting and I read:

My Dearest Son Paul,

First, let me tell you how proud I am of you. I send you away with all my love and prayers. I know I will miss you very much. You were always there when I needed you. Like Charlie, you will be in my mind and my heart every second, minute and hour of every day. So, whenever you think of me you can be sure I will be thinking of you. You know I would never stop you from doing what's in your heart. If you ever feel it's not the right thing for you, don't ever hesitate to come home. Please pray for Daddy and me. It will take me a little time to get used to it, but I will cope like everything else. As long as you're happy, so am I. I love you so much. You've always had a special place in my heart. Well, good luck sweetheart and may God bless you and protect you.

Love forever,
Mommy

I was already raw, and the letter tore my heart in two pieces. I began to cry. I wanted to hold her and console her and felt terrible that I had caused both her and my father such pain. I knew my father felt that he was giving Jesus the gift of one of his sons, but I was not sure if my mother had the spiritual maturity to think that way. This was a painful loss for her. I was twenty-four years old and pining for my mother, although does longing for one's mother ever really go away? We always shared a beautiful friendship. We held each other up.

Only a few hours earlier at home, I descended the stairway that led to the kitchen, suitcase in hand. With each step I braced myself for the angst of the "big goodbye." I dreaded the moment. How would I ever be able to say goodbye to her? The Holy Rule of the Missionaries of Charity states that when the candidate leaves home, he/she does not return home for visits, except once every 10 years. Parents and family can visit on the first Sunday of each month wherever the missionary may be stationed. This was not an uncommon rule among many pre-Vatican II religious orders. It is designed to assist the religious to uproot themselves from attachments to family and friends. We were permitted to receive unlimited mail from family and friends but could write only one letter a month. Our letters were usually opened and read by the functioning superior prior to receiving them. This was considered part of our sacrifice, and done to assist us in humility. We no longer belonged to our families and friends but were only all for Jesus—a total surrender. I was willing to accept that, but it did not lessen the pain of saying goodbye to my mother.

When I got to the bottom of the stairway, my Mom had her back to me. She wore her beat-up old apron as she fried bacon. She seemed stiff as a board, yet moved quickly in her tasks. At first I thought that she was ignoring me. I had a lump in my throat the size of Texas. Very gently, with an attempt at being light-hearted to make it more bearable for the both of us, I said, "Okay, Mom, I'm ready to go." She quickly turned, almost on auto-pilot, grabbed me, and started sobbing in my arms. She must have been fighting and dreading this moment for a long time. I was completely thrown because it was very uncharacteristic of her. I hugged her back and began to cry as well. I tried hard to be strong, but I just couldn't. I smelled the warmth of her skin and the comfort of her apron and clothes as I hugged her and wished I could fall asleep with my head on her shoulder. Being in my mother's arms was always the safest feeling in the world.

She broke the embrace and wiped her eyes and hands on her apron trying to compose herself. She took my face in both her hands and between sobs she looked me in the eyes and said, "Listen to me, there is no shame in coming home if this doesn't work out, you hear?"

I nodded as tears streamed down my face. "I love you," she said. "We're very proud of you."

"I love you too, Mom. Don't worry about anything. You know you'll be in my constant prayers."

Dad had gone to get his truck in the backyard, so I tried desperately to pull it together. I knew that time would be a great healer. I silently asked God for strength. Mom kept telling me that she loved me. She called me her "dolly" like she always did, and then quickly turned towards the oven to finish the task at hand. I truly believe that with all the suffering my mother endured in her life, if she ever allowed herself, she would fall into a cry that would last all day. I picked up my suitcase and walked to the back door where Dad was waiting for me.

———

"Please don't sit on the bed," a stern and controlled voice said. It was Father Eugene, my new Superior. "Oh, excuse me. I'm sorry." I jumped up and brushed away my tears.

"Beds are for sleeping only. Missionaries of Charity do not sit on beds or use bedrooms to be social."

I quickly hid the letter, afraid that he would want to see it or ask me about it (*my first act of disobedience*). I wanted to say to him, *Thank you for the warm welcome*. It had been less than an hour, and I was already being challenged. I tried to be mature about it, but a part of me was disappointed that the initial greeting felt a little icy.

I knew Father Eugene meant well. He smiled and tilted his head at the same time, trying to soften the admonishment. In terms of the Holy Rule, he was correct about sitting on the bed since The Rule states that beds are for sleeping only, not for leisure and relaxation. I was in a very sensitive state, having just left home. It was my first experience in turning myself over to God as a Missionary of Charity, known as an "MC." I knew that whatever suffering I endured could be offered to God for souls.

Having a strict superior was not necessarily a bad thing—it could be very beneficial to spiritual growth. It was my own choice to enter; I was there of my own free will and knew it would be difficult. I was open, willing, and ready, as challenging as it might be. I was there to sacrifice myself and to have God mold me into whatever He wanted me to be. *No longer my will but Thy Will be done, O Lord. Make me a holy saint.*

I felt alone and could not wait to see the other guys who would be in my class and who had been with me on my "Come and See" visit. There would be seven of us in my group—Clark from California; Isaac, who was a volunteer with the sisters prior to entering and a Jewish convert; Andrew from Ohio; Riccardo from La Paz, Bolivia; André from Nova Scotia; Michael from Pennsylvania—and me. I had an immediate rapport with Michael and knew that we would be good friends and support for each other.

We had all arrived by dinner time, and Father Eugene and all the other priests, postulants, and novices gave us a round of applause to welcome us. After dinner, we were instructed to meet in the third-floor library to receive our daily routine and responsibilities as the newest members of the Aspirancy.

The Aspirancy in religious life is a period, usually six to 12 months, when you "aspire" to the life of the congregation you have entered. As an Aspirant, you begin daily lessons, working with the poor, and learning how to incorporate yourself into the new lifestyle. In most cases, it is the opposite of everything you have known. It is a struggle against human nature, and the goal is to keep your eyes glued on the supernatural.

Postulancy is the second stage. This can last from one to two years, depending on the community you have entered and your progress in the Aspirancy. The Postulant is given more responsibilities and continues to study. In essence, you are aspiring to the Novitiate.

The Novitiate is the stage when you are officially registered at the Vatican as a "Religious." It is usually a one-or-two year process, during which you work less on the apostolate (the service piece of the congregation), study The Rule and Constitution of the Order in depth, and continue to pray and discern God's will. You prepare to make first vows at the end of the second year.

Once you have made your first vows (also called "junior professed"), you are an official member of the community. The vows, however, expire after one full year and must be renewed annually.

This gives you a chance to discontinue should you discern that it is not where God wants you to be. After an approximate three years of renewals, the junior professed religious may take vows for life—perpetual vows—and is "final professed."

The year prior to final vows is called the Tertianship year, where you would again return to a year of contemplation and deeper prayer, similar to the Novitiate, to make certain that this is what God, and you, want for life. Once final vows are made, should you desire to leave a congregation, a special request with the Vatican is required to be released from your vows.

This was the journey on which I embarked, beginning with the Aspirancy. I had a long road ahead of me, but this was day one, and step one. The key word was perseverance—to keep my eye on the goal and courageously overcome each challenge one day at a time.

The evening of our entrance we were given our Aspirancy schedule (as recorded in my journal):

5:00 AM: Bell Rings, rise, pray morning offering on knees, wash and get to chapel

5:30 AM: Holy Hour, meditation, Mass

6:45 AM: Breakfast in silence

7:30 AM: Personal cleaning

8:30 AM: Morning ministry (apostolate) and studies

11:45 AM: Back at home

12:00 PM: Angelus prayer, midday prayer, lunch

1:00 PM: 20 minute siesta

1:30 PM: Spiritual reading

2:00 PM: Ten minute teatime

2:10 PM: Study time/class with Aspirancy Master

4:00 PM: Study or communal duties

5:30 PM: Free Time

6:00 PM: Holy Hour

7:00 PM: Dinner

7:30 PM: Recreation in community

8:00 PM: Bell for the Grand Silence. Personal time to wash, read, or study in silence

9:00 PM: In bed and lights out for the night

There were slight variances in the schedule for each day of the week, but for the most part, this was the routine. We were expected to remain faithful to each part of our day and when we heard the bell ring to summon us to our next duty, we were to immediately drop whatever we were doing and move quickly. The bell was to be deemed the voice of God summoning us to our next task.

Isaac looked up at me after Father Eugene's talk in the library and gave me a wide-eyed stare and a half-smirk as if to say, *how the hell am I going to do this?* Isaac had a tendency of making me laugh. He had a wonderful Jewish humor, and we connected on many levels. I always knew the right thing to say to make him laugh, and vice-versa. Isaac was much older than all of us—referred to in religious life as a "late vocation"—and came with a lot of life experience. He was a political junkie, and each day he made sure he kept himself updated on the latest events.

I began my first full day with enthusiasm. The bell rang at 5:00 AM. I jumped out of bed as instructed and got on my knees to make my morning offering—a standard prayer that we were all required to pray after rising. *Oh God, I know you are here. I adore and love you with my whole heart and soul. You have created me, redeemed me by the death of your Son, sanctified me by the grace of your spirit, and preserved me this past night. I give you most humble thanks for these and all the other benefits you have poured on me . . .*

Because we were still in the Grand Silence (a period of time when we cannot speak–from 8:00 PM to 9:00 AM), I could not ask my roommate, a Postulant, which one of us should hit our small sink first to wash, so when I saw him making his bed, I took it as a hint that I should get to the sink and begin washing.

Since we were to live a life free from vanity, the bedrooms contained no mirrors, but there was a small piece of a broken mirror on the inside of the medicine cabinet where we could quickly spot check ourselves without staring in the mirror. I thought of the life I had left behind in Hollywood and how this was the complete opposite (there was no lack of mirrors in Hollywood—including my apartment). I had a full head of curly brown hair and wanted to make sure I didn't have "pillow head." I wondered how all the new Aspirants were doing, especially Michael, who tended to be nervous and neurotic. He was trendy, hip, and fun. As I washed, I tried not to laugh as I thought about something we experienced on our visit before we entered.

———

On the first night of our "Come and See" experience, after "lights out" at about 9:30 PM, I heard what sounded like rat traps going off from downstairs—something loud, like slamming against the cold, uncarpeted floors. I wasn't sure what it was. The hallways echoed loudly, but everyone in the house was in the Grand Silence, and I was curious. I snuck out of the guest bedroom on tiptoe to listen. If nothing else, I wanted to make sure no rats were running around the hall where I slept.

When I opened the door to check the noise, I encountered another candidate—Michael. Since we arrived, he had proven to be very dramatic and made me laugh. The two of us were on the same page. I thought he was odd, standing in the hallway in his pajamas wearing a pair of black Chinese slippers. Evidently, we both lived life outside the box, and we bonded. Knowing that we were not supposed to break the Grand Silence, I was concerned about the sounds we were hearing, and

I had to say something. "Pssst," I looked at Michael and whispered, "What the heck is that noise?"

"I don't know. I was thinking the same thing."

"It sounds like mouse or rat traps of some kind."

"Really? Is that what you think?"

"I have no idea; I'm just trying to figure it out."

Michael scrunched his face and said, "That is so gross. I hope not. If its rats, then they must be in the kitchen! I am totally freaked out right now. Sorry, I'm getting out of here and going to bed."

"Okay, let's not worry about it. Good night and sleep well."

"Hey," Michael interjected, "How did you feel about Father's talk tonight? Do you really think you can leave your family behind forever?"

"I don't know—that's a tough question. It scares me to think about, but I feel like I am willing to try."

Michael laughed. "There is so much to think about. It's actually stressful."

"I know, but we have two weeks. Just enjoy it and let God speak to you."

"True! Okay, goodnight, Paul."

A few months later, we found out that the sound was some of the more advanced brothers taking themselves to "the discipline"—an act designed to assist the soul in aligning with Christ's sufferings by hitting your back with a small stick hung with leather strings.

My friendship with Michael began to blossom after we entered the Aspirancy. We saw life through a similar lens and we usually knew what the other was thinking. We were both committed to Christ, and we both wanted to be holy. But, within the first week of our entrance into the Aspirancy, I was summoned to Father Eugene's office.

"I've noticed that you are very close with Michael."

"Yes, Father. He is a wonderful brother to me, and I am glad he is here. I know that he and I will be great friends."

"Have you given thought to the fact that perhaps you are ignoring some of your other brothers? The both of you, I mean. While it is good to love and be friendly with your brothers, our Rule does not permit us to have exclusive friendships. Jesus has to be first at all times, and in Christ we will have the strength and the grace to love all our brothers equally, with nothing exclusive. Do you understand?"

I was a little taken aback, but I said, "Yes, Father, I do. Thank you. I will try to be more open to all my brothers and be aware not to create a particular friendship with Michael. I apologize if I offended anyone or did something wrong. I didn't know."

"Very good, Paul. You will learn. You are doing well, yes? You are happy with us, eh?"

"Very happy. Some days I feel like I am in ecstasy, and other days it's hard to adjust."

Father Eugene smiled as if knowing the struggle and finished with, "Welcome to the religious life. The days you struggle are the days you grow. Enjoy the inspirations in those moments that God gives them to you. As for Michael, I will speak to him as well. You may go now."

"Yes, Father. Thank you." I accepted Father Eugene's good counsel and tried to do my best.

When our routine outside the house began, I was scheduled to do my apostolate work at the soup kitchen in the Bronx until further notice. Those assigned to the same ministry would journey together to the location either by foot or subway. We wore one of our two changes of clothing with sandaled feet, even in winter. If it got cold enough, we could wear socks. When we left the house, we were expected to pray the rosary and have very little idle chatter. When not in prayer, we were expected to remain in the presence of God and only speak when necessary.

While I appreciated our Rule, it had to be practiced and learned. I was not the best at only speaking when necessary. I had come from the stage, film, and television and it had only been eight months since I left Hollywood. I went from actor to renunciate in what was deemed to be one of the strictest religious orders in the Catholic Church. My own spiritual immaturity, along with my *joie de vivre*, needed to be reeled in as I often burst into song without thinking, looked for an opportunity to be funny, or spontaneously shared a thought. Some of the more seasoned brothers would kindly smile at me as we continued to walk but would not respond to my outbursts. They were gentle in their approach, attempting to teach me without embarrassing me. I got the message loud and clear when I was breaking the Rule. There was no need for words. Their silent admonitions showed the way.

Each morning at the Queen of Peace soup kitchen, the homeless and hungry would line up on East 146th Street and wait for it to open. Along with our sisters, the brothers assisted in preparing the food and serving the people. I was no longer a volunteer who could get away with things, but an Aspirant. I was now Brother Paul (although I had not yet made vows) and had to behave as such. I had a deep love for these men, especially the drug addicts. I watched and waited on them with great care.

How many of these men had families at home that worried about them? How many were depressed, sad, and trying to self-medicate? I could relate to these men in a way that my classmates and the professed brothers could not. The first 16 years of my life were deeply rooted in suffering. My oldest brother Charlie had been a drug addict. I was forced to grow up fast, and my perception of who and what these people were differed from the romantic visions of some of my missionary brothers. Watching the men I was feeding made me feel like I was feeding Charlie, and perhaps helping some poor parent somewhere who was home worrying about their child.

Most of the guys in my class, particularly the young ones, came from upper-middle-class families, shielded from city life. They may have had their own struggles, but I had seen so much by the age of 24 that I felt more complex in comparison to them—perhaps even a bit wiser. My experience was steeped in my brother's addiction and, later, by leaving home and becoming an actor.

As I fed the homeless, I often pondered my own life and my own internal poverty. How did I really end up here? What does this earthly existence mean? Why had I made such extreme choices in my young life? I got lost in my thoughts. I was trying to be faithful to the Rule by practicing detachment from memories, but I sometimes felt like a little boy lost at an amusement park trying to find his mother. My heart could not help but return to the deep bond I shared with my warm and loving family and our roots in the Bronx where it all began.

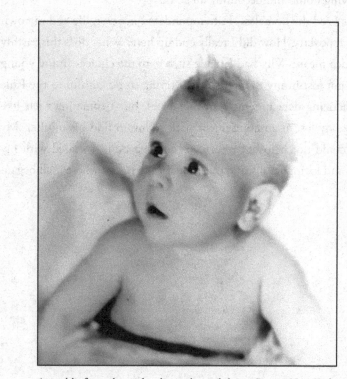

A world of wonder and unlimited possibilities. Bronx, New York, 1962.

Chapter Two

Entering the World

I have felt like an outsider for as long as I can remember—an observer, a visitor, a circle in a square. I can write and speak about my family and how I felt different, but I also think that innately, I enjoy solitude. It's who I am and in my DNA.

I landed on Planet Earth at 12:10 PM on a bright and sunny June 23, 1962, at Westchester Square Hospital in the Bronx, New York. It was Saturday and 78 degrees—just the way I like it. I am not surprised by the time of my birth since my structured, organized personality probably decided to begin my incarnation at noon, so by the time I arrived it was 12:10 PM—just in time for lunch. One of the top tunes of the day was "Stranger on the Shore" by Acker Bilk. This piece of music has always touched me and, coincidentally, its title seems to describe how I would journey through life. Two weeks after my birth, the number one hit was "The Stripper" by David Rose—go figure.

I am the seventh of 10 children born to my Dad—Gioachino Calogero LaGreca (nicknamed, Jack) and my Mom, Gloria Joan Belfiore. Both my parents were first-generation Italian-Americans. My father's mother, Antonina LaGattuta emigrated from Mezzojuso, a small village in Palermo, Sicily, founded circa 1000 A.D. by Arabs. His father, Calogero LaGreca, emigrated from Campobello di Licata, a seaside town in Agrigento, Sicily, settled by the Greek colonists of Gela in approximately 580 B.C. (Hence, LaGreca – which translates to the Greek).

My maternal grandmother, Marietta ("Mary") Montalto, was born to Italian immigrants from Cosenza, Calabria, who settled in Westerly, Rhode Island, but my mother's father, Eduardo Belfiore, emigrated to America at the age of 16 from Laureana di Borello, Calabria.

When I was born, there were already five older brothers and one older sister. After me would come three girls, bringing the grand total to 10, not including one miscarriage between birth numbers five and six. My parents learned that the miscarried baby was a boy, and his name would have been Mark. My father's goal was to have 12 children to reflect the 12 apostles, but he and Mom were two short of their goal. Dad tried to make up for it by giving the names of the apostles to as many of us as he could. We were born in groups of three with a three year gap between each group.

The first three were a complete wash for Dad's apostolic naming goal, because traditionally in Italian families, the first-born was named after a grandparent. They had Charles (named after Grandpa LaGreca, nicknamed Charlie), Jacqueline (named after Dad), and Edward (named after Grandpa Belfiore).

After my brother Edward, there was a three-year gap. Then there was John, Thomas, and James (note the names, please). After James, another three-year gap, then me, Gloria, and twin girls, Debbie and

Mary (Mary was named after Grandma Belfiore). So much for the 12 apostles.

When I asked Dad why they were going to name the miscarried boy Mark (not one of the apostles' names), my father said, "Why do you have to bust my chops? It's biblical." So be it.

I grew up surrounded by a plethora of loving aunts and uncles. My mother had 11 brothers and sisters, and my father had four. There were also a lot of cousins, but of all the families in the family tree, my immediate family won for the largest tribe.

Our small house on Revere Avenue in the Bronx had three floors. On the first floor were the "active" kitchen and our "TV room." Like most good Italian-American homes of the day, ours had a "show" living room and kitchen, located on the second floor. The whole floor was off limits; no one was permitted in these rooms. They were used only for special occasions. The chairs and couch in the show living room were carefully covered in New York's finest plastic. If we kids were caught in the show living room without permission, we were threatened with Mom's wooden spoon.

The third floor contained a bathroom and three bedrooms. The six boys and Gloria shared the first room at the top of the stairway since it was the biggest. My parents had the second bedroom with the crib, usually housing the most recent arrival, and the third and smallest bedroom was for Jacqueline, the oldest of the girls, and the twins. Jacqueline, who was in her teens when I was young, helped my mother as an additional pair of hands. Jacqueline, for the younger ones, was like a second mother. It is no wonder that all these years later Jacqueline has seven children and is now up to 10 grandchildren. She took after my mother.

We lived in a corner house with a wooden fence surrounding a small yard to the left of the house, and a big enough backyard to run around and play. It had enough room for a small plastic children's pool and a round three-foot deep pool for the older kids. The front of the house had a long concrete stairway to the right of the front door. It led to an upstairs door on the second floor which was used if Mom was entertaining and wanted guests to enter the show living room, as opposed to the downstairs kitchen.

At the top of this stairway was a small porch that extended past the big living room window to the left. This porch always scared me. I have, to this day, a horrific fear of heights, and always feared that I was going to fall over the black wrought iron fence or that the porch was going to collapse. I think part of the reason for this fear was my Aunt Flo, one of my mother's oldest sisters, who didn't want the little ones up there for fear of us falling over the railing. She used to scare us by telling us it would collapse if we walked on it. The upstairs porch railing extended to the concrete stairway and down to the street. The bottom of these stairs, or "the stoop," as we called it, would be my favorite spot in the coming years to create, imagine, and people-watch.

My earliest memory in the Bronx was watching my brothers run around the kitchen like madmen, toys in tow, while I stood in my crib. I was an extremely sensitive and impressionable child and would often feel sorry for my mother, who sometimes cried as she tried to feed us and control the chaos. As far back as I can remember, I desired nothing more than to help her and I developed, simply by observing her, a deep sense of responsibility for her. I think I was irritated by the chaos on the other side of my crib. Over the years, I have carried with me a disdain for anything too loud and chaotic. Large families are great, but they can be loud. When the volume was too much, I curled into a ball under my blanket and fell asleep regardless of what was going on around me.

I did love those comforting moments when my father used to take me out of the bath and wrap me in a big warm towel as he held me close. Nothing felt safer.

At some point as a toddler, I began my career as a professional thumb sucker. I not only sucked my thumb but as I sucked, I was able to perfectly tuck the top of my ear into the ear's interior and then by pulling on the ear lobe, it would pop out. It became my claim to fame. My thumb sucking was constant and there are even some home movies of siblings pulling the thumb out of my mouth. My parents tried everything they could to get me to stop, but their attempts did not work. It would be a habit and a source of comfort in the darkness that would descend on my family and last well into my childhood and grammar school years.

My father was a butcher and owned his own shop, Jack's Meat Market, in the Soundview section of the Bronx. He worked like a dog. His day started at 6:00 AM, when he would call in his order to the Hunts Point Market, and end when he got home at 7:00 PM. When Dad came home from the butcher shop after a long day at work, it was as if Santa Claus walked in. We all ran to the door to greet him. We would climb up his legs, jump on his back, and challenge each other for his affection. When he ate his dinner, long after the rest of us had eaten, it was normal for one or two of us to be sitting on his lap. He never rejected us. We were loved and cherished by Dad, and he looked at our obsession with him as a gift, not as a burden. If I learned anything about unconditional love, it was from my father. The love and warmth in our small house in the early to mid-1960s was above and beyond how most families expressed affection. The love was palpable, and the air was warm and inviting. The number of children was met with joy.

Christmastime was also magical for us! There was a frenetic excitement in the air during the season, and even more so on Christmas Eve when some of my mother's sisters came over to help prepare the traditional Italian fish dinner. My Aunt Mary would run through the house to tell us that Santa Claus was spotted in Brooklyn, or somewhere close by. The adults participated in the magic and helped to create childhood memories that my siblings and I still cherish.

When I was about three years old, two things happened that would forever change me: I fell in love with the cross at my church, and I saw the film, *The Wizard of Oz*. The two experiences were so diametrically opposed that I can say, in all honesty, a battle began within me—one that would last for the rest of my life: the battle of light vs. dark, worldliness vs. spiritual, saint vs. sinner. As an impressionable child, it did not take much for the smallest thing to haunt me.

I was raised a Roman Catholic and, customarily, my parents would take me and my brothers and sisters to Sunday Mass. We attended Saint Frances de Chantal, only blocks from our house. If you did not get to Mass early enough in those days, you were left to stand in the back.

I was a toddler when I profoundly experienced God for the first time. My father held me in his arms as we stood against the back wall of the church. I am not sure if my father pointed out the crucifix above the altar to teach me who Jesus was, or if I was already familiar because of the religious symbolism in our home. The cross which contained the corpus of the Crucified Christ that hung above the altar was extremely intense to my young mind. I remember the feeling I had at the time, but I can only attempt to express what I experienced.

I was in complete awe of Jesus on the cross. It was amazing, shocking, sad, and scandalous. It was also the most beautiful thing I had ever seen. I remember staring at Jesus' face against the dark back-drop on the altar. It felt like an abyss of silent communication. I wanted Him and I felt that He wanted me. Nothing else existed. There was only this unexplainable "thing" that entered my heart. It was as if a small light within a well of darkness was placed into the center of my being, and it was Him. All I had to do was close my eyes to feel it.

The cross and my experience were profound, startling, astounding, deep—this man on the cross. It was just so beautiful . . . and I knew, for some reason, that He was mine and I was His. We were one. I fell deeply in love with the Crucified Christ that day. I wanted to fall into the blackness of the altar, to stare at Him all day. I felt a glowing love—love for Him who was nailed to the cross. That image! I will never forget it. It is forever carved into my heart and memory as I was held in the arms of my own loving father. I wanted to wrap my arms around Jesus on the cross and stay with him forever.

The second experience began on a Sunday night when my family gathered together in the show living room for a special television event. All my siblings and my parents were convinced I would love the program. As we sat there on our plastic covered furniture, me on my father's lap, the lights were turned out, and as the show began, I was instantly mesmerized at the opening credits and music of *The Wizard of Oz*.

Infatuation would be a weak choice of words to describe my obsession. The film was to become the preoccupation of my childhood. My heart broke at the end, it was so full, and I was speechless. My family stared at me to see if I liked it, but by the end I had to work hard not to cry. I remember thinking, *How could this happen? How did she get so lost? Where were her aunt and uncle now? Where did they live? Were they okay? Were they happy now that she was home?* I was devastated. I went to bed picturing Dorothy's three friends alone and sad without her wherever they might be. My heart was heavy, and I cried myself to sleep.

I was preoccupied with big and important questions. Did the Scarecrow, Tin Man, and Lion stay together and take care of each other after Dorothy left? And most importantly, now that Dorothy was home again, was Miss Gulch coming back for the dog? I was a broken-hearted three-year-old.

What *The Wizard of Oz* did, I would discover more as I got older, was plant in me the seed of becoming an actor. *The Wizard of Oz* had been an annual family event with all my brothers and sisters excited and vying for the best seat in the house. Having been indoctrinated into the tradition, I was hooked.

When I reached age four, I made good with Santa, and I landed my first record player. Coincidentally, my friends and neighbors who lived a few doors down gave me a copy of the original soundtrack recording of *The Wizard of Oz*. On the cover was Dorothy standing over the Scarecrow, Tin Man and the Lion looking scared, wide-eyed and straight ahead above a fence. The artwork was against a yellow background and the colors bounced off the album cover. Again, it was magical and mesmerizing. I would stare at the cover for hours and turn it over to gape at the black and white pictures, particularly of the witch melting. I did not like her, but on some level, I also felt sorry for her because I was convinced she could have had such nice friends. I thought she was lonely.

I would play the record over and over and over again until, by the age of five, I literally had every line on the album memorized. Relatives would place me on top of the kitchen table to act out the movie. I became a hit and a sensation. I sang, I danced, and I inhabited each role—from the Tin Man to the Wicked Witch. I began to understand what it meant to be an actor, and I craved it. I discovered that performing made me feel alive. I had to sing and dance and act—there was no choice. I had to go where *The Wizard of Oz* was—whatever that meant. Many years later at M-G-M Studios in Culver City, California, I knew exactly what it meant as I ran my hand across the yellow bricks from the yellow brick road piled in a heap at the back of soundstage 23.

Singing and dancing for relatives and neighbors became my contribution to life. The wonderful part of discovering my gift was that it "put me on the map." It was something I was good at and no one could take it away from me.

I also discovered the art of impersonation. I could imitate relatives perfectly. I was able to capture the smallest nuances of each person and have the whole family roaring with laughter. They sought me out at family gatherings to entertain, so I knew I had to be good.

I was getting older, and with that came the task of trying to fit in with the boys. Growing up in the Bronx consisted of street games such as stick-ball, kick the can, rumbles, whiffle ball, and whatever else city kids get involved in. Being the youngest of six boys, there was a three year gap between me and my brother James. I had to be able to prove myself as a fighter, a baseball player, someone who could rumble and do all those things that defined a young boy growing up in the city.

Sadly, I was none of the above and keenly felt for the first time in my life that I was a circle trying to fit into a square. I realized that I was trying to figure out how to survive. It became more and more difficult. I had to start defending myself. My position and where I fell in the family line—seventh child, youngest boy—did not help. I felt weak and unable to live up to expectations. It was no one's fault; it was just the way it was.

My older brothers were not keen on my entertaining aunts and uncles by singing songs on kitchen tables. Dancing and singing around the house was "sissy stuff" by Bronx boy standards. When they saw me performing or coloring with my crayons, they felt an obligation to stop me and indoctrinate me into their world, but I wanted nothing to do with any of it.

My brothers tried to be playful by attempting to teach me how to box or wrestle. I wasn't a fighter by nature, so I always felt awkward and uncomfortable. They had good intentions and did not quite understand, nor did most adults in the Bronx at the time, what it meant to be a "creative"—someone who, by nature, lives "out of the box" or walks a path less traveled. When their attempts to toughen me up failed, they told me that I was ugly and would never get married if I couldn't fight. When you hear those words often enough, you start to believe it.

My younger sisters, Gloria, and the twins, Debbie and Mary, became my playmates. We were, and still are, referred to as the "four little ones." In reality, I grew up with the girls. Our big sister Jacqueline, who was eleven years older than me, was like a second mother. She babysat us, diapered us, and played with us.

Over time, I developed into an overly sensitive, sentimental little boy and felt that I had no place to go. If I continued playing with the girls, it was not good in the eyes of the boys. If I played with the boys, I got hurt and couldn't keep up. But I did find a place to go—inward—deep within.

I began to create my own world and space. Upstairs in the "show kitchen" where no one was permitted, there was a big china cabinet that was positioned caddy-corner to the kitchen table. If I carefully slid behind the china cabinet, there was plenty of space to sit and hide and to keep all my things safe just in case anyone got hold of my things and broke them, as they sometimes did. I had discovered the joy of art and was amazed by the beauty of a box of crayons—the smell, the assortment, and the colors. I loved to color, and I had to be very careful that my crayons were not taken and broken, or my hula-hoop dented because someone played rough with it. I hid these things for safe-keeping behind the china cabinet, along with my phonograph, *The Wizard of Oz* record, and books Mom had bought me. No one knew where my little treasures were. Hiding myself and my things was the safe thing to do.

The daily frustration of not knowing how to defend myself, punch back, or meet the challenges that confronted me caused me to invent devious methods for survival for those times when I was not behind the china cabinet. I had to be creative about how I got revenge, because I couldn't fight. I would observe something happening or hear something and then tell my parents what I'd seen and heard. I became the family snitch, and really, who wants to be a rat? But I knew I was getting back at them, and I used tattling as my revenge. "I'm telling

Mommy on you," became common words from my mouth. As we say in New York, I became a professional ball-buster.

Being a snitch to get revenge caused things to go from bad to worse, of course. My brothers' threats escalated to, "If you tell Daddy or Mommy about this, you are DEAD and I'm not kidding." And they meant it!

Being alone felt safe and was commonplace. I enjoyed it. I had peace. There was nothing more relaxing than sitting with my things behind the china cabinet and just listening to what was happening around me. Gathering my things and going into the solitude of my own private world is something that I learned then and would carry with me for the rest of my life. No matter where my family moved subsequently, or where I lived as an adult, my private space has always been my sanctuary—safe and protected from the world.

Regardless of how tough it might have been to keep up with the others, I would never underestimate for one second the love that was alive and well in my family. Outside of our safe haven of home, my brothers were very protective of me. They knew that I did not have it in me to fight, so they always had my back. And my little sisters became my best friends, particularly Gloria. When we were small, everyone thought that there were two sets of twins—me and Gloria, and Debbie and Mary—that is how close in age we were, and how well we bonded.

The fun, laughter, music, and heart that we all shared in that small Bronx house were the stuff most people dream of having. Our world was beautiful, and each child had his or her distinctive personality. Something, however, was about to change—something so powerful that it would disrupt each of our worlds for the rest of our lives. My isolation would go deeper, some of my siblings would act out in their own way, and my parents were about to suffer heartbreak. In the turbulent sixties, my oldest brother, Charlie, was introduced to drugs and became severely addicted.

My brother Charlie in his high school years, 1966.

Chapter Three

Charlie

By the time 1967 came around, I was five years old and starting to understand the world around me. I became acutely aware of the elephant in the room, which my parents hid so well from all the younger children—my oldest brother Charlie's drug addiction. Charlie was born March 24, 1950 and was seventeen years old.

Psychologists would agree that a child's most formative years are their youngest—from birth to six years old. Charlie's drug addiction, and the behavioral traits associated with those who live with an addict of any kind, took root with me and my siblings as day after day, week after week, and month after month, his addiction intensified. I was developing behaviors that I would spend the rest of my life working through in order to make healthy decisions.

1967 may go down in history as the wonderful and infamous, "Summer of Love," but for my family, it became the summer from hell.

What began as pot smoking in his early teens morphed into harder drug use and experimentation. By the time Charlie was 18, he was deemed a "finished addict." In clinical terms, he was classified as a poly-drug user, meaning he would take anything he could get his hands on.

Unbeknownst to me and some of my other younger siblings, my parents had sent Charlie to counseling, rehabilitation centers, priests, or anyone they could, hoping to find a way out for their oldest son between 1965-1967. He had quit Monsignor Spellman High School in the Bronx and was constantly in trouble. My father tried to take him under his wing and insisted that he learn the trade of being a butcher—as all the boys would be required to do in the years to come.

A house full of rambunctious, playing children often gave way to silence and frightened stares as my older brother would visibly change before our eyes. We only became aware as his addiction worsened, and it could no longer be swept under the carpet. Life with Charlie was unpredictable since we never knew on any given day what drug he was on, how much he took, or if he would come home at all. His life and problems had become our life and problems. When he was home, there was an air of constant uncertainty and insecurity. The house became Charlie.

The drug issues were not only in my family. It appeared that, overnight, every other house on Revere Avenue was struggling with one or two young family members who had become addicted. My father was sharing stories with his customers who were also experiencing the epidemic. Drugs were everywhere—in the schools, in the music, and on the streets. The sixties mantra to "turn on, tune in, drop out" was prevalent, and a nation of parents, including mine, struggled to learn how to deal with it. My parents had nine other children to worry about, but Charlie's issues had taken over our lives and were wreaking havoc in our home. The joyful chaos of running, laughing and happy children at play morphed into negative chaos—a Charlie chaos.

When my parents had to leave the house for an evening event, usually my older sister Jacqueline, who was 16 at the time, would babysit.

In their absence, I would be filled with anxiety. I remained nervous and frightened until they returned, because you never knew what might happen with Charlie, despite having Jacqueline on standby.

Charlie was brilliant. He was crazy smart, and his IQ was off the charts. He was as street smart as he was book smart, and over time the seedier street element became the prevailing personality. He was also super creative and an extremely talented drummer. He even gave lessons for extra money. He was in a rock band called "The Showmen Four" and they met some success in the New York circuit.

One hot summer evening, Charlie received permission from my parents to practice with his band in the upstairs living room. The rehearsal was out of the way and they wouldn't be disturbed since my siblings were all downstairs either watching TV or doing homework. Like my older brother, I too had an ear for music, and I was riveted by it. Even today, if I am in a crowded room and music is being piped in, I will always tune in to the music.

That evening, I heard the music coming from upstairs and I wanted to listen. I slowly crept my way up the kitchen stairwell to listen from the top stair. His one friend, Joe, a handsome guy who had a Beach Boys surfer look, saw me spying on them. There were four guys rehearsing, including Charlie. His girlfriend Desiree was listening to them practice on the stairway that led to the third floor.

My brother scolded me and asked me what I was doing there. He came over to me and started showing off in front of his friends, some who also had drug issues. He picked me up and with both hands lifted me over his head. He started to spin me as fast and hard as he could so that I would get dizzy. In my big brother's eyes (I will give him the benefit of the doubt), I was supposed to be laughing like a little brother would be and say, *Wow, this is fun!* Being overly sensitive and embarrassed, however, I cried instead and begged him to stop and put me down.

At that point, rather than put me down, they decided to have a catch—with me as the ball. I was thrown through the air one by one to each member of the band and all I can remember is how much it hurt each time I landed in someone's hands. I was as skinny as a rail and each landing hit hard on my ribcage. Jacqueline was downstairs and I couldn't scream for help because I couldn't catch my breath. My brother's girlfriend saw that I was upset and stopped it.

Desiree had long, straight black hair and looked like the quintessential hippy. She always looked strung out, but she still retained her natural beauty. She grabbed me from my brother and told them to knock it off. She took me to the stairs and rocked me in her arms. My distrust and fear of Charlie began to grow.

Charlie's odd behavior sometimes included my brothers and sisters and many times turned into a real humiliation for me. He used to enjoy playing with us by lining us up facing him in a straight line. He would tell us to act out a TV commercial and if you failed, at what was in his estimation, a good performance, he hit you with his belt.

In one instance, he lined up Johnny, Tommy, Jamie, and me. We were told to reenact the M&M's commercial: "M&M's melt in your mouth, not in your hand" and when you said the word "hand" you had to extend it exactly as they did in the commercial. I was so nervous when he got to me because I knew that it would be wrong, even if it was perfect. By the time I got half-way through the sentence I started crying, tensed my shoulders and prepared to get whacked. My estimation was correct.

When we began school a few years later, he also enjoyed having spelling bees. He would give each of us a word that was spell-able for our age group—house, lock, play, run, etc. By the time he gave me a word to spell I knew it would be an impossible word, like chandelier, or ostentatious. He wanted me out of the game from the start. Though in my own secret way, I was tough. He taught me humility and while he may have thought it bothered me, it didn't. What he deemed to be important, I didn't. It would have been fun to play, but I did not have to be competitive or win a spelling bee to be happy. Quite frankly, it removed me from the "forced-fun" obligation and allowed me to be alone and read.

Charlie, of all my brothers, tried to toughen me up the most. As well-intentioned as he was, he would smack me around and tell me to stick up my fists and defend myself. He tried to teach me to box. He was genuinely concerned because he understood the streets, and ultimately, because we lived in the city, did not want to see me get hurt. He thought nothing of hitting me or kicking me hard enough to make me fall in the hope that I would fight back, but instead, I crawled into a ball on the floor or ran crying to my parents.

While these were my issues with Charlie, each of my siblings can probably write of their own experiences. What made Charlie so difficult was the fact that I did not live up to his standard of how a boy should be and act. I was too sensitive, and with "tough guys" like Charlie, along with the overall reality of growing up in the Bronx, kindness and gentleness were viewed as weaknesses—unless you were also tough enough to throw a punch. Charlie often treated our cousins who were about my age much nicer than he treated me. When my cousin Eddie was around, Charlie made a fuss over him. Eddie was tough, could throw a punch (later in life he competed in the Golden Gloves).

Charlie was also a living paradox. While he could be abusive, he also defended me when he needed to. If any of my other brothers upset me, he would think nothing of giving them a good whack. I knew the good and benevolent side of Charlie. He wanted to be a good brother and spoil us. He used to take Gloria and me by the hand to the candy store in Throggs Neck and buy us whatever we wanted. During those moments, I got to spend time with the real Charlie, my real brother, and to feel the love that is shared between siblings. The kind, lovable, healthy, handsome, fun-loving Charlie is the brother that I always longed would walk through the door—the brother who didn't call me "punk" but "pal."

I wanted Charlie to get better so that life would return to normal for everyone in the house. As his addiction went from bad to worse, with no treatments working, my parents instructed my older siblings to hide their money and any personal things that would tempt him to steal for drug money. The worst of it was keeping Charlie's behavior a secret from the relatives.

We were instructed not to say a word to anyone, so when aunts and uncles came over, most of us would fall into "pretend mode"—Charlie did not have a problem, and everything was normal. I continued to do what I needed to survive as my brother's addiction worsened—and that included burying myself with my little hidden treasures behind the china cabinet.

—————

My small, hidden collection of 45 RPM phonograph records started to build (Jacqueline would occasionally give me her older records). The first record she gave me was "Rhythm of the Rain" by the Cascades. I remember staring at the purple Valiant label which I found to be beautiful. It was the same color as the grape Italian ice the ice cream man would bring as we sat on the stoop each afternoon. I would spoon my grape ice and watch the record turn on my record player. I loved the color purple for years. All my hidden treasures were safely stored in my hiding place.

When relatives came over, I made sure I used every opportunity to entertain. I would sing for them and imitate whomever they requested. I found refuge in the arts and was even obsessed over my parent's Bell and Howell home movie projector. I used to touch the film in wonder, loving the smell of the projector and the sound of the film clicking. My toys, music, colors, living in a fantasy world, and acting became my refuge. I was burrowing deeper and deeper into myself. The seeds of the artist were being nurtured through pain and I wanted to fall into the safe haven of creating.

I also had an intense, anxiety-ridden fear that my parents would die. I was obsessed with ensuring that my parents were all right. When I saw my mother cry or my father in pain, it was like driving a lance through my heart. I had one goal when I was around them and that was to make them happy. I became co-dependent and was not happy unless they were. I took on the role of the "savior" among my siblings. I made certain I was aware of everything that was going on so that I could dive in and help whenever necessary, from rubbing my mother's shoulders after a fight with Charlie to joining my father in the car on nights he went missing.

My siblings and I still knew how to have fun considering all that was happening. We had each other, we depended on each other, and we bonded in a way that most children do not. Even today, if any two of us argue, we cannot go 24 hours without someone saying they're sorry, or attempting to mend the situation. We played and laughed together, but we were forced to grow up faster than most children.

At the beginning of 1968, my parents began to fear for their nine younger children. They were afraid that, as we got older, someone else could become addicted to drugs. They decided it would be best to leave New York and try to find a safer haven in the suburbs. The Bronx had now become infested with drugs and Mom and Dad wanted to make the break.

My father once told me that he and my mother crossed the George Washington Bridge into New Jersey and prayed to the Holy Spirit to be led to a new home. They drove until they finally approached a small town in Bergen County called Closter. There they found a large colonial house for sale. Across the street was a catholic church—Saint Mary's, and its grammar school. The high school, Northern Valley Regional, was also less than a mile away. The Holy Spirit answered their prayers, and for a whopping $49,000 they bought the house on High Street. It was a perfect 13 room home.

September of 1968 was also when I was starting school. Mom and Dad had not wanted me to attend kindergarten in the Bronx, so they waited until we moved to New Jersey to enroll me in first grade at Saint Mary's. These were the days before kindergarten was mandatory in New Jersey. Charlie was now 18, Dad retained his butcher shop in the Bronx, and I just turned six. On July 22, 1968, 10 kids, two frightened parents, and a beat up old station wagon pulled into our new driveway at 347 High Street in Closter, New Jersey. It was the day before the twins' third birthday. Our hope and prayer was that life would get better. In some ways, it did . . . and in other ways, it didn't.

Our new home on High Street, Closter, New Jersey.

Chapter Four

High Street (No Pun Intended)

A backyard filled with fruit trees, a strawberry patch, grapevines, a barn-yard building as big as the house, a chicken coop, a cow shed, fruit trees, and a small wooded area—this was my new backyard. It was surreal.

The house smelled of cedar and old wood. There was a stairway for servants and hidden doors and compartments everywhere. Our new home pushed every creative button in me. It was like a dream. We escaped the Bronx and found ourselves in a type of Shangri-La—a huge colonial house with 13 rooms, a big front porch and a wrap-around yard. It was built in the early 1900s and it had history and a story. There was great warmth in the air in this new house.

The previous owner was a dentist who had lived there for many years with his wife and sons. Prior to that, it was said to be the convent of our new church and, before that, it was a farm. Walking distance from my front door was Saint Mary's church and grammar school.

Navigating my way through the house was an adventure unto itself. There was much to discover—a bench built into a wall that opened into a huge storage unit, buttons against walls that when pushed revealed sliding doors, wind-up ice crushers, stairways and doors that led to places not yet discovered. This was any little boy's dream house.

Our block on High Street was a mecca of children; the Connolly's across the street had 14 children, the Galligan's had five, the Burns' had five, and the Onny's had five.

City kids running loose on suburban streets can be a very dangerous thing . . . and so it was. The headlines of the local paper should have read, "Italian Kids from the Bronx Invade Small Irish Community of Closter." By the end of our first week, my brothers managed to have fist fights with most of the boys on the block. I suppose they were marking their turf, and bonding with the other boys the only way they knew how—through fighting and sports. After two weeks, though, everyone appeared to be friends. The front door of our new house that summer of 1968 was constantly being swung open, with kids running in and out.

One of the unfortunate realities of city folk moving to the country was the inexperience with landscaping. All my parents knew about maintaining a yard was how to mow a lawn. We left behind a tiny yard in New York. Mowing the lawn took on a new meaning in Closter. They had the front lawn, two side lawns, and the backyard. They also did not know how to nurture and preserve a grapevine, a strawberry patch, pear and apple trees, or Japanese maples that required special attention. Most of the fruit producing trees and vines began to die off and the dying trees were promptly removed. My father replaced them with new trees that paled in comparison to the trees that were around long before any of us were born.

I was particularly fond of the Burns family across the street. Mrs. Burns was very theatrical and she and her daughter, Bonnie, would invite me over to sit with them on their porch. They were always asking me to sing and applauded my efforts. They were kind to me and, without knowing it, nurtured my creative spirit and my love for music. They permitted me to be who I was without any effort.

Establishing a new hiding place for my things took time in the Closter house. Eventually, because there was enough space, I found plenty of safe spots in my new room—including the back of the boy's closet, which contained a place to hide behind the hanging clothes. I shared my new room with my brothers, Johnny and Tommy. Jacqueline had her own room, and Gloria and the twins, Debbie and Mary, shared the room closest to my parents. There were also three bedrooms in the attic; Charlie had his own room, Jamie and Eddie shared the second room and the third was empty.

I would get lost in that backyard for hours on those hot and humid summer days. My playmates were mostly Gloria, Debbie, and Mary. Gloria was five and the twins turned three the day after we moved. While the cicadas sang in the trees, we ran through sprinklers, swam in our small children's pool, picked strawberries in the still living patch, and explored our new adventurous backyard. We would invite newly made friends to join us—Canice and Noreen Connolly from across the street. It was sheer joy and our troubles seemed to subside (for a while, anyway).

Charlie, even though he still struggled, tried to work for my father at the butcher shop. Jacqueline had one year left at Preston High School in the Bronx and begged my parents to allow her to finish with her friends; eventually my parents complied. Eddie had two years of high school remaining and had to continue at the local public school, Northern Valley Regional High School in Demarest. Johnny, Tommy, Jamie, and I would cross the street and attend Saint Mary's: Johnny in seventh grade, Tommy in sixth, Jamie in fourth and me in first grade. Gloria was heading to kindergarten at the public school since Saint Mary's did not have a kindergarten program at the time and Debbie and Mary, of course, would stay home with Mom.

It was the end of our second month in Closter, and with friendships established and most pieces in place, two notable things happened—school began at Saint Mary's and Charlie started getting into trouble with the law in New Jersey.

The Crucifix above the altar.
(Photo courtesy of Louis Scarpa).

Chapter Five

The Bells of Saint Mary's

In September 1968, I was very excited to start school. While I had a very private and contemplative nature, I also had a type of exuberance that, if given permission, allowed me to perform for hours. I loved to make people laugh and could not wait to make friends. Most of all, I wanted to meet the interesting and beautiful sisters I saw walking in and out of the convent on High Street.

My experiences with religion in my six years of life consisted of Sunday Mass and having a deep affection for the crucifix, which began at Saint Jane Frances de Chantal. In general, I had a natural disposition to God and all things spiritual. It was not uncommon for my father to engage us in deep spiritual conversations at the dinner table. He was a staunch Catholic, and the Catechism of the Church always came first, but he would also discuss the meaning of life and where we

came from. He wanted to know our ideas and what we were thinking. Was there such a thing as reincarnation? What exactly was meant
by the eastern religions in their teachings on the cycles of death and
rebirth? What does it mean when Jesus said, "You shall do these things
and greater?" or "Eye has not seen, ear has not heard what God has in
store for those who love." What does it truly mean to love? Do we love
one another as we should?

These were the thoughts that were instilled in me. As Italian-
American and streetwise as my father could be, he was deeply religious and on his own spiritual journey. He invited us on his path. My
brother Charlie was also very spiritual, but he was on a non-religious
path that felt dark. It was sometimes frightening to listen to his ideas.

He delved deeply into mysticism, psychic phenomena, mind control, ESP, and mediums. I did not want to hear things about satanic
possessions, or how to use the mind to summon spirits, or his disserta-
tion on the book "Seth Speaks"—a book of trance-channeled material
that made a great impact in the sixties and seventies. Charlie's spirituality frightened me. My father's filled me with peace.

While the other children would leave the dinner table, bored with
spiritual talk, I sat there and absorbed it all. I had arrived on my own
spiritual journey, but did not know it. Charlie and I were so much
alike and yet on opposite ends of the spiritual spectrum. My father,
being the wise owl, allowed us to share and express what we believed.
After he was done listening, usually with his head down and nodding
as we spoke, he would then look up and provide us with his opinion
as to where we may or may not be wrong. He would quote Scripture
and provide the speaker with the necessary evidence to dissuade us
from error.

Sometimes the spiritual talks became very deep between Charlie
and my father and the debates morphed into shouting matches.
Through all this, my mother would just listen. She never contributed

to these conversations. I, however, began to understand deep within myself that these were important questions and conversations. I started to understand what was meant by the phrase, "God is within you," the power to change things through prayer, and a merciful God of love.

The juxtaposition between Charlie and me was amazing. He was the oldest of the boys and I was the youngest. One was a fearless daredevil and the other played it safe; one was tough as nails and one was gentler; one had a leaning to religion, the other to the dark arts. Charlie was born the day before the birthdate of our maternal grandfather (March 24th), and I was born on the day before the birthdate of our paternal grandfather (June 23rd). We were identical in looks, however, and both artistically inclined. We were both obsessed with music—particularly, The Beatles. We were opposite polarities and yet we were one. It felt as if we were both intentionally placed in the same household to do battle, and felt that I was his greatest nemesis and he, mine. While my other brothers and sisters had their own issues with Charlie, ours was a gnawing friction that was deeply rooted in resentment and, most likely, how we were wired.

Around this time, I began to get very severe abdominal cramps. They would come upon me hard and fast and would last for hours. I would hold my stomach and lay on my bed until the pain went away. My first conclusion was that my pain was fostered by the cigarette smoke in the house. Whenever I smelled cigarette smoke, I cramped. Back then, smoking in the house was not a big deal and both my Dad and Charlie smoked. Charlie would call me a "sissy" and tell me to shut the hell up every time I complained about the smoking. I would beg him to move his ashtray away from where I sat, and he would intentionally blow the smoke in my face.

The abdominal cramping I experienced as a child has been a problem my whole life. I believe it is due to stress—not just cigarette smoke. When your stomach is in constant knots, the manifestations in the body are inevitable. My parents took me to the doctor, but they couldn't find anything wrong.

By the time I started first grade, I'd seen too much and behaved older than my age. As often as I heard, "you are so funny and talented," I also heard, "you are far too serious for someone your age." But with joy and excitement, I ventured to my first day of school.

I kissed my mother goodbye on my first day with no tears. She left me at the side door of Saint Mary's after introducing me to Sister Terence, my first-grade teacher. I smiled up at Sister and she knelt down and said, "Hello, and welcome, Paul." She gently hugged me and took me by the hand. I felt safe. Mom was good to go.

There are those who relay unfortunate scenarios when it comes to having nuns as teachers, but not me. The order of sisters at Saint Mary's was Felician Sisters and they were beautiful. Many were guitar-playing types like in the film, *The Singing Nun*. They loved music and welcomed it. Their only requirement was to be obedient. I was so in love with them, and so committed to pleasing them, that I would do anything.

There were a few "old school" nuns who were sterner and expected nothing less than perfection, like Sister Dorothea, but I quickly learned that if you did what you were told and humbled yourself, there would be no problem. I observed their every move and was in awe of them—women who gave up their lives to follow Jesus and to emulate his mother, Mary. It was beyond comprehension that there could be something so beautiful on the earth.

I began to correlate my new teachers to the priests from Saint Frances de Chantal in the Bronx. I suppose we take it for granted when we are raised with something we do not understand, but I now understood that priests were also sacrificial and gave up their lives and will to follow Jesus. I remember thinking, *why wouldn't everyone want to be a nun or a priest?* I wanted to give my life to God in first grade and

I wanted the sisters to know. I wanted what they had—I wanted God. I was happy and full of joy.

An early dichotomy developed within me: the struggle to serve others as a priest, or as an actor who could make people happy through song and dance. There is exuberance and creativity in both. Sometimes the love of God and the joy of performing can be confusing to some. While most people would view the two choices as opposite ends of the spectrum, I never saw it that way. To me it was the same. God is joy; performing is joy—it all stems from the same place—creative "God-energy." When thinking in "worldly" terms, God and acting are separate. The common error is that most people make the two options black and white without considering the gray. If we contemplate a career mindset: Hollywood or entering religion, it differs in terms of lifestyle—they are two extremes. The result of the action of acting and the action of the priesthood, however, is to offer others a part of oneself.

From the first day, our first-grade classroom was packed. I dove into my lessons and learned instantly what I was good at: penmanship (unfortunately, a fading art due to the electronic age), reading, English, art and all things creative. On the flip side, getting me to understand math and science was synonymous with learning how to rebuild a carburetor. Both felt impossible. I simply had no aptitude for left-brain-oriented classes and therein began a great phobia of math and the sciences. It wasn't until college that I learned to love science and math.

My performing skills came to life when I made sure that Sister Terence and my classmates knew that since I had the entire *Wizard of Oz* memorized, I would gladly perform it at the asking. Sister Terence would place me before the class to perform it. I quickly had the reputation of being an entertainer. Sometimes the other sisters would pile at the classroom doorway to watch the show.

The fourth-grade sister, Sister Dulcisima, used to take me by the hand to her classroom, make me stand on her desk and sing for the class. When I was done, she gave me a piece of ribbon candy. Sister Dulcisima was older than the other sisters. She was strict and stern. She would constantly curl her tongue against her bottom teeth and when she spoke, she would spit on you. But I didn't care; I loved her.

My brother Jamie was in her class and, while I was gaining the reputation of being a singer and performer par excellence, he was trying to establish a tough and cool reputation. His little brother was not helping. It used to embarrass him when I performed for his class, and in retrospect, who could blame him?

When I began school, the results, suggestions, and mandates of the Second Vatican Council of the Catholic Church were beginning to be enforced. The Church was changing and so were religious orders. One of the many suggestions that stemmed from the Second Vatican Council was for those consecrated to the religious life to re-examine their lives and purpose. They were to put the charism (original intent) of their founders "under a microscope" and make observations as to what might be necessary to change in their order. These might be the austerity of how they were living (or lack thereof), their religious garb, and overly ornate convents and churches. Because of this reevaluation occurring in the already chaotic sixties with racial marches, women's liberation, gay rights, and other issues, many religious orders became tumultuous.

Consecrated religious, priests, sisters, and brothers, began to leave their vocations in droves. In actuality, thousands left worldwide. Some left because they felt they never had a vocation and only entered to please their parents, or because they were the unmarried son or daughter. Becoming a nun or priest was deemed a noble option for a young man or woman coming from a pre-Vatican II model Catholic family.

Still, others left because they had a new sense of freedom, including sexual liberation. They desired to be outside the walls of their orders fighting for peace and justice without the shackles of religious life. Some left because they felt that the Vatican II changes were not happening fast enough.

Sadly, there were some who left because they felt that the original intent and beauty of that first call to be a nun or priest was being watered down by the changes. The order they entered was no longer recognizable and they rejected the progressive changes. These were more traditional women and men. Sister Paul fell into this category.

When I was in first grade, Sister Paul, the sixth-grade teacher, was the first sister to "disappear" and it devastated me. Every time I passed Sister Paul's classroom, I would slow down so that I could peer into the room and watch her. Unlike the other sisters, whose religious habit skirts went down to their knees with the new reform, Sister Paul would be dressed in the old religious habit that went to the shoes. Orders that had a tendency towards progressive norms began to do away with the things they found archaic and no longer applicable to the modern world—this included traditional religious habits.

She did not wear the new modified veil, like some of the other sisters. The new veil allowed some hair to show. Her veil covered her completely. She looked like the Saints from the books we read in class. She had dark eyebrows and her eyes were filled with love and sadness at the same time. Her face was gentle and angelic and there was something about her that captured my heart. Getting a glimpse of Sister Paul always made me smile, and I had a deep love for her. We did not need to share words. When I performed, she did not respond like the other sisters with laughter and clapping. She would observe from the corner of a room and give me a slight nod of the head with a smile, letting me know that I had done well. She mystified me. I wanted what she had.

When I started second grade the following year, Sister Paul did not return. We discovered that she had left the Felician Sisters. I only recently learned that she entered a cloister that was more in line with what she sought spiritually. I will never forget her and the impact she made on my life.

One sunny morning, our school principal, Sister Adele, interrupted our class. She was smiling and tiptoed into the classroom acting very sheepish, and funny. Sister Adele had a very pronounced overbite. She was very kind but could also be tough when she had to be. She approached the front of the class and Sister Terence looked at her dumbfounded.

We jumped up from our desks and in unison, we said, "Good Morning, Sister Adele." She said, "First grade, please sit down, please sit . . . I have some wonderful news for you." Sister Terence stared at her, smiling. "I want you all to know that your teacher Sister Terence has a new name." At this, Sister Terence's jaw dropped, she went red, and put her face into her hands and began to cry what appeared to be tears of joy.

"From now on, Sister Terence will no longer be known as Sister Terence. You may call her, Sister Maria." Sister Terence, now Sister Maria, ran to Sister Adele and the two embraced like mother and daughter. Sister Maria kept crying even after Sister Adele left—she was so happy. She told us that because of some changes in the church, some sisters could return to their birth names if they chose. Sister had asked for permission to return to "Maria." The request came through and Sister Adele made it public to the class.

When some nuns, priests, or brothers enter religious life in the Catholic Church, some orders give them a new name since they are "born" into a new life. Some take the name of a Saint, male or female, and others may choose the name of someone who influenced them such as the name of their mother or father. Sister Terence was one of these. While the other children were indifferent to the news, I rejoiced with her. I plugged into her happiness, and I looked at Sister Maria as another one of my sisters. I remember beaming from ear to ear.

At Saint Mary's, not only did I find a warm place in which to express myself; I was beginning to fall in love with being in church. Our parish had a beautiful crucifix above the altar. It was life-sized and Jesus appeared very real to me. My love for the Crucified Christ was deepening—the love first kindled as a toddler at Saint Frances de Chantal. What I was experiencing internally was difficult to explain. Every religion lesson and every visit to Saint Mary's began to deepen my faith and I absorbed it all like a sponge. I wanted nothing more than to please the sisters and to be good. By being a good boy, I was also pleasing my mother and father in their time of need with Charlie. I would think, *well if Charlie wants to be the bad one, then I could be the good one.*

The sisters suggested that we always keep a rosary in our right-hand pocket to pray whenever we could and to be protected by Our Lady, Jesus' Mother. I obeyed and began a habit that has never ceased. In the best of times and in the worst of times, my rosary has always remained in my right-hand pocket—even on film sets.

I would often sit in the church after school ended and stare at the statues. One day, I stared so long and hard at the statue of Mary that I swore it moved and nodded to me. My creative mind went into overdrive and I ran out of the church to tell all my friends that the statue of Mary came to life. The church went wild with kids each day after school staring at the statue. Each time someone thought the statue moved we would all scream. The good sisters promptly put an end to the "masquerade," as they called it. Needless to say, there were no more nods from Mary.

My hiding place behind the china cabinet was replaced by the silence of Saint Mary's Church. When things got bad at home, whether my parents were fighting with Charlie or there was some unfortunate scene, I would run across the street, rosary beads in my pocket, to the altar. I loved being alone in the church, through good and bad times.

I began to develop an intimate relationship with Christ that stemmed from both my education and our family troubles. My heart was on fire, and often I could think of nothing else but the love of God and how desperately we needed to be good and loving to each other.

I loved the silence as I sat in the pews and stared up at the cross. I loved the smell, the candles, the darkness, Jesus' face cast in light on the altar, the stained-glass windows in honor of Mary, the statue of Saint Joseph. I wanted it all, but I did not know how to express it. While I played with my sisters and other kids on my block after school, my real joy was to cross the street to be alone with Christ. The church was the safest place in the world and in the deepest recesses of my heart, I knew it was my true home. I learned that nothing else in this world mattered but God. They could take all my toys, my family, my new house, everything, but God was my all. I wanted to fall into the well of His love forever.

The priests in my parish would sometimes come to our classrooms and visit us, as well as say Mass for the school each Friday. I did not develop personal relationships with the priests as I had with the sisters. I was always respectful of them and thought they were very nice. I learned through them that there was a place in the world for a kind and gentle man. Being aggressive, competitive, or able to throw a punch were no longer prerequisites for survival. I was learning a different way. Thank God for my Catholic school upbringing. It carried me.

As my grammar school years progressed, so did the problems at home with Charlie. He would disappear for days at a time and often my parents would receive phone calls from various precincts in New York City where Charlie was either found stoned in the streets or arrested. We never knew how he would come home on any given day, and we constantly walked on eggshells. His downward spiral continued.

We had to be very secretive in Closter. We had to monitor when friends and neighbors came to the front door depending on Charlie's condition. Our High Street friends were no longer permitted in the house. We harbored our secret and my parents (especially my mother) were keen on keeping his problem under the radar—this included not talking about Charlie to anyone, including relatives and teachers.

At this point in his life, Charlie was at the point of no return and did not want help. He would do anything for his next fix. He was not "hitting bottom" no matter how many times he was arrested or over-dosed. He just did not want help. As the saying goes, you can lead the horse to water, but you can't make him drink. An addict must desire recovery for it to stick.

I was only a child in grammar school, and I couldn't take any more of the constant angst. My abdominal cramping was incessant and at an all-time worst. I hoped in my heart of hearts that God would take my brother if he could not get well. I wanted Charlie and my family to have peace. At the rate we were going, I was fearful that one of my parents would die due to the constant worrying about Charlie.

One early Saturday morning, my cramps became so bad that I was burning with fever and I had been ill for a few days. I called my Dad to my bedroom very early in the morning before he left for work.

"Daddy, something's wrong."

"Where's the pain, poppa?" he said, and he rubbed his hand over my forehead and kissed it.

"It's here today." I pointed to my right side above my groin. My Dad had a gift with medicine and an uncanny ability to diagnose our ailments. He would have made a fine doctor. He looked at me and said he was going to take me to the emergency room. He feared it was appendicitis.

I arrived at the hospital with my parents just in the nick of time because as the surgeon began the procedure to remove my appendix, it burst. Dad was right. I became gravely ill and was filled with toxins. What should have been a few days in the hospital turned into two weeks. Not only did I have my appendix removed, but I developed a severe infection.

They inserted a drain from my appendix to remove toxins and I went from 99 pounds to 49 in a matter of weeks. I was a skeleton and very ill. I tried to be brave for my worried parents. When I was finally sent home, we were relieved to know what might have been causing my abdominal pain.

In the meantime, the scenes at home continued to be aggressive and at times, violent. Charlie's mood and behavior were usually dependent on the drug he took. I was young and uncertain of different drug names, but I knew that when he took "downs" he became belligerent. He would instigate fights and quite frankly, look possessed. His eyes would become dark as he took pleasure in frightening us. He would say that he had powers and could summon demons to our rooms.

He would be hunched over leaning against the wall, staring at you with a crazed, maniacal glare smiling and spewing obscenities. He seemed to know exactly what to say to push the right button to incite violence. When he upset my brothers, who were now getting older, there would be fist fights. My mother would scream, and the house would be chaotic. It was common for chairs to be thrown across a room while we all took cover. The china cabinet from the Bronx house was now in the kitchen of the Closter house and was caddy corner to the family table, so any notion of hiding behind it was obsolete.

We watched, waited and trembled, not sure what would happen next. We worried about our parents and, over time, did whatever it took to find a way to survive living with toxicity and dysfunction. After the debacle would end, he would laugh and enjoy the misery he had successfully created. Life with Charlie became a living nightmare.

During the horrific fighting, I would run into the closet of my bedroom and crawl to the back space among the shoes. I learned in the heart of the Charlie crises that incessant prayer would stop the fights.

My sister Jacqueline had a small statue of the Blessed Mother. It was a beautiful statue and I loved how Mary's face looked very real on it. I would grab it, hide in the closet, and beg God to make the shouting stop and to make Charlie go away. I began to learn the power of prayer. The harder and faster I sincerely prayed, the quicker it all stopped.

I would come out of the closet when the shouting stopped without anyone knowing that I had been hiding. As I crawled out, I inevitably wondered how it concluded—did someone die this time? Did someone leave the house? Was Mommy crying? I would crack the door open and listen—my heart pounding in my chest. Sometimes there was an eerie silence that was almost deafening. I wouldn't leave the closet until I felt it was safe.

One hot summer morning we heard loud banging on our back door. I was upstairs in my bedroom and was startled to hear the banging. I moved close to the banister to listen.

"It's the police. Open the door." My father opened the back door and two police officers barged in and asked my father where Charlie was. Police cars filled our driveway as if someone had just robbed a bank. My mother ran upstairs out of fear and hid in her bedroom holding her heart and trembling in fear of the police in our house. My mother became frightened very easily.

"Charlie is upstairs, officer," my father interjected. "Let me go get him."

"There's no need to get him; we will." They trudged past my father and made their way up the kitchen stairway into the attic. I had no idea what my brother could have done but moments later as I peered out of my bedroom, I saw him being dragged down the stairs by his legs. My mother started to scream from her bedroom, and I ran to protect her.

My little sisters were all crying, as well as my father. He was told to come to the station where they were going to arrest my brother for writing fake prescriptions. My father immediately complied and left the house. Charlie was thrown into the backseat of the police car as I watched from my parents' bedroom window.

My mother lay on her bed holding her heart in a state of delirium. She was mumbling and made no sense. The fear gripped her so tightly that she shook and rocked herself into the fetal position on her bed. I held her in my nine-year-old arms. For a few moments, it appeared as if she had gone temporarily insane. She kept rambling to herself, "Shhhh momma, it's okay momma . . . shhhh momma, it's okay, don't worry momma." She stared ahead at no one, with her eyes wide with fright, as she rambled. I wasn't sure what to do. It frightened me to see my mother like this, and I held her in my arms and rocked her while she cried and muttered unintelligible words.

Eventually, she calmed down and was able to pull herself together. She sat up on the bed, then, between sobs, stood, wiped her tears, and made her way to the kitchen. She had been cooking and still had her apron on. Her motherly duties were interrupted by the unimaginable. I stayed strong for my mother in these times and temporarily switched roles. My tears were usually hidden and saved for the right moment.

Charlie was released on bail and returned home which was a disappointment. It felt like he would never go away and that his nightmare would be ours forever.

On another sad occasion, when I was about eleven years old, and after my oldest sister married her husband, Burt, my mother invited some of her family over for a summer barbeque. It was a beautiful and sunny summer day. My sisters and I were excited to see our relatives, swim and have hot dogs.

Before my relatives arrived, Charlie came downstairs from his room. He looked crazed and no one knew what he had taken but it was clear he wanted to start trouble. My mother had warned him the day before to be on good behavior in front of her sisters. He was hunched over and spoke belligerently to my mother. He again looked possessed and frightening. My father got very angry and tried to get him under control before my relatives arrived. Because it was a sunny day, the back porch door was open and neighbors could easily hear the shouting.

"What the hell did you take this time?" my father shouted.

"You gotta lend me ten bucks," he mumbled, barely able to stand.

"Ah, look at you! You're ruining our lives." Charlie laughed and cursed at my father.

Burt and Jackie arrived at the house and walked in the back door. They heard the shouting and asked what was going on? Burt was a Vietnam vet and served in the navy—a tall, German, Nordic type who was also a bodybuilder. Charlie respected Burt's physical attributes and would never consider fighting with him. He was from the Bronx and close in age to Charlie, so they were friendly and often spent time together. I was relieved to see Burt, since I knew he could control Charlie. His presence was synonymous with feeling safe.

Charlie turned towards Jacqueline and Burt like a madman and stared at them. Burt saw my parents' concern and picked up the cue to help. Burt gave his usual half chuckle as if to say, what are you doin' now, Charlie?

"Come on Charlie, let's go for a drive." Burt pulled him out the back door. It was uncharacteristic for Charlie to challenge Burt, but while on the porch, Charlie decided to take a swing at him. My mother and father got nervous and ran to the porch. My sisters heard the scuffle and ran to the porch from the TV room. I stood on the sidelines steeped in the angst of the moment and I felt in my heart of hearts that disaster was looming.

"Oh my God, Jackie," my mother cried to my father, "Get him to stop fighting."

After the first swing, Burt tried to get Charlie under physical control as best he could, but after trying to slug Burt again and missing, Charlie took a knife out of his pants pocket, at which point my mother started screaming. Charlie continued to fight, knife in hand, as Burt tried to restrain him.

My mother started screaming and went to grab Charlie's arm. He was so hell-bent on trying to get at Burt that he pushed my mother, who standing at the top of the porch stairs. She toppled backwards down the wooden stairs and hit her head on the concrete walkway. We all started crying and screaming for my mother, and the scene went from bad to complete bedlam. I wanted this madness to stop. My mother was lying on the ground in a state of shock while Burt had to resort to more violent means to get him under control. He slammed Charlie against the porch wall and knocked the wind out of him. The knife fell from Charlie's hand and my father grabbed it.

Burt literally picked Charlie up and put him into his car. Burt and Jackie, selflessly, took him away for the day. My mother, still crying and in shock, pulled herself up and tried to gain composure. She sobbed like a little girl as she walked defeated into the house to continue cooking for her family who would soon arrive. My father was crying as well and was so frustrated and upset that he punched the hard mahogany wall in the hallway and split the wood.

I stood there watching them both. I was at a loss and didn't know what to do for my parents. My father looked at us with tears rolling down his cheeks, as he had pity on his frightened younger children.

"It's okay kids, go ahead and play. Daddy and Mommy are okay. I am so sorry you had to witness that."

My mother said, "Go outside and play, it's a beautiful day. We'll be all right. Thank God he's gone. Go ahead. Go play in the pool."

The girls ran away to play, but I was in knots, overtaken by anxiety and fear. I wanted Charlie dead, gone, out of our lives. I couldn't take it anymore—none of us could. My heart weighed a hundred pounds as I made my way upstairs to pray. I begged God to make the day bearable with my relatives coming.

One Sunday afternoon in the same timeframe, my parents left us to go to a wedding. Jacqueline was there to monitor Charlie so that my parents could leave for once, and have a little peace. Dad said that Charlie had taken a handful of barbiturates and was likely to be asleep for the rest of the day. He was wrong.

After they left, Charlie came half-falling and half-walking down the stairs to the kitchen. He stumbled and fell face down on the kitchen floor. My sisters were in the TV room and did not know what was happening. But I witnessed it and was so upset and angry that I did not call Jacqueline for help. I just watched him. I saw it as an opportunity to hurt him, or even create an accidental death.

He was lying on the floor, face down and unconscious. I looked at him and with all the strength I could muster; I kicked him as hard as I could in his side. He didn't move or flinch. I kicked him again, and he slightly stirred. I then went to his head and grabbed as many of his black curls as I could in my fist and pulled his hair and head back so far that I had a clump of hair in my hand. As I did it, I whispered in his ear, "Why don't you just die already. You're killing us."

He stirred and came to for a moment. I backed up out of fear thinking he knew exactly what had happened, which would have meant I would get a beating. He looked at me with a half-smile and whispered, "Hey pal." My heart sunk. The moment sickened me. His greeting was so sad and pathetic considering what I was doing to him that I felt heartbroken. My heart swelled with love for him in the midst of my confusion. I began to cry because I hurt him. I didn't mean to hurt him—I just wanted the pain to go away. He rested his head against the floor and fell asleep, as I pulled myself together so no one would know what had happened.

The twins came into the kitchen and saw him lying on the floor. Rather than react with fear, they "hopscotched" over his body to get to the pantry for a snack—we were used to jumping over Charlie on the floor.

This dysfunction is what our lives had become, and I wanted it to end.

I was aggressive with Charlie only one other time. No one else was in the kitchen as I watched him settle down at the kitchen table to eat a bowl of soup. It was evident that he was on opioids—he was nodding out and waking up, nodding out and waking up. As he was eating, he began nodding out into his soup. I decided to get behind him. I looked around to make sure no one was coming and decided that I would kill him and try to make it look like an accident. I grabbed his hair from the back of his head and pushed him forward into the soup until he was face down. I held it there. In a fit of frustration, I went up and down several times. When I heard him gurgle, I got scared and lifted his head. I caught myself in the insanity of the moment and felt remorseful for what I had done.

I immediately played it off in case he came to his senses, even though I knew he was so messed up that he would not be able to speak. I said, "Hey Charl, be careful, your face went into your soup!" I wiped his sad face clean and I held him up even though he couldn't eat. I stood by him as he sat—a poor, pathetic twenty-two-year-old lost somewhere no one could find him. I decided to try to feed him to make sure he ate and didn't hurt himself. I wondered if deep down inside he knew what he was doing to us. If he did, I am sure it pained him as much as it pained us.

I was forced to grow up fast. Besides the fact that, by nature, I enjoyed seclusion, these experiences removed the folly of youth. I was not interested in going out and playing. I preferred not to interact with others and wanted to be alone.

In union with my alone time at Saint Mary's, I became a regular at the Closter Public Library taking out five to seven books at a time. I lost myself in books and they became my obsession. I sat in the library for hours picking up book after book about Hollywood, the lives of movie stars, and stories about drug addicts, such as "Go Ask Alice."

I was also a regular at our small town bookstore, The Written Word, and spent hours after school, week after week, picking up books, smelling them, holding them, and reading the back covers. I couldn't get enough. I became an avid reader and knew all the weekly bestsellers and what was due to come out.

I also dived into the arts. I loved drawing, working with clay, paint, colors, music, and dance. My creativity was expanding, and I was finding those things that brought me peace. My father and brothers, however, made feeble attempts to incorporate me into their world by enrolling me in farm league baseball (baseball for third and fourth graders). I wanted them to leave me alone with their unrealistic expectations. Charlie was bad enough, but their insistence on forcing me to fit into their mold caused me great angst. In addition to Charlie, I had secondary struggles to battle.

Dad and I comparing guns.

Chapter Six

———

"Be a Man"

The baseball came flying at me full force. I didn't know what to do. I stood there like an idiot. *Oh God*, I thought, *please let this humiliation end*. The ball flew past me and hit the metal net that captured me within its cove. I was a prisoner of a farm league baseball field and for the time being, I was trapped. After the ball hit the net, I heard the jeering of fathers and teammates around me. The sound of aggressive voices reverberated in my ears. I was scared. I couldn't move. I could not swing at the ball and I couldn't turn my head. I was literally frozen stiff. The team had a few weeks of practice and now we had our first game.

During our practices, I often pretended, when in the outfield, that I did not see the ball coming at me, or that I was blinded by the sun. I stood in the field reveling in the sunshine. I was amazed by the beauty of the yellow daffodils against the green grass under an umbrella of blue. I wished I had my crayons to draw with or even to just sit on the grass to think or sing.

"What's wrong with him? Why can't he just swing?" they shouted.

But little did they know that I was in survival mode. I had years and years of survival practice. I acted as passé as I could about my ineptness. I stayed in that stiff position until I could make my inevitable third strike. Again, I looked up at the pitcher and tried my best to swing at the ball. I prayed to God and pleaded for his assistance to get me through this new challenge. There was so much going on at home and my family had bigger fish to fry. I could not believe I had to contend with this! It all felt silly, ridiculously immature and quite frankly, boring. I just wanted to be alone.

I looked at the pitcher. He looked at me with a smug, bully face with all the confidence in the world that he would strike me out and be Mr. Tough Guy for doing it. I held onto God and prayed He would get me through this. In an instant the ball flew past me and I heard the ump shout, "Strike two." I looked over at my teammates and wished I could just get kicked off the team. I hated baseball. The only good thing about it was that I wore a uniform and in wearing it for a few hours, people might think of me as an average little boy playing ball at the park. They didn't have to see the boy that didn't fit in—only the costume.

I heard one of the guys on the team behind me. He was admonishing the other boys for screaming at me and for saying cruel things. He said, "Leave him alone, he's trying. I'd like to see you guys do better." Someone else replied, "My sister could do better." The others laughed, but that didn't satisfy him. He looked at me with empathy and care in his eyes and genuinely felt my torment. I have never forgotten that. I learned that a simple act of kindness could stick with someone for the rest of their lives.

The third pitch came at me with such force that I panicked for a moment and in a weak attempt to hit the ball, I swung the bat. The ball smashed against my thumb into the bat. It hit so hard that I saw stars and couldn't choke back the tears. I wanted my mother and I wanted to go home. I had enough. ENOUGH!

My world stood still as I silently cursed my father and brothers for signing me up for baseball. The pain was excruciating and the nail on my thumb instantly turned purple and black. I began to panic and decided to leave the field. I looked around at all the shocked faces, some grimacing, some concerned, and I threw the bat, against my prison cage. I bolted off the field without giving the adults a chance to help me and ran and ran. I was heading home. I heard nothing behind me. I blocked it all out. All I could hear was my labored breathing as I cried and ran.

I ran past the public school and then made a concerted effort to pull it together and control my tears. I had to get home as soon as possible, but I did not want my mother to see me crying. I knew she would feel sorry for me and I didn't want to cause her any more pain. I wiped away my tears when I was far away from the field and gained as much control as I could. I passed my school, Saint Mary's, where life was safe and pure, and cruelty was not allowed. I looked at the statue of the Blessed Mother through the glass doors of the school entrance and was reminded that God loves me. All would be okay. *Ah, connected—that peace!*

Finally, I walked through my front door, hand outstretched, and nonchalantly said, "Oh boy, Mommy, look . . . I had a little accident. I think I might need some help, but it's okay, I'm fine."

She wiped her hands on her apron and looked at me. I could see she had pity in her eyes—my mother was not naïve. She made me sit on the toilet bowl seat in the downstairs bathroom. She bandaged my thumb, kissed me on the forehead, and told me to rest. I could tell she felt bad. My mother didn't say much, but her expressions always gave her away—she wore her heart on her sleeve. She hugged me and said that I didn't have to go back to the field if I didn't want to and not to worry.

I surrendered the quest to be who my father and brothers wanted me to be and hoped they would leave me alone once and for all. I was never going to be a baseball player, I was never playing football, I was not going to fight and there was no way I was remaining in the Boy Scouts (another failed shove-it-down-your-throat venture they imposed on me). The athleticism I did enjoy was outdoors, in the sunshine and alone—running, hiking, swimming.

I felt like a circle in a square and the more they tried to force their ideals on me, the more I receded into myself spending time at the library, listening to music, and creating fantasies. The alpha New York Italian male stuff that was smeared in my face since I was born was something to reject. I had to count the days, months, and years until I was liberated, and it was a long way off. I lived in the hope that one day I would run—the same way I did off the field that day—run so fast and so far, that I would never return, and no one would know where to find me. I often wonder if I would have ended up like Charlie if I was a teenager in the sixties.

A bit of a rebellious nature was beginning to take root. I even secretly liked misbehaving—even though I tried my best to be good. Two girls from the public school who were my age, and an annoyance to everyone, Wendie and Pat, would occasionally walk through the Saint Mary's parking lot on their way to school. When they did, they would scream at the top of their lungs as if they were being murdered—just for laughs. They tried their best to irritate the sisters and would shout, "HEY PENGUINS" at the top of their lungs (a slang expression for a nun in black and white) or "GOOD MORNING, SAINT MARY'S FAIRIES," and then laugh hysterically. What was it about those two that drew me?

At the public library, they were worse. They used to try and knock as many books off the shelves as they could without getting caught. Although I hid my amusement, I found it hysterical. I think I was living vicariously through them, and their antics became a cathartic experience of acting out. Once I arrived at high school, Wendie and I became very close.

While it has its humorous side now, I did make one attempt at running away. I heard that children who were unhappy at home ran away to New York or hid in friends' houses. The frustration I was experiencing was so real and physical that I chose to give running away a shot. I wasn't sure how I would do it or where I would go, but I knew no other way to express my disdain. I wanted my parents to know how much I hated being bullied.

I packed a large Hefty garbage bag with some clothes. I stormed out of the house and at ten years old, made my way down High Street, garbage bag in tow, waving to neighbors as I passed. After five full minutes, I was exhausted from lugging the heavy bag, so I decided to turn around and make camp in my backyard. I chose not to run away but I wanted them to see that I was upset and not happy.

When I arrived in my backyard, I sat under a tree and when I looked up at the kitchen window, I saw my parents and a few siblings laughing as if it was a show—so much for running away. I schlepped back into the house and had to bear the humiliation of only making it 500 feet from the house. When I walked into the kitchen, my mother was laughing and took my face in her hands, kissed me and said she loved me. If running away made my mother laugh, it was worth it, regardless of the jeers. I had to tuck away my angst. Mom was on my side and I couldn't place a price tag on it. Mom protected me. I never felt shamed by her. It was unconditional love. She was my bud.

———

Dealing with testosterone and the survival of the fittest also began to rear its ugly head at Saint Mary's. I had my first "man-to-man" confrontation, though I did not have the time or patience to think about a fist fight. All the pathetic notions that defined what a boy should be seemed so childish and immature. I placated my opponent so that we could fight and get it over with—as I'd done with farm league baseball.

The big scheduled fight was with Sean Duggan, a classmate of mine. He was one of my closest friends and we often played after school. We were also rivals, however, when it came to the attention of the girls in class. He had a tendency of getting jealous when the girls surrounded me to sing or dance, and one day he couldn't take it anymore. He looked me dead in the eye and told me to meet him after school in the parking lot in the Giordano's backyard (a family whose backyard faced the parking lot of Saint Mary's and was adjacent to the woods). I had to show up for this big fight since all eyes were on me. I was being called out, and I knew my credibility was at stake. All my friends promised that they were going to come and cheer me on. The week before, Sean and I had spent time goofing off in the basement of his house so the whole confrontation totally confused me.

On the day of the big fight, when the dismissal bell rang, my heart nervously sunk into my chest as I headed for the exit doors of the school, and quickly told all my friends I'd see them tomorrow. I broadly smiled hoping that Sean would see me and that my smile would help him change his mind. No way! I could see that he was committed to slaughtering me. There was no way of getting out of it.

As I left the side door of the school, he followed me retaining eye contact, and as soon as we got outside, he abruptly pushed me against the brick wall to remind me of the fight. I played dumb and said, "Oh yeah, I forgot—sorry." We began our trek to the Giordano's backyard. Other students joined the pack, with me walking in the center, and Sean staring me down as if he was a starved dog who found a bone (with meat on it). I felt like I was outside of my body and watching a scene from a movie. I was so nervous that I did not know whether to laugh or cry.

Our friends stood on the sidelines and watched as Sean and I gathered on the lawn. One of the older Giordano girls came out to watch. The Giordanos were tough Italian kids from New York City and loved fights. Getting help from them was nil to none.

I never had a fist fight with a friend, and I did not know how to start. As I stood there feeling foolish, Sean pushed me to the ground as hard as he could and knocked the wind out of me. This guy meant business. I remember thinking, *what could I have possibly done that could elicit such anger in a person?* The cheering started with the biggest ones coming from the Giordanos who encouraged me to punch him in the face. They were my paesani (fellow Italians) and wanted me to beat the hell out of the "Irish punk." It all felt so mean.

I felt helpless, and finally lifted my fist to punch Sean in the face. He had me on the ground and was sitting on my chest, with both legs straddling my side. He looked down at me, and before I threw the punch that was organically coming from the center of my being, I thought of his mother and realized I could not hit him. All I could see was Sean going home to his mother with blood on his face telling her that he had a fight. I suppose I thought all mothers had the same heartaches as my mother. I felt bad for her. By hurting Sean, I was hurting this wonderful woman who baked cookies for us just last week. I also felt bad for Sean as I looked at him with the eyes of a parent.

I went deep within myself for a moment as I looked up at Sean. My heart welled, because I realized how much I loved my friend. I tuned out the shouting around me and sunk into a black hole seeing both Sean and his mother in my mind's eye. I did not want to hurt Sean or Mrs. Duggan. It sounds crazy, but this was my reality—my world was being colored by Charlie and his effect on my family. Besides the fact that I was feeling these things, I was also convinced that I couldn't win the fight anyway, so I lowered my hand and chose not to hit back. I surrendered and gave it all to God.

At that point, the cheers and jeers got louder, and I snapped back to reality only to hear my friends screaming "hit him Paulie, hit him." I thought that the entire situation was insane, and with that, Sean punched me in the face over and over and over, until a stream of red ran down my face. I was called names and teased because I didn't hit back, but I did not care; something deep within me took over. I felt God's love and knew no harm could come to me. Once again, God let me know he was with me every step of the way. I smiled inwardly. I allowed Sean to win. When blood was exhibited, I knew it was over.

Sean was pleased—pleased that he clearly won and then with a big smile pulled me up, shook my hand and said, "That's what men do, they shake after a fight." *Oh, gee, Sean, thanks a lot. I have to remember that for next time.*

I was glad and relieved that we had peace between us, even though the Giordanos looked disappointed that I let Italy down. He was satisfied and our friendship continued. I never wanted to have another fist fight again. And I never did.

Happy days at Saint Mary's School.

Chapter Seven

Who Am I?

It should not go unsaid that when Charlie was clean and sober, as brief as it may have been, he was kind and loving. It always pained me to know this about Charlie, because even as a child I innately understood that he had potential. When he was clean, he would call me his "pal" or "little buddy" and would enjoy the fact that I could sing and dance, when only a week prior he hit me for the same things. I learned that it was the drugs that made him ugly—it was not who he really was.

He often called me "Hollywood" (his nickname for me) and could be protective when he wanted to be. How I wished *this* Charlie would be around more, but it wasn't to be. Living with an addict is unpredictable. We never knew which "personality" would show up when he walked in the door—a high and abusive Charlie, or a loving big brother.

My school days were usually filled with angst as to what might be happening at home. I feared that my mother would be home alone with Charlie if he was not in the Bronx with my father. I had constant knots in my stomach and lived with the fear that something terrible was going to happen. Impending doom loomed over my young head. At lunchtime, I would walk to our classroom windows and strain to look down the block to see if I could get a glimpse of my house.

I wanted to share with someone what was happening at home but knew that I couldn't. I began to provide hints so someone would hear me. I verbally slipped a few times in front of relatives (thank God, my father's sister, my Aunt Annie, and her husband, Uncle Joe, already knew. They were a great support to my parents). I even wrote a book on index cards in fourth grade entitled, "The Family That Tried to Make It." It spoke of a fictional family with an addict brother. I even illustrated it. My great literary masterpiece was discovered by one of the strictest teachers in the school—Mrs. Nancy Lione—a teacher who dryly told us her middle initial was "P"—for PERFECTION. Fortunately, Mrs. Lione, while she scared the heck out of the students, was friendly with my Mom and Dad. I didn't know it at the time, but she also knew about our situation at home.

She came to my house one evening. I was scared to death. She was friendly with my parents, but it wasn't her habit to come over. I thought, *what is Mrs. Lione doing here?* I was upstairs in my pajamas and did not want Mrs. Lione to see me ready for bed—it felt creepy to think of your teacher seeing you in your pajamas. I slowly snuck down the kitchen stairs to eavesdrop on their conversation and braced myself for the worst. I had a feeling it was about me.

Mrs. Lione was every student's worst nightmare. She was a hybrid of Ruth Bader Ginsberg, and Bella Abzug. She was tall with jet black hair, and her face was always stern. She favored the smart kids and her fuse was short with those who struggled in class. You were supposed to pick up on the material and pick it up quick. Rumor had it that she even left her son Salvatore back in the third grade just to prove that she was not to be messed with. When she told us to use a ruler to under-line our names at the top of the page, it better be a sharp, crisp line with no swerves, or you were toast! My older brothers were lucky and started Saint Mary's in the higher grades, but Gloria, Debbie, Mary and I had to endure the wrath of Mrs. Lione. Her husband Paul, how-ever, was very small and thin with wiry glasses. He always smiled and waved to us at Sunday Mass. He was a cross between Woody Allen and Mister Rogers. He was also our mailman.

I tried my darndest not to make the stairs squeak as I approached the bottom of the stairwell. And then I heard them, ". . . And did you know he wrote this little story about your situation? I feel compelled to tell you because you know I care about you both and did not want this to begin circulating. You know the gossip mill at Saint Mary's."

"Thank you, Nancy. You have no idea how much we appreciate it," my mother replied.

She handed them my best selling work of non-fiction which I was preparing to duplicate and sell for ten cents a copy. When my parents saw the title, "The Family that Tried to Make It," they all laughed. My mother said, "He's such a character. Thank you, Nancy."

"There is one more thing I need to bring to your attention. He is talented and has many gifts, but I heard him insult me by imitating me with one of his classmates. He did everything he could to get a laugh at my expense." She sounded hurt and I went numb. *Oh my God*, I thought, *how did she find out? Did she hear me imitate her? Where was she listening? Yes, I imitated her—but I imitated everybody*. Now my parents sounded angry.

"Paulie," they shouted. *Crap!* I was supposed to be upstairs and now I was at the bottom of the stairwell. They would know I was lis-tening if I responded straight away or if one of them turned around to shout upstairs. I froze. I waited. I could not respond.

"Paulie!" they shouted louder. Nothing. I tried to think on my feet, but as I feebly thought of a plan to deceive them by making my way back up the stairs silently and then descend loudly in response to their calls, my father turned the corner to the stairway, looked up to the top of the stairs and then looked down to see me on the second step. *Gulp!* He made direct eye contact with me and looked surprised.

"Were you listening this whole time?" he asked.

"No," I lied, "I was just coming down for juice." I stood up and decided to brave what was coming to me. I turned the corner and made eye contact with Mrs. Lione. She eyed me up and down in my pajamas and a little part of me felt gross. I held my father's hand and I knew he didn't believe me. He said, "I know you heard. Apologize to Mrs. Lione for imitating her and promise you will never do that again." I started to get a lump in my throat and was scared. Coughing back tears, I said I was sorry and then started to cry. I ran to my mother who comforted me. She rubbed my back as I saw her wink to Mrs. Lione and said, "He won't do it again, Mrs. Lione. He's a good boy . . . right, Paul?"

"Right," I sobbed.

They told me to give Mrs. Lione a hug. I gave Mrs. Lione a warm hug and what passed through me was not a beast at all, but a loving woman. I smelled the warmth of her skin and the good intentions of her heart. She smiled at me but proceeded with one more topic.

She encouraged my parents to enroll me in art school since she thought I was a gifted artist. The fact of the matter is I started to come out all over the place—acting, singing, imitating, art—the need to express an overactive imagination. I welcomed the suggestion with a big smile. I needed an outlet, and Mrs. Lione recognized that.

Later on in life, Mrs. Lione became a very dear friend of mine. It was true what they said in Closter—when you have Mrs. Lione in class, it will be rough, but what she gives you will remain with you forever. She passed away a few years ago, and I think of her often.

Regardless of being scolded and trying to figure out life, things were always safe at Saint Mary's. As more and more sisters started to leave the Felician Order, post Vatican-II, the school began to fill up with more lay teachers. I was comforted and protected by the good sisters, but so many left. Two that remained became great influences— Sister Sharon and Sister Juanita. Sister Juanita was my favorite. She and Sister Sharon played the guitar and started a glee club, which I joined in sixth grade. Nothing made me happier. It was wholesome, fun, and safe, and I felt close to God in those blissful moments. We sang songs that spoke to me, such as "Hear, O Lord the sound of my call, hear O Lord and have mercy, my soul is longing for the glory of you, O Hear O Lord and answer me" or "Up with People."

Sister Juanita reflected Jesus to me, all the time, every day. She was never without a smile and her kindness was something I wanted to emulate. She was the truest example of what it meant to radiate Christ. If anyone was responsible for watering my blossoming faith, it was Sister Juanita. She had my heart and I dreaded the day that I would have to say goodbye to her and Saint Mary's. If you recall the film, *The Bells of Saint Mary's*, I felt like Patsy—a child who clung to Sister Benedict, played by Ingrid Bergman, because Sister made life so bearable at Saint Mary's. It was the same for me.

There were a few strict sisters, but I never got hit. The only out of the ordinary scolding I witnessed was when Sister Denise held Sean Duggan (yes, the same Sean that beat me up) against the wall by his tie—feet off the floor—and said to him, "You want to get smart with me punk? You want to wise off? Let's see how tough you are. Go ahead, I dare you . . . say something now, wise guy." With that, she threw him to the side. Only God knows what Sean said to warrant that anger in Sister Denise, but the next day Mrs. Duggan pulled my best friend out of Saint Mary's and placed him in our local public middle school.

By the time I was in seventh grade, I begged my parents to enroll me for tap lessons and they finally agreed. I wanted to be a big M-G-M musical star and needed to begin tapping. I did some research and found a dance school in Closter. I enrolled at the Academy of the Dance and was mentored by two old-timers from the ballet world and Broadway stage, a married couple, Grant and Kim Delaney. I was especially fond of Kim, since she had a cameo role in the Gene Kelly film, Marjorie Morningstar. She was also a graduate of the famous New York High School of the Performing Arts. Grant had been in corps de ballet with Ballet Russe of Monte Carlo. I was star-struck and in awe of the two of them. In Closter, they were the closest I had gotten to Hollywood and Broadway.

After starting my dance career, I was hooked and wanted nothing more than to spend every waking hour at the studio. I found a safe niche and was thrilled. Grant, seeing that I had talent, was somewhat harsh with me because he wanted me to improve and get to New York one day. My posture was horrible, and my shoulders were slumped. He would scream things in class like "doesn't your father correct your posture?" *My father should correct my posture?* I thought, *is he kidding me?*

Kim, on the other hand, thought that for me to make it in New York, I had to begin right away with as much dance as possible, including ballet and jazz. The acting, she said, would come later. I should immerse myself and my body in dance. By show biz standards I was already behind the eight-ball, since most male dancers start as early as four, five or six years old and I was already eleven years old.

I began to take ballet three nights a week, jazz one night and tap twice a week. Nothing else mattered—this was all I wanted. I improved with time and soon single pirouettes turned into double pirouettes and occasionally a triple. I also had an incredible ability to jump, and jump high! I believe, looking back, that the height came from the joy in doing what I loved to do. Grant was impressed with how I was advancing.

My level of sophistication began to change as well, thanks to Grant and Kim. Buying the latest 45 RPM records was soon replaced with buying albums such as Tchaikovsky's, "Swan Lake" and classical music compilations. When I was home, I would listen to the records and practice and practice. I was not naturally limber. I had to go through painstaking efforts to stretch and stay stretched. Missing class on a given day for any dancer has a price. When I missed, not only did I feel it physically, but I had to bear the wrath of Grant who did not let up on me. He demanded more discipline and practice. Grant and Kim wanted me to pursue a career in dance and be prepared for New York both physically and mentally. They did everything they could to assist me.

When I finally graduated Saint Mary's, I was blessed to receive the coveted "Rooney Award"—an award given to a student who exemplified Christian ethics, academic achievement, and was an all-around good example to other students. It was also known as the "Nun Brown-Nose" award, but I did not care. It felt great to be recognized and acknowledged. When my name was called at graduation as the recipient, I screamed in the church like I won an Academy Award. Everyone laughed.

Now that I had graduated grammar school and was heading to high school, I had four years to go before I would live the life I craved. My heart was set on one thing and one thing only—getting to New York and then to Hollywood. I had subscriptions to *Rona Barrett's Hollywood*, *Photoplay*, *Motion Picture* and others—thank God for a mother who also loved these same magazines and funded my addiction. I was obsessed with becoming an actor and a star. My bedroom was plastered with wall-to-wall photos of movie stars and movie posters.

I saved every penny I had to go to the Closter Theater which was walking distance from my house. It did not matter if I went alone. I saw every film that ran in that theater—provided it wasn't rated "R". To this day, I can recite the voice message that you heard if you called the theater to see what was playing, "This is a recorded announcement from your United Artists Closter Theater, located in the Closter

Shopping Plaza, today we are pleased to present . . ."

Also, about this time, the film *That's Entertainment!* was released. If you looked up obsession in the dictionary, my picture would have been there. I saw the film 15 times in the theater. I was a Hollywood-junkie and had to get there, particularly to M-G-M. I wanted them to sign me.

I wrote letters week after week to the studios asking them to fly me out to Hollywood to give me a chance in a movie. I knew my chances were slim, but could you imagine my excitement when letters arrived at the house from Columbia Pictures, Metro-Goldwyn-Mayer and Warner Brothers thanking me for my letters! I swear, a few times I almost needed smelling salts. As soon as I saw the return addresses, I ripped open the letter. Of course, they were "thanks, but no thanks" but I held each letter in my hands just staring and unable to believe that what I was holding actually came from Hollywood and the studios.

I also knew the story behind every major star in Hollywood—who was working on what project, relationships and filmographies, including Hollywood history. By the time I started high school, I wanted to finish as quickly as possible so that I could pursue my career.

I graduated grammar school in June of 1976 and was so sorry to say goodbye to the Felician Sisters and Saint Mary's. On the bright side, the nation was celebrating its bicentennial and I learned that there would be auditions for the musical, *George M!*, based on the life of George M. Cohan. The auditions were being held at the local public grammar school. If I could audition and get a role in the play, I would be on my way.

I auditioned and was cast in the ensemble and met my first hand-ful of friends who were just like me. My talents did not go to waste. I had a tap solo to the song, "Give My Regards to Broadway." I was so happy and wanted nothing more than to keep acting, dancing, and singing. The best part was that my Mom came to see my show and loved every minute of it. I think she lived vicariously through me. My father missed the show due to his grueling schedule, including all the plays I would appear in the future. Kim and Grant came to see me in *George M!* and all were so proud of me.

In August, the director of *George M!* notified me that they were having auditions for *How to Succeed in Business Without Really Trying* at a small church one town over. I went to the audition and was cast in the chorus. *George M!* and *How to Succeed* were my first introductions to musical theater and slowly but surely, my theatrical skills began to take shape. With two plays under my belt, my dance lessons, my books, Chopin, Bach, Beethoven, The Beatles, and a God who loved me, I was ready for high school.

Sporting my Chorus Line sweatshirt on a Search weekend.

Chapter Eight

Coming into My Own

One of the benefits of having tough older brothers is the mark they leave behind—and high school was no exception. As sensitive, outgoing, religious, and theatrical as I was, I was not messed with or bullied in my four years of high-school—courtesy of my brother Jamie. When I was a freshman, Jamie was a senior and he was part of the black leather jacket crowd, or as they were referred to at the time, "greasers." Some of my new friends feared him because he and his friends were tough as nails and were always getting into trouble. The greasers in the school were put on standby by Jamie to keep an eye out for me when he was not around. They called me "Little LaGrec's" and treated me like royalty. It was like having my own personal mafia.

High school meant I was only four years away from going to

New York and eventually, Hollywood. I was focused and nothing was going to stop me. It was also a new experience to be in a public school. My parents believed that once we had a strong Christian foundation, we should learn about other people and cultures—to integrate into the world. Due to the loss of religious vocations and incoming lay teachers, tuitions were, and are, astronomically high in Catholic high schools, and my parents could not afford it. As religious as I was, Catholic high schools were, for the most part, unisex and I could not imagine myself in an all-boy high school. I also knew that the expectations in an all-boy high school would include athletics, and there was no way I was going. It would have been a recipe for disaster.

In my freshman year, being the survivor that I am, I began to navigate well. I found that I could make friends easily from the greasers and artists, to jocks, nerds, and theatrical types. I was fascinated by the variety of people and cultures that I was encountering and enjoyed engaging them.

I was riveted by my non-Christian friends and wanted to learn everything about their culture and holidays. I related especially well to my new Jewish friends and teachers. They were smart, well-informed, interested in books, always in good humor, and our conversations consistently surrounded things that were important to me, to us, and to the world. They never scoffed at ideas, but listened intently. It was so refreshing for me. After a time, I felt like a Jew trapped inside a gentile body!

One day, my beloved art teacher, Joel Krauser, watched me drift into space, as I often do.

"You're deep in thought there, Mr. LaGreca." Coming from a strict Catholic school, I jumped up and thought I was about to be scolded.

"Yes, Mr. Krauser, I am. I'm very sorry."

He looked at me with his smiling eyes and with great paternal compassion he stated, "Never apologize, Paul. Never stop thinking. Thinking is good. Thinking is a good thing." He kept nodding his head with a knowing grin and his eyes closed. Incredible!

These were the people I was so grateful to encounter. They enjoyed my talent and affirmed my artistic gifts, citing that the arts were just as important as anything else. How grateful I was, and still am, for the intelligence and encouragement that these wonderful people provided.

I was also grateful and content that my locker was in the hallway where art classes were held. Many of the friendships I developed in high school were with the art students and teachers. Passing each of my art teacher's classrooms on my way to my "left brain" oriented studies gave me a sense of peace knowing that this was home base. Greeting Mr. Wright, Mr. Krauser or Ms. Lages at the door of their classrooms each day, let me know that everything was all right in the world. I preferred the introverted, intense ambiance that the art classrooms provided even more than the performing arts. Mr. Wright taught me that oil painting to Mozart, Bach or Chopin assists in opening up creative channels—something I still practice. He encouraged me by telling me that when he showed his wife his students' art work (she was an artist as well), she was particularly impressed by mine.

Mr. Wright was extremely humorous without knowing it. I would often have to cough back laughing when he would say things like, "See the white canvas—here it is—you can see it—it's white, it's clear—there's nothing on it. But look what happens when we paint a red line and then paint a yellow line that passes through the red line. Now look, the red line and yellow line met in the middle and WE HAVE ORANGE! They met and something wonderful happened—two lines created form and color—that's ART! YES, THAT'S ART! DO YOU SEE IT?!" Delightful!

In addition to art, my love for books, literature, and the humanities was fired up by incredible teachers, who taught me to see the world through different lenses. I began to study Hemingway, Kurt Vonnegut, Jr., and J.D. Salinger, as well as to learn how to write. I was finding my place in academia.

I also remained actively involved in my church and was part of the youth group. Now that I was in high school, I became part of "Search" weekends. A Search weekend was a Friday, Saturday and Sunday retreat experience for young adults. A series of talks would be presented throughout the weekend by other young adults who had previously attended Search weekends. We shared about God, our lives, our suffering, fears, etc. That, combined with song and breaking bread together, created a very deep love and fellowship that we all experienced by the end of the weekend. These were very intense religious experiences and continued to lay the foundation of my spirituality.

At home during this same period, Charlie had been arrested again for stealing prescription pads from the office of a local doctor and writing false prescriptions. This arrest was major and the doctor, pressing charges, made sure he was put away for a few years. He was scheduled to come out of prison in the summer of 1978. Shortly after I turned 16 and a few weeks before his release, my father and I went to visit him. He made himself very clear.

"I love the streets. I love everything about it—hustling, and getting high."

My father and I looked at each other. It was evident that he had no intention of stopping and would pick up right where he left off. It made my stomach turn. Just the thought of Charlie returning home was enough to make me sick; I think that feeling was true for everyone in my family. We had a long break from the insanity, and it seemed that it was about to start all over again.

Before his release, I got on my knees in my bedroom and prayed from the heart, "Heavenly Father, I love my brother. When he is good, he is a joy to be around but when he is bad, he is a demon. I am not asking you . . . I am begging you for an end to this madness. I pray for his healing, but if this is not what you or Charlie want, then please take him sooner rather than later. I can no longer bear to see my parents suffer. We cannot go on like this anymore. Please Lord, I am begging you. Please."

Less than two weeks after returning home, Charlie placed a large fast food soda cup in the refrigerator. He had been clean since coming out of prison, although edgy. My sister Debbie, who was now thirteen years old, opened the refrigerator and picked up the cup to take a sip thinking it was a soda from Burger King. She spit it out and screamed and when my mother asked what was wrong, she said, "What is in this?" My mother put down her ironing to investigate and discovered it had been filled to the top with cough medicine and crushed pills. My mother went wild on my brother and bedlam returned to the house. He was no longer clean and sober; he was using—and worse yet, putting his siblings in danger. That night, once again, Charlie changed before our eyes. Our hiatus was over, and our hell resumed.

Two weeks later, on the morning of August 7, 1978, my father went to work as usual and took Charlie with him. Tommy was working with Dad in the store that day. It was a hot and sunny August day and I was organizing our food pantry for Mom. The phone rang and my mother answered it. She started to cry hysterically and screamed, "No, no, no . . ."

I stopped what I was doing and ran out of the food pantry. Her sobs were intense and heart-breaking. She hung up the phone and leaned against the wall crying into a dish towel.

"Charlie overdosed again; Daddy thinks he is going to die," she sobbed.

Later I learned that my father mercifully planned to ease my mother into Charlie's death. Charlie died before my father made that first phone call. He died in the back seat of my father's station wagon as my father panicked and tried to get him to the emergency room of the hospital. He was stuck in traffic and tried to resuscitate him in the back seat while he was driving.

By the time he arrived at the hospital, Charlie was gone. This was Charlie's seventh and last overdose. He was twenty-eight years old. His nightmare was over, and so was ours. He was at peace. And now, I hoped and prayed we would find peace. Whatever emotional damage was done to me or my siblings, having lived with a hardened addict for most of our lives, we would have to work out in the ensuing years.

I felt guilty because I had trouble crying for the loss of Charlie. I was numb and any emotion I demonstrated was because I hated to see my parents so devastated. At the funeral parlor, I stared at the four walls emotionless. I was exhausted from it all. Finally, one Saturday morning, shortly after Charlie died, I went to use the men's room at the butcher shop. Charlie sometimes walked with a cane, and there it was, leaning against the wall behind the toilet bowl. I saw the cane and held it, and for the first time I allowed the flood gates to open and remained crying until I could compose myself.

I know, in my heart of hearts, that if Charlie were standing in front of me as I write this, he would have more love than I could imagine in his eyes and heart. Despite it all, I loved my brother, and I know he loved me.

We buried Charlie at Saint Raymond's Cemetery in the Bronx where my parents had a plot, and slowly we tried to pick up the pieces. I learned later in life that the damage my siblings and I had to work through was extensive. We all did whatever was needed to survive the drama when Charlie was alive, but after his death many of us acted out in one way or another.

Adult children of alcoholics and addicts have a lot to work through, and I was no exception. One role that I assumed was that of the "savior." I was there for Mom and Dad through thick and thin. Everyone had to be happy in the roost in order for me to be happy—especially my mother. If she was sad, I was sad. My joy and peace were dependent upon my parents' state of mind. Now we know the name for this is co-dependent behavior and I was one of many poster children.

When school resumed after Charlie's death in September of 1978, I dived into my work and my grades began to improve. I learned that I could focus better and started earning consistent A's and B's. I also auditioned for our school musicals and had lead roles in *No, No, Nanette, Annie Get Your Gun,* and *Bye Bye Birdie.* I continued my ballet and jazz work with Grant, and I began to have a good reputation with the faculty as an outstanding entertainer. Faculty members, remembering my last performance, would pass me in the hall and break out in a smile. It was lovely to be recognized for my acting; it was validating, affirming, and made me happy. I finally found a place to be accepted—up there on the stage. It was becoming home and I loved everything about it.

Another interesting thing happened after Charlie went to the Other Side. I began to listen to and comfort friends who had been involved with drugs themselves. I was the "just say no" guy, the "turn to God" voice and the "please call me if you need me" friend. I was shocked when friends I loved and valued smoked pot and asked if I wanted to try smoking. I would get furious and refuse to get into any car where there were drugs. I had enough of drugs and I knew where they would lead. I was disgusted.

Our retreat mistress, Sister Lorrain Quinn, asked to speak to me alone one evening after one of our Search weekends. Sister Lorraine (or

Sister "L" as we kids liked to call her), is in my top ten list of the most compassionate people I have ever met. She was the epitome of kindness and had great spiritual depth. There was nothing she wouldn't do for any of us high-school kids. She was about 5'11", had short cropped hair, and no longer wore her religious habit.

"Tell me Paul, what is it that you want to do with your life as you prepare to graduate?"

"Oh Sister, my heart is so set on becoming an actor. I love it all. I want to go to Broadway, maybe Hollywood and . . ."

"Paul," she interrupted, "I appreciate you and I appreciate all you bring to the table. But there are a few things I would like to bring to your attention and a few things I would like to share with you." I feared for a second that I had done something wrong and I got a little nervous.

She continued, "I've watched you, as I've watched Barbara, Felicia and some of the others. Have you ever thought about becoming a priest? Or a religious brother?" I got nervous and felt a little cornered.

"Well Sister, when I was younger, I used to think about it, but not lately."

Gently and with great tenderness she said, "In you, I see a fine young man—a man of God. I see a man who will never be truly happy in this world. And I am not saying that because I am trying to manipulate you, I am saying that you have a very deep hunger for God. I have listened to you and watched you for many years. I personally do not think anything in this world will satisfy you. I am not telling you to do this; I am only making a suggestion and would like you to consider it. It is something to pray about. I would be remiss if I did not have this conversation with you. You have a hunger for God, and it will never go away. You will always want more."

I was dumbfounded by what Sister shared because I hadn't considered becoming a priest since Saint Mary's. Yes, I wanted the bliss of being alive and celebrating God in my life, but did I have a calling to become a priest?

I thanked Sister Lorraine for thinking of me and for talking with me. She touched me very deeply. The fact that she thought I had the qualities to become a priest was humbling. I was glad she could see me working for God. I wanted always to be a man of God and a loving and helpful person to all who came to me. But was God calling me to consecrate my life to Him as a priest or a religious? That would take time and I was not sure.

There may be confusion for a lay-person in understanding what it means to be a priest. There are two types of priests—secular priests and religious priests, so I will clarify. A secular priest is a diocesan priest. This priest does not participate in what we call the "Evangelical Counsels"—the vows of poverty, chastity and obedience—rather he makes promises of chastity and obedience only. He doesn't take a promise of poverty, but he is expected to live simply. The diocesan priest becomes a priest in a local diocese. So, for example, if a young man wanted to be a priest in New York City, then he would apply to the seminary for the Archdiocese of New York. Upon completion of his four years of philosophy and four years of Theology, he would be ordained as a diocesan priest for New York and receive his "faculties"—permission to perform the duties of a priest for that geographic area. He is obedient to the local bishop who can move him at any time to any of the churches or positions within that diocese. Since he does not take a promise of poverty, he can save his pennies from his small salary and one day retire into a small condo on a beach if that is his desire.

A "religious priest" is one who joins one of the many religious orders or congregations within the Church. The work is not limited to a diocese—it can take the priest anywhere in the world. In most cases, the order that he joins follows the charism (way of life) and teachings of a particular Saint. The Franciscans, for example, follow the example of Saint Francis of Assisi (work with the poor), the Dominicans – Saint Dominic (educators), The Benedictines – Saint Benedict (a life of silence, manual labor, and prayer), the Carthusians – Saint Bruno (hermits), etc. The religious priest takes vows, not promises, of poverty, chastity, and obedience, and in some cases a fourth vow, such as the vow of stability (to live a contemplative life in one particular monastery), as is the case with the Carthusians, for example. The Missionaries of Charity require a fourth vow of "whole-hearted and free service to the poorest of the poor." The religious priest is devoted to the work of his congregation and, for the most part, lives in community. As previously mentioned, since the Second Vatican Council, many of these orders have undergone major changes, such as some orders of religious nuns and priests no longer wearing the religious habit. If I were to consider becoming a priest, the first thing I would need to ask myself would be, "Is God calling me to become a religious or diocesan priest?"

I have always felt that there was a battle raging within me—one for the things of heaven and one for the things of the world—a dilemma that has haunted me my whole life. I knew how much it would please my father if I became a priest. He prayed his whole life that one of his children would be a gift from him to God, "blood of my blood, flesh of my flesh," as he often said. My mother, on the other hand, always had a dream of being a dancer, a Rockette to be specific, but her father did not permit her to dance. Grandpa Belfiore believed that dancing for a living was not a professional option. I had both of their dreams in my heart—and their dreams were my dreams.

I had to process what Sister Lorraine was asking me to consider. I knew that I had to explore the arts. Coincidentally, I had always felt that perhaps, over time, I would be led to some sort of religious life, but I didn't know when, where, or what it would look like. One thing that the sisters instilled in me was true—to never give up the fight to become a saint. Maybe not a Church recognized Saint with a capital "S" but someone who goes to heaven—a saint—with a small "s."

My first headhshot.

Chapter Nine

If They Could See Me Now

In the fall of 1979, my senior class went to see the play, "A Chorus Line" on Broadway. I can only describe it as one of the most magical and life-changing events of my life. I had seen other plays growing up, but this marked something very different.

The actors on stage stood in a row, shoulder to shoulder, faced the audience and told their individual stories through song and dance. *My God*, I thought, *this can't be happening*. I related to them on so many levels, particularly the struggle to fit in and find my place in the world. I was overcome by the fact that there were people like me. I watched my own story through the actors on stage. It was a cathartic experience—from feeling rejected to the struggle of how to express oneself in the midst of opposition.

I left the show with a sense of well-being and an inner voice that told me that liberation was on the way. I had only to be patient and allow my life to unfold as it will. I would have the chance to be fully myself. "A Chorus Line" comforted me like a mother wrapping her baby in a warm blanket. I came into the full realization that night that I hungered to self-express.

I was full of peace and contentment on the bus ride home, knowing that I would soon be pursuing my dream. While classmates on the bus passed around pot brownies, I sat with my head against the window on a natural high and I counted the days until graduation. I had a goal and I already had one foot in the door thanks to the tutelage of Grant and Kim at the Academy. The closer I got to high school graduation, however, the more I inwardly moaned about the prospect of going to college. My heart was not in it. My parents insisted that I apply for college and get my degree before embarking on a career in show business, but *I* insisted that it made no sense.

Pursuing show business in one's youth is critical. For the most part, it is a young man's game. Why sit in a classroom studying economics or algebra when I needed to train full-time in dance, voice, and developing my craft as an actor? I just couldn't picture it. I wanted to begin "pounding pavement" (as we say) in New York, surrounded by her inspiring streets, museums, ballet studios, jazz studios, and acting schools. I wanted a life in the arts—nothing else. I was on fire with the desire to live a non-conventional artist's life and just the thought of four years at a learning institution made me feel anxious and panicked. Thankfully, my parents gave in.

I graduated high school on June 14, 1980 and immediately began honing my various crafts in New York. The early '80-s' was a wonderful time to be in New York. The energy and excitement in the air was palpable for those pursuing careers in the performing arts. I enrolled at some of New York's most competitive schools with the help of Kim and Grant.

My routine consisted of jazz class on Monday, Wednesday and

Friday at Phil Black Dance Studio on 50th street and Broadway. I took ballet classes at Carnegie Hall Studios on Tuesday and Thursday afternoons and ballet with Grant on Monday, Wednesday, and Friday evening back in New Jersey. Tuesday morning was voice class with a private teacher, Bernese Elkin, and acting classes at the American Academy of Dramatic Arts on Tuesday evenings.

My routine could change on the flip of a dime if there was an audition; acting work always came first. Since I did not go to college, my parents funded my lessons with the money that would have been used for tuition. I reasoned, pursuing my acting career was less expensive than college tuition.

On Saturday mornings I woke at 6:00 AM to work at Dad's butcher shop. I had been working there every Saturday since my freshmen year in high school. My Dad hoped that all his sons, regardless of college, would have butcher training skills to fall back on. I had no desire to become a butcher like my brother Eddie who followed in Dad's footsteps. I took the requirement in stride and did what I needed to do to help Dad and make some money. Thank God for Eddie though—by partnering with Dad, he took a huge burden off the other boys. Tom was entering law school, John embarked on a sales career, and Jamie was studying to be an accountant.

This was also a time of complete cultural immersion and I loved every minute of it. When I said goodbye to the "suburban mold," I entered a world of colorful people. I had led a sheltered life in a safe haven, despite the Charlie issues, and now felt free, liberated, and ready to take on the world. I began to befriend people who I would have feared years earlier—gay people, neurotic intellectuals, avant-garde types, and hippy-types. Every day I would come home and share about the fantastic people I met. When I shared some of the antics I observed or people I met Mom would stop her ironing as she watched her favorite soap opera, "Days of Our Lives," look up at me with a grimace and say,

"And you're friends with these kooks? They sound crazy. Do me a favor, don't tell me any more." I learned I had to proceed cautiously in what I shared and also to heed Mom's advice to be careful with some of my new acquaintances. I was dipping my toes into the deep end of the waters.

After the movie *Fame* was released, initial auditions began in New York for the TV series and an open call was scheduled. It would be my very first audition in New York. I showed up for the audition on a casting line that extended from the Gaiety strip joint on West 46th street and Broadway down to 8th Avenue—about a quarter of a mile. It was mayhem, but I was having fun. Dancers showed up in tights, singers with sheet music, actors practicing monologues, and musicians with their instruments. We were all newcomers. I didn't even have a proper picture and resume yet, just a cheap 8 x 10 photo that my friend Marian took in her living room. I had a resume with my name, social security number (we did that back then), answering service number, and high-school play credits.

When I finally made it into the waiting room, it was crammed with hopefuls. Everyone was bonding, sharing, singing, and stretching on whatever free spot of the floor they could find. It was like a scene from the movie *Fame*. I was home.

I found a free spot on the floor at the back of the room and was leaning against a floor to ceiling pole that emitted heat. The room by itself embraced all those wonderful artists that were welcomed since it was built.

Two dancers sat next to me who, coincidentally, were students at "P.A."—The High School of Performing Arts—the school that *Fame* was based on. I also met a girl named Leslie who was actually in the film (she played the girl reenacting the scene from *The Towering Inferno*.) She was sweet and I was so happy to meet her. Here she was on line with us trying for a part on the series. I thought she was a shoo-in given her scene in the film was hysterical.

After approximately five hours, my number was finally called. I met with one of several associate casting directors at a small desk; I was not nervous at all. I was thrilled, all smiles and determined. There was a joy in me back then that came from the heart. It was charming and sweet, and casting people responded to it.

I had a quick interview and discovered that none of us had to audition at this point, although we were all prepared. The casting director asked me a few questions, made a few notes, and that was it. I was done.

I was not immediately cast in the series, but oddly, several years later when I moved to Hollywood, I would be cast in *Fame*—but with a different casting director. My first audition would pan out somewhere down the road.

The world of the dance was extraordinary to me; I was meeting young people from all over the world cramming into broken-down dance studios that smelled of sweat and years gone by. Pianos sounded from distant rooms at the end of long halls, and the dance rooms blasted jazz, classical, lyrical, and Latin music. The classes were jammed with diverse talent: African-Americans, Puerto Ricans, and Europeans. I was living my dream in my newfound paradise. I loved everything about my new life—the creativity, the people, the challenge, and that incessant desire to succeed.

The energy of those young talented people was exhilarating and exciting and challenged each new artist to get to the next level. The competition, however, was sometimes extreme, but it was all worth it. It was not uncommon to see dancers trying to trip each other in class. Even in my old Phil Black jazz class there was a tough cookie named Joyce. If you dared to challenge her, she would think nothing of nailing you in the shins in the middle of a routine, so you didn't want to mess with her. Thank God she liked me and found me to be funny.

My classes also contained kids who would one day be famous—

Sarah Jessica Parker, Erica Gimpel, Danielle Brisebois, Eddie Mekka—to name a few.

It was a wonderful time; a time of exploration, of living life with passion, of dance, of singing out after years of being pent up from Charlie, of learning the craft of acting, of being young and having the whole world ahead of me and discovering who I was. *Nothing was going to stop me*, I would think as I walked proudly to the Port Authority Bus Terminal at the end of a long day to return to New Jersey. I was so excited to wake up in the morning with the hope and expectation that each day held unlimited possibilities. I would work as hard as I could to achieve my goals. With my dance bag over my shoulder, I was coming into my own and it felt great.

I also wanted nothing more than to make my parents proud, especially after convincing them I could be successful even without going to college. Despite Charlie, I hoped to make up for the sadness and disappointment they may have felt with their oldest son.

At our local mall in New Jersey, Paramus Park, there was an ice-cream parlor called "Farrells." I would go there with my friends after an evening of shopping. One night, my friend Miriam thought it would be funny to tell our good looking waiter, Jack, that it was my birthday (it wasn't!). At Farrell's they had a tradition of bringing you an ice-cream sundae and singing "Happy Birthday" if it was your birthday. As soon as the words came out of Miriam's mouth, I panicked.

"Please Jack, don't bring me a birthday treat. She was only joking. Seriously, it's not my birthday. I mean it."

"Oh, so it's your birthday is it?" He laughed and thought it was hysterical.

"I don't want to be humiliated. Please! I'm serious!"

He walked away smiling, and under his breath he mischievously said, "Don't worry about it."

Five minutes later, three waiters surrounded my table and began their rendition of "Happy Birthday to you . . . Happy Birthday to you . . ." I wanted to die. I was so embarrassed that I half-slid under the table. Jack kept laughing and was happy to be in on the joke.

A few days later, as my early morning bus to New York passed through the town of Tenafly, a familiar face embarked—Jack! It turned out that he lived in Tenafly just a few towns away from Closter. I was so excited to see him.

"Jack!" He looked up and saw me in my seat.

"Hey, it's the happy birthday guy from the ice-cream parlor." We both laughed.

I introduced myself formally and he sat next to me. I learned that he was an actor and model as well. He was doing more modeling than acting which made complete sense. He had a big manager in New York and had been pursuing his career for a few years. Jack's demeanor changed with me when he discovered I was a pursuant actor.

"You have to be real careful about the roles you accept. Don't just take anything. It can ruin your career. You have to be willing to wait." I was willing to take whatever advice he had to offer.

In the ensuing months, we looked for each other's company on the bus and we shared from the heart on those trips to New York side by side in the rain, cold of winter, and heat of summer. We shared about everything from drug use, to God, to Hollywood.

I also found Jack to be extremely sensitive and vulnerable. There was a sad side to him. On a deeper level, I felt that it wasn't me he was warning to be careful in show business, but himself.

One day, after we arrived in the city, we headed down the escalators of the Port Authority Bus Terminal and he said, "Hey, can I speak to you for a second."

"Sure." I got nervous because he looked very serious. I wasn't sure what he was going to say.

I put on my best face; he pulled me to a corner and said, "I like talking to you. I think you are great, and I am so glad we met . . . but uh, I hope you don't think I'm gay and trying to hit on you." I was so bewildered but wanted to put him at ease. I offered him a big reassuring smile.

"Absolutely not, Jack. I never got that feeling for one second." And, I meant it.

"I hope so, because there are so many people in this business who try to take advantage of nice people and I just wanted to let you know that is not what is happening here. And please look out for yourself in this business. If you ever have any questions, I am here for you."

What a kind and special person, I thought. *This world is not meant for people like you, Jack. You're a good soul—too good.*

Jack left New York shortly after that to go to Hollywood. He was being screen tested for a new TV series called, *Voyagers* and ultimately, he got the part. Jack, as I knew him, soon became known by his full name, Jon-Erik Hexum. I was so proud of him. We lost contact when his career took off but reconnected later when I got to California.

In the dance studio dressing rooms, I always tried to remain focused. I moved in haste so that the other male dancers would not watch me get dressed. I was very self-conscious and, being raised to be extremely modest, it was important to be prudent. I was young, naïve and many of the dancers, men and women, were sexually aggressive. Jack's advice rang true for me.

After three months of intense study, I was doing great. I had a terrific dancer's body, long curly hair, and confidence in all three areas of study—acting, music, and dance. I knew at this point that striving to be a ballet dancer was moot. I hadn't grown past 5'7" and I started too late—most professional male dancers started as small boys. Ballet, however, conditioned and disciplined me. It laid the foundation for jazz dancing, which basically meant I would be able to audition for musical theater.

Each Thursday morning, "Backstage" and "Show Business" were released at the newsstands. These were the industry trade newspapers and contained all the auditions for the week. I would go home each Thursday night and scan each open job. If it was right for me, I would clip it out of the paper and tape it into my appointment book. Sometimes I had three auditions in a day. I was ecstatic when I booked my first job—a trial run of the play, *You're a Good Man, Charlie Brown*, which would briefly run at the Town Hall Theater for backers (Producers are sometimes given the task to raise a certain percentage of cash to fund a show. Backers are individuals who invest in a production through the producer). I was cast in the role of Linus. It would be my first paid acting job.

It was also the first time I experienced overt sexual harassment. After finishing our last rehearsal, my director asked me if I would be interested in going out to dinner with him. I had a sense that something else was underlying his request and kindly refused. He persisted in asking me out and I continually rejected his invitations. It became clear that he wanted something more from me and it made me very nervous. He would not let up.

One day after rehearsal, he cornered me backstage against a wall when no one was looking. He got close to my face and said: "I think you are gorgeous, and I'd love to give you your first sexual experience." I was petrified and began to shake.

"How do you know that I've had no sexual experiences? I think you've made a terrible mistake."

He laughed and seemed to enjoy the cat and mouse situation. It was turning him on but causing me to panic. I had to think of another tactic to get him off me.

"Look, I am pretty religious and at this point in my life I have no intentions of doing anything that I think would be displeasing to God." He laughed in my face and let me loose.

"Well, I'm Jewish, so all that stuff you just said doesn't mean any-thing to me. Just know that one of the reasons I hired you was because I like looking at your ass." With that he smirked and walked away saying, "The invitation is open." I was scared and wanted to go home. I knew these encounters were coming and I had to learn how to handle them without letting it affect me or my work. I had to grow a tough skin fast.

I also began to experience life in front of the camera and was thrilled when casting director, Sylvia Fay, hired me for my first "extra work" job. New York was a great place to do background work because it wasn't stigmatized there and allowed for a lot of on-camera experi-ence. Background work can sometimes be frowned upon in the indus-try. There is a misconception that the "serious" actor should never be seen doing extra work, or the actor could be pegged as a professional extra. This is because there was once a Screen Extras Guild (which began to dissipate in 1990). Up to that point an extra was an extra, and nothing more. Extra work is a terrific way to learn the ropes on a set, observe how films are shot and gain comfortability before a camera. Extra work also pays the rent. It can supplement an actor's income between jobs.

My dream of being on film sets was coming true. The first film I worked on was *So Fine* with Ryan O'Neal. I played a dancer in the Studio 54 scene. You can see my feet moving on the catwalk in the final cut, but it is one of those "do not blink" moments or you'd miss my feet. Fortunately, my friend Susan Wuchter, another Phil Black dancer, also booked the gig so we got to spend the day dancing at Studio 54. Susan was from Westwood, New Jersey and lived five min-utes from my house—we were two peas in a pod and when we were together, we did nothing but laugh.

On set, I was excited to work with my first stars—Italian actress Mariangela Melato, Richard Kiley, and even Farrah Fawcett, who was on set with her then beau, Ryan O'Neal. It was an amazing experience and beyond fun.

After *So Fine*, I worked on the Woody Allen film, *Broadway Danny Rose*. I had a "featured" extra role—meaning it required more than just walking by. The camera would be on me for something specific. I stood next to Woody Allen in a synagogue scene. He was praying and doing his comedy thing by exaggerating rocking back and forth as he was praying. I was standing to his right in prayer wearing a yarmulke and a prayer shawl.

The big issue on the set was, in fact, the extras. Woody had shipped in about 50 residents from a Jewish nursing home to fill the synagogue. They were the sweetest and most adorable people I had ever met. They were clearly instructed to remain silent, look forward, and to not look at the camera. Each time we began rolling, they would all turn around to watch Woody working—smiling—and so thrilled to be there. They would blurt out comments during takes such as, "Oh, look at him," "He's so funny," "Move over, I can't see him."

"CUT!" the Assistant Director shouted.

"Please ladies, no speaking. Stare straight ahead and don't turn around. Okay?"

We proceeded with the shot, and slowly, slowly, one by one, the heads turned and watched the scene. The only thing they were missing was the popcorn. We cut over and over again, and one lady tapped me on the shoulder to ask me ask me if I made my bar mitzvah yet. I was in love—but not Woody. Unfortunately, the scene was not in the final cut of the film.

I also had the privilege to work more intensely with the late Sidney Lumet on the film, *Daniel*. I was hand chosen to be a patient in a mental institution (I have wondered what distinctive quality jumped out at them to identify me!) In the scene, Amanda Plummer is confronting Timothy Hutton after her character tries to commit suicide. Watching

Sidney, Timothy, and Amanda work was incredible. I found Amanda to be mesmerizing. Her takes were never the same. Her acting was organic and fascinating. At one point when we cut, I smiled at her across the room, looking so alone and almost frightened. I waved to her in a very small, impish kind of way. She beamed at me and waved back the same way. She stayed in character and interacted with me as if we were really in the institution. It was a moment I cherish.

At the end of my first year of acting classes at the American Academy of Dramatic Arts, I was nineteen years old and had already landed a few acting jobs. I was happy and living the life I dreamed of for so many years. On our last day of class, we went to a pub not far from the school to celebrate. If you get a bunch of actors together at a table with alcohol, chances are good it will get loud, and everyone will vie to be the center of attention. One of our teachers showed up and sat at the head of the table.

Jason, as I will refer to him, was a great guy with quite an eye for talent. He was a successful actor himself, having appeared on Broadway and in feature films. As the night rolled on, we had our pitchers of beer and wine refilled and we got louder and louder. Everyone now wanted Jason's attention and eventually, we all became intoxicated.

Lena was an opera singer taking acting to support her singing. She was the loudest in the bunch, sat closest to Jason and tried to make others feel that whatever you said to Jason was being said to her too. She was, in plain English, obnoxious. I tolerated her in a spirit of patience, but I wanted her to shut up already!

My favorite of all my classmates was Wanda. She was a six foot tall black woman from New Jersey who dyed her very short hair blonde. There were times when we walked to the Port Authority Bus Terminal together after class. Black men would come up to her and say things like "Hey, Star." She'd say stuff like, "Hiya baby . . . you know that's right . . ." She was a riot.

Then there was Sadie Horowitz who changed her name to

"L'Oréal"—she thought she was a beauty model, but she looked and sounded like Shelly Winters in her final moments in *The Poseidon Adventure.*

I was introduced to the land of needy show business people and found it all very irritating. I learned that I did not like most actors. Everyone was always "on" and no one knew how to keep it real and when to turn it off. After spending one full year with these people, I was looking forward to class ending. I was preparing to study over the summer with private coach, Jon Christopher Bua, in his class of 10 students. It included actors from Broadway and New York soaps.

Seeing annoyance on my face at some of the overly dramatic antics at the table, I looked at Jason who smiled at me. He knew exactly what I was thinking. I stood up and announced that I was leaving and wished them all a good summer. I was drunk and had to get to the Port Authority Bus Terminal to catch the last bus back to New Jersey at 11:50 PM. Jason jumped up and said, "Wait, I'll go with you. We can grab a cab together." It sounded like a great plan, and together we hailed a taxi.

Jason asked me if it would be okay if we dropped him off first since he was on the way. I said of course, no problem. I wanted to be alone because I was intoxicated, and everything was spinning. I was not used to drinking and I felt a little nauseous. I just wanted to put my head down and fall asleep on the bus.

As we headed up Madison Avenue, Jason asked me if I liked cats. He said he had a big furry cat that was his best friend. He liked to put the cat on his lap and read—sometimes when he was naked. I looked at him and started to sense that he was a little creepy. *What an odd thing to share*, I thought. He proceeded to laugh and he was intoxicated as well. He then turned to look at me.

"You know, I am very comfortable with you. Unlike the others, you put me at ease."

"Thank you, Jason."

"I also appreciate your committed hard work in class. I think you have something special and will be successful."

"Oh, wow! Thank you, Jason. That means the world to me. And I just want to thank you for everything you've done for my acting."

He stopped smiling and leaned forward. He put his hand at the back of my head and began rubbing my scalp with his thumb. He then took my face in his hands, looked at me intently and very seriously said, "And you are also very beautiful. I love looking into those big brown eyes." Then he kissed me. A million thoughts were running through my mind and I thought I was dreaming. *Did he just kiss me on the lips? My teacher?*

I was stunned and couldn't move. I felt stupid, awkward, and I was afraid. I did not know how to respond to what had just happened. I had never been kissed by a man before. I was a virgin and felt like a complete and utter idiot. I did not know what to do, or how to respond, so I just looked at him as if I were made of stone. I tried not to swallow because I wanted to spit his saliva from my mouth.

We pulled up in front of his building and he whispered into my ear, "Would you like to come up?"

"What? You mean to your house? I mean apartment? Um, well, thank you for the kind invite but I can't—my parents would worry about me, and I have a bus to catch. Did you know it's the last bus to New Jersey?"

He chuckled and was amused by my childish response. "Come on, you can catch a bus in the morning."

"No, the Red and Tan bus line is very confusing on a Saturday morning. They have this weekend schedule and it can make anyone mashugana."

He laughed again, and quickly kissed me on the forehead as he stared me in the eye and rubbed his thumb across my cheek.

"Get home safe." He jumped out of the taxi and waved goodbye. I looked to the front seat to see if the driver had seen or heard what had just transpired. If he did, he did not make it obvious. I leaned my head against the back seat. I was shocked. *How could anyone be so brazen?* He also never seemed gay to me and always appeared masculine (another lesson learned).

I was nineteen years old and feeling very insecure. I wanted to go home as quickly as possible. I was stuck with the bizarre image of Jason sitting naked in a rocking chair with a furry cat on his lap. The experience sobered me. I opened the taxi door to spit as fast and furiously as I could before the driver pulled away. I wanted my mother and father.

With Patricia Place in *On Golden Pond*,
Mountain Playhouse, Jennerstown, Pennsylvania, 1981.

Chapter Ten

Sweet Smell of Success

September 1980 through June 1983 in New York delivered a nice string of success. Working on my acting, singing, and dancing and attending every audition I could began to yield great results. When I completed *You're a Good Man Charlie Brown*, one of former acting teachers at the American Academy of Dramatic Arts (not backseat Jason) informed me that some friends of his were casting a play for the Mountain Playhouse Theater in Jennerstown, Pennsylvania. They requested a student who was 18 or older who could still realistically play mid-teens. They were preparing *On Golden Pond* and could not find anyone to fill the Billy Ray, Jr. role. He thought of me instantly and on his recommendation alone, I was cast in the role—no audition was necessary.

I could not believe my luck. I was ecstatic. My hard work paid

off. I had one issue, however; I was not in the theater union, Actors'
Equity Association. I had to join immediately. On one hand, many
actors spend years honing their craft in non-union theater until they
can get into the union. Actors work on their craft so by the time they
enter the world of union theater (Broadway, Off-Broadway, etc.),
they are prepared. On the other hand, there is a camp of actors who
believe when an opportunity comes along, you must grab it. Well,
I did. My Dad shelled out the money for my Equity card and in
less than a week, I took a leave from acting class to join the cast in
Pennsylvania.

The woman playing my grandmother, Patricia Place, was driving to Jennerstown and she offered to pick me up and drive me to
Pennsylvania. It was a terrific drive with Patricia. She shared her tricks
on how she dodges the camera while doing extra work so she won't be
recognized. She was a very kind woman and we had an instant rapport.

I arrived in Jennerstown very excited. I was full of life and had
great energy although somewhat naïve and trusting. I also believed
that everyone in show business was happy; after all, we were doing
what we loved. We had jobs; we were on stage and getting paid for it.
My experience at the Mountain Playhouse would prove otherwise. For
the first time in my life, I saw the ugly side of show business. I experienced a little of it with *Charlie Brown*, but this was different.

The living arrangement was an old barn that was converted into
actors' housing. As charming as it may have been, it was toxic. Many
of actors knew in advance how I was cast, and I met cold opposition
to my presence. When I was initially introduced to some of the actors,
one of the first things they said to me was, "Oh, you're the one playing
the kid? You had to join Equity overnight to take the gig, right?"

"Yes, can you believe it?" Wrong response. I thought they would
have shared in my good fortune.

"Yea, well it took me 10 years of hard work to get where I am in the theater, so don't be so free to brag about it." *Brag about it?*

The jealousy was palpable. I instinctually knew that the world of show business was competitive and felt I had to tread lightly. I did not want to anger them, or my life would be made a living hell over the next four weeks.

I did not give up on my fellow actors, though. I remained gracious and kind to the point where most befriended me. I had to remember that it had nothing to do with me, per se. They had their own issues and hang-ups. I observed a lot after one week. Some of these frustrated thespians were full of gossip and venom. When one walked out of a room, they gossiped about that person. The only people I trusted and appreciated were Patricia, Charlie Crain, who played my grandfather and lovely, David Garwood. They were consistently kind to me from day one.

When religion came up, particularly my faith in the Church, most of the other actors would strike at me: "How could you believe all that garbage?" . . . "Are you serious?" . . . "You still subscribe to all that?" They tried to hammer me into silence and made it very clear that my faith represented enemy territory. Thus, I had to learn to monitor what I shared if I was to survive.

My parents were supposed to drive out to see the play, and deep down I didn't want them to come. I did not want them to witness what I was immersed in because it would only give them cause to worry and I did not want that—but man, was I happy when they arrived. All of a sudden, everyone was nice and reached out to my parents. I was glad; better that they faked it for my parents. They could return to their vicious behavior after my parents left. In the Bronx, we had a name for these type of people—phonies!

The play ended after a two week run (two weeks rehearsal, two weeks performance) and I was home with my Equity card in hand and an outstanding credit for my resume. I was slowly replacing the high school plays with important theater credits.

I was fortunate enough, at the same time, to sign with a child man-ager—Shirley Grant. Shirley was a tough Jewish momma—the first of my many Jewish mothers yet to come. She was aggressive, sometimes crass, brutally honest, but always nurturing and kind to all her "kids." If she believed in you, you were going to get out and audition. That was her reputation.

After signing with her, she immediately told me that I had to work on developing a more "street" persona—a tough Italian street kid.

"But Shirley, that is not who I am. I hate that stuff. Please don't send me out for tough guy roles. I see myself as the sensitive guy, like Timothy Hutton in *Ordinary People*, or something funny, but not the tough kid."

"Listen to me bubala, I know what I'm talking about. Now stand up mommy and let me take a look at you. You see, you have darker skin, dark hair—you're ethnic looking, hunny. You have to begin to market yourself for how you are going to sell. I'm telling you, for you it will be street. Street, street, street. Trust me." I sighed because it was not what I wanted to hear.

"Okay, if you say so, but can you at least still submit me for the other stuff too?"

"Of course, don't worry about that. Just leave it up to me and keep working on your acting, singing, and dancing—all three. I'm going to sell you as a triple threat." A triple threat is someone in show business who can do all three: act, sing, and dance.

I immediately began auditioning and after two auditions, I landed my first commercial. But once again, I had a dilemma. Shirley sub-mitted me for a Screen Actors Guild commercial, but I was still non-union. Auditioning is tricky with union stuff. You have to be union to get a union audition, but to get into the union, a producer had to offer you a union job—a big catch-22.

The audition was for a famous gum product. It was a voice-over spot. Well, I knocked it out of the ballpark, and they wanted me. They called Shirley the same afternoon and booked me. I could not believe it. My father and mother were thrilled, which made me even happier. It was my goal more than anything else to thrill them and make them proud.

Shirley called me, however, and said, "Listen hunny, you have to get over to SAG right away and join."

I went into a panic. "Wait, what? I thought this was a non-union job?"

"Hunny, sometimes you have to white lie. I told them you were union to get you in. I did it intentionally because they were in a tight spot and I knew you would nail it. But you have to join SAG today. You're delicious baby, delicious."

I did not have the $1,000 plus dollars to join! I just asked Dad for the $800.00 to join Actors Equity. By getting the role, I was "Taft-Hartley'd," which meant giving a SAG card offer to a non-union actor at a producer's request and joining the union. They could have just as easily dismissed me and moved on to the next actor, but they didn't. The benefit was not so much for the voice over, as much as it meant that I now had my SAG card, which was a big deal. Being a SAG member meant that Shirley could submit me for bigger things. I would be able to audition for television and feature films.

I humbled myself to Dad and asked him for the money. He wrote me a check without hesitation. We were not rich by any stretch of the imagination, but we were rich in love. Dad always found a way if it was for something good. The man was amazing. As he used to say, "God is watching over us. Don't ask me where the money comes from; it's just there when we need it. I don't understand it."

I joined SAG and successfully completed the voice-over. I was thrilled. Some people wait years to get their SAG card, but I was able to get mine in the first year of acting. It was a big break and a big credit. Even though I loved the theater, I enjoyed the world of television, and film much more. The actors in film seemed different than theater actors. In my experience, they felt less needy.

I next landed a small role on the soap opera, *Search for Tomorrow*. It was my first TV job with lots of exposure, and I was nervous as hell. The scene I was doing was with a young actress named Stacey Glick. In the scene, she was diagnosed with diabetes, and I played a young counselor in the hospital who was trying to encourage her to stay positive in spite of her new illness. I memorized my lines inside and out, even with one big speech. I was ready to go. One thing I learned early in my acting career: the more prepared you are as an actor, the more confidence you will bring to the set.

I enthusiastically reported to the studio bright and early. I was given a dressing room and proceeded to hair and makeup. While waiting to be called on set, I had the opportunity to chat with some of the other actors. Cindy Gibb, a regular on *Search for Tomorrow*, was memorizing re-written lines that were handed to her only minutes before her first scene. *What a drag*, I thought. *Poor thing! Imagine having to relearn your lines before shooting?!*

After I got dressed one of the Assistant Directors came into my dressing room and said, "Hey Paul, we have a few changes to your dialogue." *What?* I tried not to show it, but I went into a silent panic. He handed me the new scene and my heart sunk. I had a limited amount of time to learn a new monologue. Sentences were rearranged and some were entirely different. I tried to remain composed and immediately began to work on the new material without panicking. *I could do this!*

In the new speech, I had to recite a list of famous people who had diabetes so that this newly diagnosed child would be encouraged. It would have been easier if the names were movie stars, but no, they were sports figures—and I had no idea who any of them were. *Oy vey!* I had to get their names right and the only one I knew on the list was Bobby Orr.

I closed my eyes and begged God to come to my assistance—to infuse me with the ability to learn these lines. By the time my scene was called, I felt calmer and regained my excitement and peace, even though I was somewhat sketchy with the memorization. We rehearsed and staged the scene. After 15 minutes, I felt that I had been on the sound stage all my life. It was very natural for me. I loved every single minute of it. This was my new world. I adjusted to the crew and my surroundings like a pro.

As for my new big speech, I tried not to worry, but continued to beg God to be with me. I was good with lines, but not last minute. In the world of television and film, rewrites come with the territory. Over time and by exercising that muscle, the actor learns to develop the memorization skill, so that rewrites become less of a challenge. Being a novice, I could only do my best.

It was time for the first take, and I pulled it off. I was so happy. I got through it with no mistakes. I silently prayed that we would move to the next set up, but we didn't. The director called for another take since Cindy Gibb went up on a few lines. We did it again and this time it was my turn to mess up.

When we did the scene a second time, I said, ". . . and in hockey, there's Bobby Orr and in baseball there is Ron Santos and in . . ." "CUT!" The director said, "Paul, it's Ron Santo not Santos. Okay, let's do it again."

I maintained my composure and apologized. Cindy gave me a look that said, "Don't worry, it happens all the time." We did it a third time, and as I recited the names of the athletes I started to think, oh my God is it Santo or Santos? I forgot what he said! I began again, ". . . and in baseball, there is Ron Santos." I did it right this time . . . CUT was not called, and I was happy. Santos, it was! It was a "take" and they were moving on.

The director pulled me aside and pointedly said, "It's Ron Santo, not Santos, but don't worry about it. We'll use it."

I wanted to cry and felt so stupid. I was utterly confused . . . Santos, Santo, Santini . . . *what the hell?!* Couldn't John Travolta have diabetes, it would have been much easier. They were moving on; so much for my credibility. I shook everyone's hands, maintained a professional demeanor and left the studio.

A few minutes later as I sat on the A train to head home. I looked up from where I was sitting and saw Michael Corbett, a regular on the show. We had met earlier in the day. He held onto the rail strap above me and gave me a big smile.

"Hey! Good work today." I thanked him and felt warm inside. I took it as a little gift from God that I did not have to beat myself up. What I had done on the set was fine, or they wouldn't have moved on. I just needed to learn from my mistakes. When the episode finally aired, nothing was cut. If I should ever meet Ron freakin' Santo one day, I owe him an apology, but knowing me I will probably shake his hand and say, "Mr. Santos, it's wonderful to meet you."

In the summer of 1982, I booked an Equity TYA contract (Theater for Young Audiences) at the Penny Bridge Theater in Brooklyn Heights. I was signed to do two children's plays. I was a working actor going from one project to the next.

One evening, after rehearsal, a cast member asked me to take a walk with her to the Brooklyn Heights promenade where one could have a terrific view of the Statue of Liberty. Clare was very bohemian, and very much a hippy. She looked like she could have been one of Charles Manson's girls, long black hair, big eyes that looked like she was far away on a perpetual acid trip and, to top it off, she walked through the streets of New York barefoot. She was an excellent and uninhibited actress and I was intrigued by her. I loved her sense of freedom and being somewhat bohemian myself, we bonded and became very good friends. She was dating one of the band members from the sixties rock band, The Left Banke, who recorded one of my favorite songs—*Walk Away Renee.*

I was beginning a new stage in my life. My judgments of what was right and wrong were beginning to fall away. I became more comfortable with people who were gay, bi, straight, in open relationships and less apt to run away out of fear. People were doing drugs around me, proselytizing about politics, religion, art, and, over time, avant-garde behaviors felt comfortable. I was veering away from any conventional type of living. I fell into a mindset of *everyone do your own thing and just be beautiful. Express yourself. Be you.* Sounds corny, but the fact of the matter is I, too, had started to adopt a hipster style. I loved the inner freedom and appreciated not having to care or worry about every little thing. I enjoyed drinking, but I had never done drugs, although I became curious.

Clare and I arrived at the promenade, and she asked me if I smoked.

"No, I hate cigarettes. They gross me out."

"No, not cigarettes man, do you smoke weed?"

"Uh, sure yeah . . . I've smoked before." I lied.

"Cool. I have a joint. Wanna share it with me?"

"Okay." I wanted Clare's acceptance, and on that balmy August night, with an amazing moon, barefoot and overlooking the East River and a view of the Statue of Liberty, I prepared to get stoned for the first time. I decided that I wanted to experience this once and for all. I hoped that I wouldn't cough and give myself away.

I watched Clare and just did what she did. I inhaled and held in. I did not cough—so far, so good. Slowly, I blew it out. I repeated, and the second time I began to cough like I was choking.

"Are you telling me the truth, guy? Have you really smoked before?"

"Yes, yes," I replied as I turned purple. "Why would I lie to you?"

Clare smiled and knew I was full of it as we walked together to the A train. Clare was heading to Hell's Kitchen and I was heading to dirty

Jersey. I was waiting to get high, but I felt nothing. I was not stoned. I'd been told that you don't get high the first time, but now that I had done it, I wanted to know what it felt like to "get stoned." I promised myself that the next time it was offered, I would do it.

I smoked again with Clare and finally experienced getting high. I usually stared into space and went into my own world. One night I stayed at her apartment in Hells Kitchen. There was no bed—just a pile of clothes she made me sleep on. The apartment was infested with roaches. When I opened her refrigerator door, they were in everything. A year earlier, I would have been scandalized by the dirty apartment and roaches, but at this juncture in my life, I greeted the critters and honored them as living things. My time with Clare and other post-hippy era friends began to change me. I smoked whenever it was offered.

Meanwhile, at Jack's Meat Market, I decided to go vegetarian and protested against animal abuse and meat-eating while at work. In retrospect, I deserved some of the under the counter punches I received from my brothers. Commenting out loud about what customers were ordering was simply, rude. I would hold my breath when pulling hog maws (pig stomach), or chitterlings (pig intestines), from the respective barrels. I would shout out loud when the blood splattered when I sliced liver. I was being rebellious for the first time in my life and now that I had friends that supported me, I thought I didn't need my family, or even the Church. All I wanted was my art. I was beginning to "feel my oats," as the saying goes.

My brothers thought they were comedians and would stick ground beef in the pages of my book or throw chopped meat at my face from across the store. They also thought it was fun to take sharp butcher knives, make a semi-circle, and slowly walk towards me like the centurions of Rome. They would corner me against the wall and tell me to renounce my faith as a Christian, or I would die as the blade tips were pressed against my stomach. It's funny now, but back then it annoyed the hell out of me.

I began to answer my brothers back and stopped fearing their blows. It took many years to stop flinching when a few of them walked by, but over time, that got better too. Push me and I'll push you back. I may not win, but I will do it. Throw a piece of chopped meat at my face and you'll get it right back in yours. I was losing my fear and coming into my own. I was fighting back. This caused issues because I was no longer the silent peacemaker, and fights flared in the shop where normally there were none.

My father would get very upset, so I reeled in some of my comments and tried my best to refrain from reacting—for him. My father almost always took my side—except when I humiliated him by offending customers.

Because of my ballet training, classical music became my favorite. I had a hunger for all of it—Rachmaninoff, Bach, Beethoven, and Chopin. I would stretch night after night in my bedroom and blast Swan Lake, Vivaldi, and Mahler. Along with the music came literature. I craved books, and I could not get enough of the classics. Dickens, Dostoyevsky, Jane Austen and D.H. Lawrence became staples on my bookshelf. I always had a book with me wherever I went.

I was constantly changing the radio station in the butcher shop to classical music or I would pick up my book and start reading whenever I wanted. There was something gratifying in being rebellious. I suppose it felt like I was sticking it to them while being faithful to myself. My father would have to say, "Put the book down now . . . NOW." I would sigh, and put the book down with no sense of urgency. I intentionally moved like molasses because I knew it would annoy them, although I didn't want to upset my father.

I simultaneously harbored a huge resentment with the entire Italian-American experience. I did not relate to it. Masculine success for the average Italian-American male was measured by how tough you were. Some guys even dressed the part and tried to give the appearance that they were wise-guys or in the mafia. It was all so annoying and, quite frankly, ignorant.

I despised their manner of speech ("Yo, Paulie, you gettin' laid yet?"), found it all to be corny, and it embarrassed me. I also resented cigarette smoke (all my uncles smoked in those days), how they objectified women, and all the phony machismo garbage that goes with it.

My rejection and lack of participation with the boys and men in this circle became glaringly evident. I heard my father and uncles say on quite a number of occasions, "Where the hell did this one come from?" referring to me. It was repulsive and in a strange way, it all represented Charlie—the prototype of this kind of behavior. It was my turn, my chance to be me, and not give a damn what anyone else thought or said. I was older and no one was going to stop me. I did not have to participate. I also knew I wanted to bail out of Dodge and get as far away from the Italian-American experience as soon as I could.

After accumulating some beautiful credits in New York and having been screen tested for some major films, I wanted to leave for Los Angeles. I was hungry for success. The time had come. I would be twenty-one years old on June 23, 1983, and I hoped and prayed my parents would understand.

I came up with a good plan. I contacted my friend Lesley, the twin sister of my sister Gloria's fiancé, Jimmy. Lesley was a rebel, and after she graduated high school in 1974, she got into her VW bug and drove cross-country. She was married and lived in Santa Ana. She was very chill, and I knew she and her husband Steve would be more than happy to host me until I found a place in Los Angeles. I knew Les from childhood. She graduated with my brother John, and was also one of the summer's arts and crafts counselors at Closter's Memorial Field.

Lesley was thrilled that someone from home was coming out to

Cali and told me I could hang up my hat as long as I wanted. Her husband, Steve, was awesome and had no issue with my stay. I promised to leave as soon as I got on my feet. I would commute by bus from Santa Ana to Hollywood so there was no need to worry about transportation.

The big day came when I had to disclose my plan to Mom and Dad. I was so afraid of causing them pain. I took them to the Closter Diner and gently gave them my plan and asked for their permission and blessing. They were very concerned and looked worried but agreed to let me go.

Having lost a son a few years earlier, and now having a child leave the nest to be 3000 miles away in a city with a seedy reputation scared them. My mother knew how badly I wanted to act, and a part of her wanted me to go. My father, on the other hand, humbly supported me, but because Dad wore his heart on his sleeve, I knew he did not want me to leave. I also knew in my heart that nothing would have brought him more joy than if I chose to become a priest. He feared for me, and it was all over his face.

I begged them both not to worry and promised to take it three months at a time. At the end of each three month period, if things were not working out, I promised I would return home. This is the caveat that provided comfort for all of us—it removed the permanency. I had their blessing, and now it was a matter of making a plane reservation. On June 7, 1983, just weeks before my 21st birthday, I was heading to Hollywood. Finally! I was dizzy with excitement. It was Hollywood or bust!

My heart skipped a beat when I saw the Hollywood sign for the first time.

Chapter Eleven

—

Hooray for Hollywood

I should have known I was heading to "Lala-land." It was my first time on a plane. I wanted a window seat so I could look down on the country I was about to fly over. No luck—I was stuck on an aisle seat. Next to me was a short man with a thick Russian accent. He was bald and had a handlebar mustache. He had earphones on and as we flew, his hands were flexed in front of him with palms facing outward as he danced in his seat to whatever he was listening to. His shoulders rocked rhythmically as he made circular motions with his flexed palms. I couldn't take my eyes off the spectacle and tried, nonchalantly, to spy on him. I glanced over. Eye contact. Yikes! With a big smile on his face, he removed his earphones, turned to me and said, "I love flyyyy." He replaced the earphones and continued his little dance as he downed plane sized bottles of vodka. I was oscillating between annoyance and amusement and I couldn't wait to land.

Finally, after five hours of flying, I spotted palm trees outside the window as we began our descent into Los Angeles International Airport. I'd never seen one before and was thrilled. Lesley was picking me up on her lunch break since she worked at a bank in Long Beach, which is not too far from the airport. I counted the minutes until I was away from the vodka-induced dancer sitting next to me.

Santa Ana wasn't the most Hollywood-like place in the world, but heck, I was closer to my dream, and I was with Les and Steve. I could take a bus to Hollywood, the beach was 15 minutes from the house, the weather was beautiful, and the town had palm trees—who was complaining? Santa Ana is only an hour south of Los Angeles (with no traffic) by car. By bus and with traffic, it can take anywhere from two to three hours one-way. I learned this after my first two bus rides to Hollywood. It was worth it just to get a glimpse of the Hollywood sign as the bus pulled into L.A. each day. The first time I saw the Hollywood sign, I thought I would need smelling salts.

I began to apply my game plan. First, I would mail 75 to 100 pictures and resumes to agents with a brief note telling them I was new in town. Second, I would search for a part-time job that would support my acting. Third, I would keep my eyes open for a cheap car, since you had to have a car in Los Angeles. Unlike New York, Los Angeles has less public transportation options. Lastly, I would keep my options open for any affordable housing in Los Angeles. All systems were go!

In a moment of weakness and desperation to stop taking the bus, I purchased a car on impulse—a real junky jalopy. It was a '73 Ford Maverick. I never bought a car before and did it all on my own. When Lesley came home from work that evening, she asked about the car in the driveway. When I told her I bought it, Lesley became irate (and rightfully so) being the daughter of a mechanic.

"Paulie, you bought a piece of shit. You didn't do it the right way, dude. Why didn't you ask me for help? Did you at least take it for a test spin?"

"No."

"Did you have a mechanic look at it?"

"No."

"Did you get the price down? That thing is not worth $900 dollars."

"No. I just said thanks and handed him the cash."

"Shit, Paulie. They screwed you. They sold you a piece of shit lemon. Dammit."

Les knew a lot about cars and would know if it was a decent deal or not. She was disappointed and concerned, but I made the best of it.

When I registered the car, the letters on my new license plates read, GOI. I was a goy driving in GOI! When I drove through Beverly Hills, people would drive by me and laugh. Goyem, in Yiddish, are non-Jews and the term can sometimes be used derogatorily to refer to a gentile. GOI, was light blue, with scraped paint. The interior smelled like a car from the seventies. She served her purpose, and successfully got me back and forth to Hollywood from Santa Ana. Each time I drove it, however, I had to pray that I made it each way. Every now and then, the old girl would break down to catch her breath.

After the car debacle, I mailed my pictures and resumes. Unlike New York, it was difficult to work in Los Angeles without an agent. Within three days, I heard from 10 agents. It was very, very exciting. I schlepped to Los Angeles in GOI and began the interview process.

The feedback, overall, was good—not excellent—but good. My New York/New Jersey accent was going to be a problem and I had to do whatever I could to lessen it, if not get rid of it completely. The odd thing about my regional accent was that some heard it and others didn't.

On my 21st birthday, I went for my tenth interview. It was with Selected Artists Agency. Most of the agents I met wanted to sign me, but I wanted to wait to meet them all before making a final decision. I was set to meet with Flo Joseph, an agent who formerly worked for the Merritt Blake Agency (big) and left Merritt to start her own agency.

Flo wanted to meet over lunch, which was different, and I appreciated it very much. The restaurant she chose was "Tail of the Cock" which was walking distance from her office on Ventura Boulevard. Flo stood at about 5'2", was slightly plump, in her mid-50s to early 60s and had a face that radiated goodness. I had an instant connection with her and knew in my heart of hearts that she was the one for me. We had a lovely lunch as I shared my story, my dreams, and my aspirations. She smiled through the whole meeting as if she was listening to one of her children.

"Well Hun, gee, I think you have a lot going for you. You have some great New York credits, you're young, adorable, and can play younger which is real big here in town. I would love to have you come on board. I think there's a lot I can do for you."

"Well," I replied, "I couldn't have asked for a nicer birthday present."

"It's your birthday, Paul? Truly? Well, doggone!" She giggled. "See, it sure seems like this was meant to be, dunn'it?"

"It sure does, Flo. I don't have to think about this one. I would love to sign with you." I was later criticized by actor friends, because I was offered contracts with bigger agencies, but Flo was special, and I listened to my heart.

"Fantastic, kiddo. Well, here's what I want you to do babe. You bring me 50 pictures and resumes as soon as possible. I'm going to start submitting you right away." It was my two week mark in California, and I had an agent and a car. I was floating on air.

When I returned to Santa Ana that night, Les and Steve took me out with some of their friends to celebrate my 21st birthday. We went to a western barbeque place that had sawdust on the floor. I was now legal to drink and Lesley, who is known to enjoy her brews, ordered the first round. It was a night to celebrate and I felt that I was on top of the world. I was so happy.

In my third week, I also secured a job at an answering service, Actorfone, at 6565 Sunset Boulevard in Hollywood. Prior to cell phones, when someone such as an agent or a casting director needed to reach an actor right away, the answering service was the solution. If actors were not home to answer a call, an agent would call the service and leave a message. Actors would check in for messages frequently throughout the day. Some of our clients who were not yet household names included George Clooney and Demi Moore.

I also rented my first apartment with a new friend, Beverly. Bev had smiling eyes and all we did was laugh when we were together. When she proposed looking for an apartment together, I couldn't think of a better roomie. Since the commute from Santa Ana to Los Angeles every day was getting impossible to deal with, I needed to settle into Los Angeles once and for all. Bev and I found a perfect two bedroom apartment on North Verdugo Road in Glendale.

In September of 1983, after being in L.A. for three months, and having met quite a few casting directors, I landed my first acting job. Flo sent me to meet DeeDee Bradley, a casting director who worked at Bob Morones Casting. DeeDee had eyes that sparkled. I had an instant crush on her and thought she was beautiful—inside and out. She was very sweet and kind. I was reading for a mini-series that was to air on the Playboy channel called *Erotic Images*. The show was not pornographic, but it did contain some risqué scenes where there might be brief nudity and simulated sex. The star of the series was Britt Ekland, and I was reading for a supporting role as her son's best friend.

After reading for DeeDee, and then Bob Morones, Flo and I received a phone call a few days later telling me that I was cast. It was very simple back then. You went in, you read, and sometimes casting directors made the decision. I was very excited, but even though they wanted to cast me, Flo proceeded to share her thoughts.

"Hey Hunny, now listen, you gotta understand something, it's good to get out there and meet people and audition as much as you can, but I don't want us taking this job. You met DeeDee and Bob and that's great, but this is a role we want to pass up."

"Why, Flo? I don't understand it. If you sent me up for it, then how bad could it be?"

"Now listen kid, I only just got my hands on the script. There is a lot of stuff that is not desirable, and I don't want any of my clients appearing in anything that could mar a reputation that hasn't been developed yet. If you got this role, you'll get other things. It's only a matter of time. And besides, Paul, you and I have spoken about God. Is this really the direction you think He wants you to move in?"

"But Flo, Britt Ekland is in it, how bad could it be?"

"I don't care who is in it. I'm telling you, I read the script and I think we should pass. Listen, the decision is yours, hun. I'm not gonna tell you what to do, you're a big boy, but I want you to pray and think about it . . . for me and for God. Okay, can we do that?"

"Okay."

I think I waited all of two hours before I called her back and said, *"I'm in!"* She was disappointed, I could tell. Deep in my heart, I knew she was right, but my stubbornness prevailed. I wanted to be on a set and to act. An opportunity came along and I wanted it. The only thing that made me nervous was how to properly explain the show to my parents.

Flo had my best interests; there is no doubt. She may have also tried to sabotage the job because when I got to the set the first day and met a production assistant, he said to me, "Wow that agent of yours, she really likes to argue. She was fighting us regarding your contract."

"She's just looking out for me. Don't think badly of her; she's a wonderful person."

"I guess so," he shot back. I found out later that the production assistant, Radames, was on the old *Kung Fu* TV series when he was younger. He played Grasshopper. It was such an exciting time for me—you never knew who you were going to meet.

When I arrived on set, I was taken to a small trailer that would be my personal space for the next few days. Radames had the responsibility of getting the actors from their trailers to set, so I was psyched when he knocked and said those infamous words, "We're ready for you." The last time I had heard that, my lines were changed—Ron Friggin' Santos or Santo or whatever!

I met Danny, the actor who was playing my best friend. He was a good looking blonde haired guy, about my age, and had a snotty, preppy, Beverly Hills rich kid look—great casting. He was dressed for the part, since Britt Ekland played a successful author who lived in a rich town. The other star of the show was Edd Byrnes, who played Kookie in the television series, *77 Sunset Strip*. He was tall, handsome, and could easily play the rich Beverly Hills exec type.

When I arrived to set, Danny told me that in the next soundstage they were shooting a porno. I was so shocked and said, "What?!" My stomach dropped.

"Just stay with me today, dude, you'll see everything. I got my finger on the pulse dude . . . my finger on the pulse. Yesterday, I saw Marilyn Chambers getting her legs waxed next door. They didn't know I was there, but I saw everything."

"Who is Marilyn Chambers?"

"Dude, where have you been? She's a big name in porn. She's supposed to be this hot babe, but I think she's a real dog, man."

The frankness of such a shocking conversation began to scandalize me. Flo was right. I got scared and I wanted to leave. How could I tell Flo that I didn't want to be here? He was so nonchalant about pornography, and so mean about Marilyn Chambers. Even though I was now open to new experiences and did not live such an insular life, I was still a virgin.

In times like these, something very spiritual happens to me. A spiritual well opens up in the deepest recesses of my heart and takes me over. It is the only way I know how to describe it. It is a feeling of truth, of love, of something not of this world, and I am filled with a type of temporary wisdom. A veil of some sort lifts, and I can see things for what they are. I wake up from my selfish self and I can see things supernaturally. Perhaps this is a grace from God, I do not know. The best way to describe it is that I fill up with wisdom.

Something was wrong with the whole show—it was not just Danny—it was the show, the stars, Hollywood, and the nauseating self-seeking. Now that I occasionally smoked pot and relaxed some of my stricter morals, taking this role added to my ever-growing list of "giving in," and I clearly saw it for what it was. I knew I had to bite the bullet, close my eyes and stay close to God. It was too late to turn away.

Danny was starting to irritate me, and I felt he was showing off. I hung out with him because I had no one to speak with, and because I played his best friend and was trying to develop a rapport.

"I think there might be some DeLorean floating around here."

"What's DeLorean? You mean the car dealer that is in trouble? You saw him on the set too?"

"No dude, where are you from? DeLorean—it's the buzz word for powder, dude." *Oh*, I thought, *cocaine. Got it!*

As we continued our conversation, Britt Ekland came on set in a short nylon robe. She was beautiful and seemed very sweet. I smiled at her and she returned a half smile. She seemed to be the type of person that would be fun to share a glass of wine with. After a few minutes, she summoned our director, Declan Langan.

"Where is the mirror? I need to check my hair before the shot. I don't understand why one is not here when I have asked before."

"Oh boy," I said to Danny, "she seems angry."

He looked at me with a face of disgust. "Yea, she's all right, but you know she does that star thing to let you know she's the star."

Before she shot her bedroom scene with Edd Byrnes, she looked at Danny and me—two twenty-somethings staring on the side-lines. She said loud enough so that we could hear, "What are they doing on the set? I want them off . . . everybody off. I want a closed set for this."

Declan sauntered over to us and said in his Irish brogue, "Sorry fellas, gotta ask ya to exit the set. Thank you."

"Screw her, who the hell does she think she is?" Danny whispered to me.

I understood, though. Perhaps if I was the star, I would feel the same way. So, out of the sound stage we went.

Over the course of the next few days, I shot my scenes—one with Britt and Edd, where I say "hello" to Britt from her bedroom door as she and Edd are both lying in bed and the other when I look down her robe in the living room while she is scrambling on the floor through a garbage pail.

I liked Britt. She worked very hard and was a pleasant person to work with. She and I enjoyed each other's company, and I could tell she wanted to laugh when we did our scenes. I think she got a kick out of the "young boy with a crush" stuff that our scenes encompassed. I respected both Britt and Edd Byrnes. It was a pleasure working with them.

The second thing I learned is to listen to my agent. Flo knew best. It was embarrassing for me to get a call from my older brother Eddie and his wife Vickie who saw me on a "dirty show" on Playboy and ask, "Is that you?" Ugh! I also regret, as someone who has always had a deep love for Christ that I allowed myself to take his name in such a profound way in one of my lines—just for money and fame. We live and we learn.

I finished the project and received payment through Flo, but I did feel like a hypocrite. How could I be so upset and guilty about the show and my lines when I was smoking grass, regularly drinking with friends, and had even tried cocaine? It didn't follow. But something was alive in me that was not letting me go. It was gnawing—a hunger for something deep—and I never knew when the "well" would open again.

I shared about what I was experiencing spiritually with my new set of friends. They were convinced that "Catholic programming" marred my sense of reality. They suggested that rather than holding on to any more guilt, I needed to free myself by going down roads that I would not have normally explored and allow myself to be open to everything without judgment. I thought, perhaps they were right. My new goal was to try and not to be so hung up about everything. But deep down, no matter how cool I tried to be, I refused to let go of God.

Determined, focused, and living my dream.

Chapter Twelve

A Seed of Kindness
and the Birth of Tino

The next month, I was sent to Universal Studios to audition for a non-speaking role in a new CBS pilot called, *Airwolf*. In the scene, a young Arab boy is being used as entertainment. As the boy stands in a swimming pool, a sheik shoots at him with the goal of shooting coins out of the boy's raised hand. A bullet then grazes the boy's finger at which point he freaks out. The role was for "featured" billing credit, and the pay was great for only one day's work.

When I arrived at Donna Dockstader's office, she told me to stand against the wall where she was just going to pretend to shoot me. She wanted to see my reaction as I was being shot. I have always found the game of make believe to be simple. It resonates with me. I was confident that the moment was real and was proud of the audition. She dismissed me, looked down, and thanked me with a half-smile; which could mean, "He stinks" or "He nailed it."

As I was exiting from the casting bungalow, I noticed that the receptionist had her head down and appeared to be sad. She looked like she was crying. I had the impression of a lonely person. She had a cat calendar and cat photos around her.

"Thank you so much for everything," I said on the way out. "By the way, are you all right?" I asked smiling. I stopped and stood over the reception desk. No one else was in the waiting area.

"Well, things could be better I suppose. I'm a little upset today because my oldest kitty is ill, and we're not sure if he is going to make it."

"Oh, boy! I'm real sorry to hear that. Well, I'll be sure to say a prayer for you and your kitty. Try not to worry." She looked at me with tear-filled eyes and seemed appreciative for that small moment.

"How did your audition go?"

"As well as can be expected, I guess. You just go in there and do your best."

"Well good luck! I hope you get it."

As I was speaking with her, I heard a voice behind me say, "Excuse me." A handsome African-American man came towards the reception desk. He had a big broad smile, and I felt he was going to ask me to move along so that the receptionist could return to work.

"Hey there, my name is Mel Johnson. I am one of the casting directors here at Universal Television. I assume you were here to audition?"

"Hi Mel, nice to meet you. Yes, I was here for *Airwolf*. I met with Donna Dockstader."

"Ah," he replied, "great. Well, I gotta tell you, we're in a little bit of a rut. We're about to shoot an episode of *Knight Rider* on Monday and the actor who was supposed to guest star on the show has the flu. When I saw you, I was a little taken aback because you resemble him and may be very right for the role. Did your agent submit you for this role?"

"No, I don't think so. It was never mentioned."

"Would you be interested in reading?" *My heart skipped a beat. A guest star spot!*

"Sure! I would be honored." I grinned from ear to ear.

A guest-starring role on a major prime time series is huge. Once an actor has a guest-star credit on their resume, he or she can leverage for big roles, including recurring roles or series regular.

"Who is your agent?"

"Flo Joseph at Selected Artists."

"Ah! Flo—wonderful lady, good friend of mine. I will give her a call. I need to introduce you to April Webster first, so if you wouldn't mind, can you wait right here for a second?"

"Sure!"

I looked at the receptionist wide-eyed, and she winked at me and nodded her head with a pleased grin. I felt so happy and had a sense of well-being both for lending an ear to the receptionist and for the warm-natured kindness that Mel Johnson demonstrated.

"Good luck, Paul, you deserve it. You'll get this, you'll see."

Mel came back to the lobby after a few minutes and gave me thumbs up and escorted to me to April Webster's office. April smiled at me very warmly. She stood up to shake my hand. She was also very pregnant. I was instantly endeared to her. Unlike other casting directors I'd met, both she and Mel exuded kindness. I instantly felt safe with April. She asked me for my resume, and saw that I had only done featured roles, but was pleased that I was getting seen and being called back for major productions.

April had to be careful, because the last thing any casting person wants to do is place their reputation on the line by hiring an actor who has no idea what they are doing. A guest-star is required to "carry the show." That means they have the skill, craft, and professionalism to stay focused on their character scene after scene. They cannot be thrown off their game if there are set glitches or odd camera angles. In other words, they must have experience. The investment by the studios in a new actor who cannot handle the work or the role could cost a production a lot of money. The *Knight Rider* role was not a silent bit role or a few lines, as in *Erotic Images*. This was big time and I would be in a large chunk of the episode.

She placed her hands behind her head. In her eyes I read that she had found her kid—a fluky " being in the right place at the right time" replacement hire that showed up out of the blue. On the flip side of the coin, I had to come through for her. There is an old expression in show business, "success happens when chance meets talent." Luck fell in both of our laps. If I pulled through this audition with my talent and gave her the confidence she needed to see, it would be a win-win. She handed me a few pages of the script and said, "Let's do this cold, okay?" She then looked at me to see how I would respond to that suggestion. I was glad because I was skilled at cold readings from acting classes.

The character was a rambunctious gypsy boy named Tino, whose father had just died. He had run away from his sister and was alone on the streets, living in an abandoned shack. He accidentally witnesses a bank robbery and becomes a key witness of the crime. As he witnessed the crime, he was able to lift a dangling gold watch from the pocket of one of the thieves. The thieves notice and start to run after Tino. Michael Knight (David Hasselhoff) is driving down the road in KITT when the kid accidentally gets hit by the car. Voila! Michael Knight to the rescue and the pursuit is on.

I said a silent prayer before we started and tried to hide that I was nervous. We began. The words were meant for me. They poured off my tongue with ease. I related to Tino and how he spoke. Tino was very "New York" in nature. I knew who Tino was. He was a wise-ass and a conniver. He was also lost and trying to find his way. Tino was a little bit of Charlie and a lot of me—running, hiding, escaping. Tino was a boy behind the china cabinet. He resonated with me with the first sentence.

April put down the script and stared at me. She took a deep breath and said, "Okay. You did great. Do you think you can handle this? Be honest with me. If you say no, I will remember you for other things."

"I have no doubt in myself, April. I can do this and I'm not just saying that."

"Well, it's late and we shoot on location Monday morning. Do you think you can have the lines memorized by then?"

"Yes, I can start right away and memorize all weekend. I can do this."

"All right. Okay. I'm going to call Flo and fill her in. I know it's last minute, but can you come back to the main gate of the studio tonight to meet the show's producer, Glen Larson? The director will also be there. His name is Bruce Kessler."

When April said that, I knew I had done something right. I was beaming on the inside and tried to contain my composure. "You bet," I said.

She handed me a copy of the script and told me to go home and read it. Flo would be provided with the details of the callback. I couldn't stop thanking her and refrained from hugging her. I floated out of the Universal casting bungalows. I couldn't help to think that if I did not stop to ask the receptionist why she looked sad, I would have never had this opportunity. Mel would have walked down the hall, business as usual, and I wouldn't have been there. It was one small act of kindness. The stars were aligned. Synchronicity!

When I came back, the guard at Universal's main gates let me through; the lot was empty. It was autumn, and the air was balmy with a slight scent of eucalyptus: a smell I love in Los Angeles. I felt surrounded by love. All was right in the world. I got out of GOI and stood alone in the lot. I looked around and took in the moment. Universal Studios! Universal! Here I was. I reflected on all those years as a child when I wrote letters to this same address—the fantasizing, the imagining, and the excitement of believing that one day it will happen. Had I manifested this moment and experience in my desire to be here? I was filled with gratitude and indescribable joy. I breathed in the moment and savored the experience through my whole being. It was me, alone in the heart of Universal Studios on a lovely Friday night and it wasn't a dream.

When I arrived at Glen Larson's office, the nerves kicked in. I was slightly inhibited. I noticed that there were two other young actors there, so I was not a shoo-in, as I suspected. I learned later that Glen always wanted options just to be on the safe side, so April had to call in a few other actors just in case. I knew that April was rooting for me.

April greeted me at the door; I was the last of the three actors. When it was my turn, she escorted me in and gave me a reassuring pat on the back. She was lovely and an angel. The room smelled of cigar smoke with the jiggling of cocktail glasses. Glen shook my hand and looked very dapper and in charge—a polished, no-nonsense, Hollywood executive. It was something out of a movie. I also shook hands with Bruce—man to man—to exhibit confidence and star presence. I sat in a chair facing the couch and lounge chair where Glen and Bruce sat.

As I started the first scene with April, I noticed out of the side of my eye that Glen chuckled here and there. He was either laughing at me or liked the New York, tough kid vibe that I was bringing to the role.

When I finished, Bruce made eye contact with April and gave a quick nod before giving me instructions.

"Okay kid, good job, very good job. I'm just going to give you a slight adjustment." An adjustment at auditions is when you are instructed to redo the scene a different way or to add or remove something in your acting choices. It can also be a test to see if an actor can take direction—some actors cannot. I was a big gamble, and they had to make sure.

"Good approach. I like the tough thing, but try to pull back on being too punky. Just let the punk reveal himself through the words without forcing it. Got it? Can you do that?"

"Sure. Let's do it," I said.

"Do you need a few minutes?"

"Nope, I know exactly what you mean."

"Okay, good."

I knew that Tino and I were one, so all I had to do was say the words, because when you think about it, Tino was a vibrant color living in my crayon box. He had only to be summoned forward.

April and I read the scene again. When I was done, Bruce looked at Glen and they smiled at each other. Glen chewed into his cigar with a shit eating grin. I could tell he liked Tino. They both stood and shook my hand and thanked me for coming in so late. As nice as they were, was as hard ass as they were. Bruce said, "This is a big spot, kid. If we hire you, do you think you can handle it?"

"I sure do, Bruce. I am not worried."

Glen chimed in, "You're gonna do all right in this town, kid. Thanks for coming in."

"Thanks, Glen. And as Tino would say, 'Piece of cake . . . I'm outta here.'" They both laughed, and I left. On the way out, April said she'd call Flo that night with the decision and to be on standby. It felt meant to be. The whole thing was too much of a coincidence.

As I opened my apartment door in Glendale, I heard the phone ringing from my bedroom. My hands were shaking, and I ran to the bedroom to answer it. I lifted the receiver.

"Hello?"

"Hey Hun, it's Flo. Guess what, babe? They want you! April said you nailed it." She continued speaking, but my head was spinning. I didn't hear anything else she said. I booked a guest-starring role on *Knight Rider*. I was so happy that I got choked up. It was my first big acting gig and I thanked God on my knees. I couldn't wait to call my parents to tell them the good news. I wanted to make them proud.

That weekend, I began memorizing my lines and working on my character. Because of my *Search for Tomorrow* scare with line changes, I was mentally prepared for re-writes, so there was minimal fear. We were shooting the first scenes in West Covina on Monday morning, and my call time was 6:00 AM. That meant I had to be up at 4:30 AM, take a half an hour to get ready and be out the door by 5:00 AM to be in West Covina with time to kill. I also prayed that GOI would behave and get me there on time.

The benefit of working at Actorfone was that it employed actors, so if you were cast in something, you would be able to take the acting work without losing your position. The other actors would fill in for you. It was ideal. My boss, Ruthie, was thrilled for me and told me to "knock em' dead and break-a-leg, little boy."

Steve had a sister, Kay, who lived directly across the street from Universal Studios. We became very close while I lived with Steve and Les. Kay and I spent a lot of time together at the beach, eating out, and sharing good times. Her roommate, Joy, became a friend as well. Since a large chunk of my episode was shooting at Universal, Kay and Joy were nice enough to allow me to stay with them at their house in Universal City rather than leave for the set each day from Glendale. The ladies were also a security blanket in the event anything happened. Each evening, Kay and Joy had dinner on the table and tutored me with my lines. I felt safe and secure staying with them. They were big sisters turned best friends.

When I arrived at the set on day one, I was escorted to my trailer to settle in. I was nervous, and it was hot! The temperature was going up to the high 90s. I didn't have an appetite for food, but I did decide to have an apple and a cup of coffee to wake me up. The episode, named "Silent Knight," was a Christmas episode, so the wardrobe department dressed me in winter clothing. My outfit included jeans, a t-shirt, and a corduroy jacket. Wearing corduroy in ninety-degree heat was a nightmare, but without grumbling, I surrendered to what was being asked.

I was summoned to the set by the first Assistant Director and we blocked the first scene. In it, I tell the three thugs who capture me, played by Stephen Liska, Robert Miranda, and David Provol, that they should let me out of the car because I am going to be sick. My character, Tino, was faking it, of course. I wanted the thugs to pull over so that I could escape the abduction. I beg them from the back seat of the car, "Please! I'm warning you; I am going to be sick."

We began the very first take of the episode. Well, I am not sure if it was method acting training or the psychology of repeating the same thing over and over again, but with the heat, acidity of the apple, coffee, lack of sleep, nerves, or a combination of all the above, suddenly, in the middle of the third take, the lines became real. I started to feel nauseous and I needed to vomit. They say if a creative lives in the right side of the brain, that hemisphere has trouble determining reality from make believe. I have no doubt that I convinced myself that I was going to puke.

I began to panic as we repeated the scene over and over again and thought *what am I going to do?* Sometimes between takes there is small talk between the actors, but I did not have the strength to talk with them. Stephen asked me if I was all right.

"Yeah, yeah I'm fine," I said.

Take four . . . here we go again.

Tino: Pull over, I'm gonna be sick.

Casey: Shut up, kid.

I started to moan in the back seat (not in the script). Panic . . . *don't panic . . . don't vomit. Dear God, please help me.*

Finally, I couldn't hold it in any longer. I could no longer say those words. It was too real. I surrendered. I gave in. I begged them to pull the car over and then I shouted, "PULL OVER - I mean it" (not in the script). Bruce shouted, "CUT" and with that I opened the window of the car, stuck my head out and vomited. *Oy vey iz mir!*

My first day, my first hour on a prime time set, my moment to impress and I was sick to my stomach. If you watch the scene today, what you will see is real. No acting.

I opened the car door, and ran into the bushes to continue vomiting on all fours. Bruce Kessler came over to help me, while the crew just stared at me. Some of the crew were tough and hard as nails and were not nice about it. Some laughed at me, and others were pissed that they had to clean it up. One nasty crew member snidely said, "There goes your spin off-series, Tino." *Asshole.*

When I finished, I stood up. Bruce put his hand on my back.

"Listen kid, there is a flu going around. That's how we lost our first guy. Do you think you have it? Because if you do, we can replace you while it's still early."

"No way, no way, no way," I adamantly said. "I'll be fine, really! It was those damn lines. How many times can I say I'm gonna puke, Bruce, and not puke? I just need to put my head down for half an hour. I need to settle after that scene. I am so sorry." I don't think Bruce believed me.

"Okay kid, okay. You go rest, and we'll shoot around you. Let's see if it passes . . . and when you come back, no method acting—this is TV!"

I tried to smile, "Thank you, Bruce."

I made my way to my trailer, mortified and humiliated beyond words. Moments later there was a knock at my door. It was David Hasselhoff.

"Hey, Tino, I'm David, welcome to my set."

"Hi David, it's good to meet you. I am so sorry. I got sick. I think it was the scene."

"I heard you had an upset stomach. Don't worry about it, it happens to me too, pal. You just rest up and we'll work around you until you are well. Don't listen to anyone else. In the meantime, these little suckers help me when I am in the same situation." He handed me two pink Pepto Bismol lozenges. I thanked him, took them, and fell into a deep sleep.

I woke from a loud knock on my trailer door. It was the first AD again. He was checking in to make sure I wasn't dead and if I felt well enough to continue. I stopped shaking, but still looked pale. There was nothing more in my system to throw up, so I was okay to return to set. There was no way I was getting replaced on this job. I asked for 10 minutes to brush my teeth and freshen up, and then headed back to set. They were going to use the first shots we already finished, so there was no need to worry about repeating my reenactment from *The Exorcist*. Why should they? It was as close to reality as they were going to get. As a dancer, I know my body very well. I knew what I needed physically and felt well enough to get the job done. I also prayed to God to see me through the day.

The next shot was simple. I was to sit in the driver's seat of KITT after KITT had taken me for a joy ride. David comes up to my car window and says something like, "You satisfied now?" I respond, "Yea, yea, it was nothing." I get back into the passenger seat so he could take over. I still felt weak, but well enough to continue. David knew though. He kept saying to me between takes, "just keep breathing, you're doing fine." He knew what a gig meant to an actor and he sided with me.

After about an hour or so, I started to feel myself again. The gray in my face was replaced with color and, like a trooper, I finished the day's work. Bruce gave me the thumbs up at the end of the day and said, "Good job, kid. I like you New York types. You're tough and don't baby yourselves." I was very grateful, said thanks and headed home. I could have easily been fired that day—Hollywood is not compassionate. I was grateful—I got through it with the help of God. I credit my work ethic and perseverance to my father and the grueling work in the butcher shop, as well as the discipline of ballet.

I woke up the next day feeling terrific and ready and raring to go. My fellow actors were all supportive and asked how I was feeling. I also met the actress playing my sister, and she was very sweet and concerned.

I grew very fond of David. I spent a lot of time with him in KITT between takes, and we had some intense conversations. My vibes told me he was overly-sensitive with a deep rooted sense of insecurity. Outside of his rough exterior, I saw a good-hearted man who, perhaps, couldn't get out of his own way. He was genuinely kind and there was nothing he wouldn't do for anyone on the set.

While we were between takes one day and being "dolly pulled" from the front of the car through a main road in West Covina, we were having idle chit-chat. Our windows were down and someone from the side of the road shouted, "*Knight Rider* sucks." David's face dropped and he looked stunned and hurt. It was painful to witness. He lifted his head and shouted out the window, "So do you!"

"Pay that garbage no mind, David. You know to expect that, right?" I chimed.

"The asshole."

"It's just not worth the aggravation. People are jealous. This can't be the first time you experienced something like this? I would imagine it happens often. They *are* assholes. Just let it go. They wish they were you. Trust me."

"You're right, I will. It's just annoying as shit. The prick."

"I hear you."

We drove on in silence and as we did, I sensed deep loneliness in David and a desire to be comforted. I felt that he was a little boy who became a big boy, not a little boy who became a man.

The week finished with a bang and so did our last scene. Our last shot, and my favorite scene in the episode, was the fist fight in the cornfield. David picked me up and put me on his shoulders after we fought the villains. I love any kind of physical acting—probably from my dance training. The last shot of the fist fight that becomes a freeze frame at the end of the episode of David and me summarizes my experience. Triumph and joy! I did it. Even Kay and Joy came to watch me work on the last day.

Walking off the set, Bruce turned around to look at me. He

stopped in his tracks on the dirt road and said, "Hey Kid, you pulled it off. Welcome to L.A.—you're gonna do just fine." That comment was better than my salary.

Besides working with David Hasselhoff and my three villain buddies, the role of Uncle Stefano—the head gypsy, was played by the opera singer, Giorgio Tozzi, who sang the lead role in the film, *South Pacific*. What a lovely man! He was a gentleman and I was very sad when I heard he passed away in 2011.

Knight Rider was quite the experience. Despite my obstacle on the first day, I was able to carry the episode, and I learned how to remain focused in the face of adversity. I learned what it was like to be treated like a star—to have someone at my feet for my every need, to get me what I wanted when I asked, to tell me how I was doing, to dine and work with celebrities, to have breakfast, lunch, and dinner waiting for me, and to have people line up for my autograph between takes in West Covina.

For many actors, it is a horrible feeling when a gig ends. You return home and you wonder if it will ever happen again. You were handed a new life on a silver platter for a week and then it is taken away. There are always people around you, and then there are none.

I sat in my apartment the following Monday and cried. I had to return to the day job at Actorfone and I felt like I was in mourning. Where did it all go? I had no idea the impact my episode would make on fans of *Knight Rider*. Later, it became a fan favorite and even today, people reach out to me from all over the world. It is truly amazing.

After *Knight Rider*, I couldn't figure out how to transition from a dream job back to the day job. It seemed like a mean joke. While Actorfone was convenient for the working actor, it was seedy and not a nice place. It surrounded me with those who were only hopeful after I had a taste of success. I felt as if it slowed my momentum and I put it in my head, more than ever, that I had to remain focused and get out of there.

On the set of *Big Trouble* at Columbia Pictures.

Chapter Thirteen

Oh, the People You Will Meet

My experience on *Knight Rider* was a metamorphosis for me. Something shifted professionally, and I wanted more of what I'd just experienced. I wanted to move out of Glendale and live closer to the studios. It felt like I lived in the far reaches of Egypt in Glendale—too far from everything. After three months with Bev, I decided to move out of the apartment. Several irritating factors, including listening to her having "chicky-chicky" with her boyfriend, made me understand that I was better off living alone.

I could finally afford my own place and found a small studio apartment on Aqua Vista Street in Studio City. It was $550.00 per month and 500 square feet. I was finally living alone, I had a day job, and I started to have a better social life.

In the autumn of 1983, word was spreading rapidly in Los Angeles about a new type of pneumonia that seemed to be striking gay men. The buzz started in New York and spread across the nation. I heard it referred to as a "gay flu" and if you contracted it, it was a death sentence. As newspapers and television broadcasts started circulating data about the new disease, people I knew started to contract it and die. The names of actors that I knew from New York started appearing in the Memorial section of the Actors' Equity Association newspaper. Even at Actorfone, there was talk of friends and friends of friends contracting it.

I was a red-blooded Italian male whose hormones were alive and well, but with all the talk of sexually transmitted diseases I became frightened and rejected invitations from women (and men). The new disease sealed my decision to remain faithful to what I believed God wanted of me—to remain pure.

I was also a strong believer that what anyone did in the privacy of their bedroom was their business and not to be shared. In Los Angeles, it seemed like everyone shared sexual antics as if it were nothing. If you expressed alarm at any of the overt sharing, you were perceived as being "hung up." It all went against my grain and I thought it best to remain silent.

As annoying as the environment at Actorfone could be, it was also fun. We laughed and joked throughout the day and I developed a few strong friendships, but very simply, the office, the antics, and working in downtown Hollywood felt sleazy to me. I prayed for more acting work so that I could get out of there.

Flo called me exactly one week after I wrapped on *Knight Rider*. She informed me that she heard from Donna Dockstader and they wanted me for the Arab boy in the pilot of *Airwolf*. I was ecstatic. It was two days' work at my day rate (once you begin working in the industry, you can begin to name a price and negotiate wages). I was summoned back to Universal for a wardrobe fitting. This time it was not a rush job as with *Knight Rider*.

In my scene, I had to wear a loincloth since I was playing a young boy in a pool being shot at by the sheik. It was killing me to have to wear it, especially since I would be in a pool. We were shooting in the small town of Carpentaria, just south of Santa Barbara. I was instructed to park my car at the studio and from there I would be shuttled with the other co-stars to a large mansion that looked like it could be a mid-eastern castle.

When I arrived, I was immediately pulled into makeup. They wanted me in the loincloth so they could darken my skin with makeup. When we were through, and I left the makeup room with only my loincloth on, Ernest Borgnine was standing there. He looked at me and smiled, hesitated, looked down, lost his smile and said loudly, "What the hell kind of show is this?" The crew all laughed, and I was embarrassed—so much for introductions. Ernie and I were both represented by Flo and I wanted to properly introduce myself to him. I felt stupid at that point but knew I would have the opportunity later.

There was a lot of waiting around on this set, and I was cold in the loincloth. It was November and the temperature was in the low 50s. The costume department wrapped me in a warm terrycloth robe and made sure I was looked after.

When it was time to shoot, I went into the pool; it was freezing! I was anxious about shooting the scene because I get cold very quickly—even in the summer. My hands and feet can easily turn into ice blocks any time of the year. I started to shiver, and someone suggested that I do laps to get used to it, but as I did, I felt my loincloth rising and kept reaching around me to lower it as I swam. I was very self-conscious. I decided to just stay still in the shallow end.

The producer and director, Don Bellisario, came on set and introduced himself to me as I stood in the pool. At the time, Don was a big deal at Universal having produced *Tales of the Gold Monkey*, and *Magnum, P.I.* It was a pleasure to meet him. I awkwardly made my way to the side of the pool to shake his hand. He seemed like a real nice guy. I was hired by Donna herself with no callback, so I didn't meet him during the audition process. Booking the guest starring role on *Knight Rider* probably helped in booking *Airwolf*. Flo told me that the word on the street at Universal was that "the LaGreca kid bailed us out of trouble with *Knight Rider*; he's talented, and could be trusted." I gained the reputation of being a safe bet at Universal television.

I shot my scene with British actor, David Hemmings, who played the sheik. David was an old pro who made dozens of successful films in the U.K., so I made sure I was on my game. The takes were fast and successful. I was pleased with my work. There were no lines as it was a silent featured role, so the work was mostly internal. I had to ask myself the following questions: *What does it feel like to have a gun pointed at you? What if he misses? How does that make me feel physically and emotionally?* I layered my choices with missing my parents. Everyone on set seemed pleased with the scene.

On the way out, I finally introduced myself to Ernie, who said, "Hey kid, pleased to meet you. Good work and good luck in town." He was abrupt, but a nice guy. He had a very New York Italian vibe and reminded me of my uncles. I also met Jan Michael Vincent who I admired. He had his head down a lot, and was very quiet and shy. He was someone with whom I would have liked to converse.

When I wrapped on *Airwolf*, I once again began to experience depression. The gig had ended, and I felt lonely, abandoned, and frightened. I was nurtured and looked after for a few days and now I felt let down. There was also a dichotomy occurring within me.

While I hungered for my next acting job and dreaded going back to the answering service, I also started to develop a small resentment with Hollywood. I resented the way they did things—how they applaud you and put you on top one day, and the next day toss you to the side. I resented the fact that crew members and other actors felt comfortable saying anything they wanted to you—and got away with it. I wanted the attention and success of an actor, but I did not want to fall into the dregs of the business. It was my observation that the "muck and mire" was ever present—and looking for one good moment to initiate you.

It was at these times that I missed my family. My older siblings were married now and starting to have children. We all went through so much together with Charlie that there was an unspoken bond and devotion. I was not home to revel in the joy of my newborn nephews and nieces; rather I was going to work and returning to a small, hot, empty apartment feeling lonely and sad. I had friends that held me up, but I was learning that in Los Angeles, one had to stay on top of friendships, or they easily fizzle. Everyone seemed to have an agenda. I wanted full time acting work. The time in-between was torture.

The quality time I spent was with Kay, who was like family to me because of Les and Steve. Weekends were often spent at the beach, partying and having fun. New friends from Actorfone—John, Rochelle, and Colleen lived in the same apartment complex, so almost every weekend, Rochelle, who was the oldest, would turn into a good Jewish mother and make us some delicious soup on a dime. We'd all get comfortable on her futon and watch movies together. It helped during lonely times.

Because I started making good money as an actor, rather than saving every penny for the dry times, I started treating these same friends to dinner or lunch. Things were tight for us struggling artists and I saw no reason why I shouldn't share in my good fortune.

By the end of 1983, I made major strides with my career. I established a positive reputation at Universal Studios and casting directors were getting to know me. I felt like I was on my way. I returned to New Jersey for the Christmas season; I hadn't been home since I left in June. My family was so happy to see me, and my heart swelled with love—especially to see Mom and Dad.

On December 18, 1983, my *Knight Rider* episode, "Silent Knight," aired. My family watched the episode together in the TV room but I couldn't bear to watch it with them. I locked myself in my parents' bedroom and paced as I watched it on their television set.

Like other actors, I do not like watching myself on film. It is an overwhelming experience. I become filled with anxiety and hate the way I sound and look. I nitpick at every acting choice I make. I become self-deprecating and convince myself that I will never work again. To this day, I have not seen myself in quite a few projects. When I do, I have to be able to react to my work alone, not in front of other people.

As the episode aired, all I could hear downstairs from the family room was cheering and laughter. It warmed my heart that I was making them happy, in light of all we had been through.

When the episode finished, I sheepishly went downstairs. My mother was beaming and when she saw me at the bottom of the stairs, she gave me a big hug and kissed me over and over again, telling me how proud she was of me. The phone started ringing once the credits rolled, and all night my father spoke to aunts, uncles and friends who were all so impressed and happy. My Uncle Frank, my father's older brother said, "Jackie, how special was it to see the LaGreca name in the credits?" I was thrilled with the impact on the family.

The next day I had to start my Christmas shopping. Mom and I went to the Paramus Park Mall. I suppose I never expected or thought about it, but as I was shopping people were stopping and staring at me. I kept saying to myself, *what the heck? Is something on my face?*

Then two young girls passed us and one of them said out loud, "Oh my God, it *is* him." My mother noticed and said, "Paulie, I think they're recognizing you from last night. You're being recognized." She was beaming and getting such a kick out of it. She was right. It never dawned on me.

But then my Mom started annoying me because I wanted to be

cool about it. You gotta show some swag in these situations. I was taking the behavioral lead from my time in L.A., but Mom didn't know better. I wanted her to refrain from overt excitement and when I mentioned it, she told me to "shut up." *Welcome home!*

At the mall, I did notice that Jack Hexum's former day job, Farrell's Ice Cream parlor, was no longer there. It was replaced by a McDonalds (go figure). It reminded me that I never phoned him when I went out to Los Angeles, and that I should do so when I returned. He would probably ignore me, I thought. He was the star of his own television series, playing the role of Phineas Bogg on *Voyagers* and probably wanted nothing to do with me at that point. I hesitated to contact him because I thought he would think I wanted something from him. How sensitive and silly we actors can be—we can overthink ourselves to madness.

For the next few days, it was actually fun to be recognized. When I was on the A train heading into Manhattan, a guy turned to me and said, "I can't help it man, sorry to bother you, but was you that punk on *Knight Rider*?" I smiled and nodded.

He let out a good and hearty laugh.

"Damn, bro! I knew it. I was looking at you and I be like, I know that kid." He asked me for my autograph, and then told me he thought I was great. And then it came, the infamous question that I would get repeatedly until today, "What was it like to drive KITT?" It thrilled me that I was able to answer his question and to touch his heart. It did more for me than for him. It made me feel good that my talent could touch others.

I returned to L.A. in January. 1984 started out slow, but the residual checks started coming in from *Knight Rider* and that was a great help financially. I was informed that the *Airwolf* pilot, "Shadow of the Hawke," was made into a feature film in Europe, in addition to being the pilot in America. So, I was cashing in nicely from that experience.

Humbling myself and going on an audition for a non-speaking role yielded television and feature film income. Again, if I had not stopped to speak to that receptionist . . .

As I was getting older, life wasn't just about Hollywood and acting. I continued to ask the big questions. Who are we and why are we here? I began a phase of intense spiritual searching. Rochelle and John were also receptive to the spiritual quest, so it was a common thread that bound us. I was open to new ideas and absorbed anything spiritual like a sponge. I was not going to Mass on Sundays, however, nor was I much of a practicing Catholic.

I regularly went to my favorite metaphysical bookstore, The Bodhi Tree, on Melrose Avenue. It became my home away from home. When you walked into the store, you were greeted with wafts of sweet smelling incense, and piped-in music that could be chants from a Christian, Tibetan or Buddhist monastery, ocean sounds, or classical music. They also offered hot herbal tea while you shopped. The patrons were all very hip and on their own spiritual journeys. I loved it.

I purchased books that resonated with me at the time: the writings of Edgar Cayce, The Wisdom of the Mystic Masters, the writings of Paramahansa Yogananda, books on near-death experiences, lives of Saints, and books that explored the next world. My quest was a sincere one, and this new path—outside of nothing but Catholic literature—was exciting; I had the opportunity to explore without guilt or shame. I had the right to think and make decisions on my own. That is not to say that I entirely rejected the Church, quite the contrary. I began to compare what I knew and what I learned against what other writers and teachers were professing. I dove in headfirst and my spiritual quest became first and foremost in my daily life.

Rochelle, of all my friends, appreciated The Bodhi Tree and the spiritual quest. Together we would have intense spiritual conversations. Ro had befriended one of our clients, a young actress from the soap opera, *General Hospital*, named Demi Moore who, at the time, was gaining nice momentum as Jackie Templeton. I only knew her indirectly as a client from Actorfone.

One evening, I met Demi at a party. She arrived with Rochelle. She was a knock-out, and extremely nice. We took to each other immediately. Rochelle and Demi had recently joined a Buddhist chanting group called NSA—Nichiren Shoshu of America. The basic tenant of the practice is for one to chant daily to a Gohonzon (a sacred scroll that the Buddhist hung in their house that reflected your life energy), and to recite specific chants from a daily chant book each morning and evening. This was called Gongyo.

The premise behind chanting to a Gohonzon is that the chanter who focuses and concentrates on desired things would, over time, clear up the negative karma of many lifetimes, allowing those things that you desire to pour into your life. It was explained to me like this: if you attach a hose to a water spigot at the end of winter and turn it on in spring, the first water from the hose would come out dirty and murky but as it continues to flow, the water becomes cleaner and purer. It was also the same with chanting. In the meantime, you were also chanting for world peace.

For example, if one chants for a new car, you would chant for it each day until it manifests itself. You might experience some unfortunate things at first like your old car dying and breaking down or maybe even a car accident, but eventually the karma would clear until the new car manifested. Ultimately, the practicing chanter would no longer chant for material things but the higher virtues such as wisdom, or tolerance.

I was introduced to NSA by Rochelle, who was already a member of the Santa Monica hon (group) – the biggest in the USA and one that contained a few celebrities: Tina Turner and Patrick Duffy, to name a few. I was very reluctant to consider chanting to a Gohonzon because it felt like idol worship, and even though I was not going to Mass, I still felt that it was breaking the second commandment: Thou shalt not place false idols before me.

I appeased Rochelle and decided to go with her to a meeting. Sheila, another Actorfone client, spoke to me about her Catholic past, and explained that her brother was a priest. She told me that he practiced chanting as well and that chanting does not mean that you are denying your belief system, but simply attaching an additional spiritual practice. She continued by saying that many nuns and priests belong to NSA and that I was in good company. I temporarily let down my guard.

After hearing what Shiela had to say, and with a bit of coercion, I gave in. I tried not to be negative about it and thought I would give it a shot. It felt like I had nothing to lose, so I began my practice. My Gohonzon was installed and my chanting began. My Buddhism and my continued spiritual search were very gratifying. I felt happy and good about it.

Another place I frequented was the Self-Realization Fellowship Shrine—a lake shrine built by Paramahansa Yogananda—that honored all the great religions of the world. It was in Santa Monica and was an oasis of peace in the heart of Los Angeles. I would go, read on hidden benches that were placed between trees, and enjoy the beauty. A giant statue of Jesus with His arms extended stood over the lake representing Christianity. There were even some of Gandhi's ashes in the Hindu section.

As I continued on my spiritual journey, I received a phone call from Flo telling me that Mel Johnson at Universal wanted me to come in and read for a possible recurring role on the TV series, *Whiz Kids*, starring Matthew Laborteaux—famous from the television series, *Little House on the Prairie*. According to Mel, the part was mine for the taking, but I had to meet the producers. Unlike trying to prove myself at some of the other studios, Universal knew me and liked me. Flo told me that once I hit a certain level, it was only a matter of time until they would consider me for a series regular. In her words, "Hold on, hang tight and enjoy the ride, baby." And, I did.

God bless Mel Johnson, I ended up booking the role of Sid, one of the school bullies. I shot two episodes of *Whiz Kids* but, unfortunately, the series was canceled soon after that. It was a shame because the character could have easily rolled into a series regular.

Even though I was doing well as an actor, I had to be careful with money and I wanted to ultimately get out of Actorfone. My friend John invited me to apply at a new restaurant in Beverly Hills where he now worked. The famous director, Dino De Laurentiis, was opening an international food market and restaurant called the "DDL Foodshow" on Canon Street off Wilshire Blvd. The retail section was downstairs, and the restaurant was upstairs. The place would cater to top celebrities and industry moguls. I applied and was hired to work in the bakery, chocolate, and pizza area (all one long counter) and John was across the aisle from me in the "gastronomia"—hot foods and cold salads. Most of the DDL employees were struggling artists, so a major perk was being able to purchase these magnificent foods at a 30% discount; it was wonderful.

Dino made us put on white gloves and he wanted to inspect us and give us a pep talk the evening before we opened. He kept telling us how pleased he was and when in doubt with anything, we should just "smile, smile, smile and everything will be all right." Everything that night would be free for the guests, since it was a promotional event for all the invited VIPs.

At the end of the evening, Dino told us it was a great success and because the next day everything had to be "fresh, fresh, fresh," he told us that we could take home what remained in our areas. Well, the second he walked away, it was as if we turned into a herd of starving cows. With French café music playing in the background, we began to pull at each other like animals and began grabbing the bread, the pizza, anything. Breadsticks were breaking and falling on the floor and employees were climbing over each other to get to higher shelves. The whole scene was like something out of a movie. I began to laugh and couldn't stop. My friend Cheryl turned to me as she filled her bag and said, "C'est magnifique, eh Paul?"

John and I were both actors and film and theater buffs. He was great to have around, because besides constantly laughing, he had an uncanny eye at spotting the famous. We could be walking down Sunset Boulevard deep in conversation and, out of the blue, he would spot a celebrity in a car at a stop light, 10 cars from where we were standing. He was amazing. As for me, if Tom Hanks himself came toward me to say hi, it would still take a moment for it to register who he was, if at all! So, to have John at DDL meant we would know instantly who was who.

John, besides Kay, quickly became a close friend, and there was very little that we did not share with each other. He too had a Roman Catholic background, and we spiritually understood each other without having to explain. Even though John was no longer a practicing Catholic, he had a statue of Our Lady of Fatima in his bedroom, which I secretly was very pleased he displayed. John became a stalwart in my life.

I was happy to be working with him at Actorfone and now the DDL Foodshow. The fun started for us almost the minute we started working there. He would occasionally abandon the gastronomia to quickly walk past my area to say something like, "go over to the cheese section quick, it's Dionne Warwick." It was so much fun. This was the life I lived at DDL. The managers also understood that if any of the hired actors had an audition, they had permission to go. It was ideal.

The DDL Foodshow itself was outrageous. It had an espresso bar, a fantastic international wine section, a cheese counter with products imported from all over the world, a cold cut area with the best of the best, and other delicacies, including caviar and rare pig truffles. The bakery had various kinds of fresh bread and pizza made daily—not Italian-American pizza—but the pizza one would buy at a piazza in Italy.

The breads were also spectacular—every shape and size—breads with different vegetable fillings, rosettas, breadsticks, and on and on. At the end of my section was an international chocolate section where we sold Moreau and Koenig chocolate. Outside the chocolate counter there was a cove built into the walls with an array of international coffees—from chocolate coffee to African, French, and Brazilian blends—all ground fresh for the asking.

The place was incredible, and people would come into the store just to "ooh" and "aah" at everything around them, often asking for samples but having no intention to purchase. These folks became easy to spot over time. The piped-in music was a combination of sexy Bossa Nova, French café, and Italian music. It was pure class, and a delightful place to work.

I became enamored with my surroundings and desired to be a part of it, not as a servant but as one being served. I began to gain an appreciation for the employees who were hired from all over the world—the French were hired to work in the cheese section, the Italians were the chefs, bread and pizza makers, along with a few chefs from England. Many of the employees were educated and spoke multiple languages.

I spoke a little Italian at the time both from my youth and from studying in high school, so I was able to communicate well with Anna Maria and Ciccio Mariano, a married couple from Italy who were our bread chefs. I was very comfortable with Anna Maria and Ciccio and would get very silly with them. Anna Maria would yell at me and say to me, "Paolo, tu devi imparare ed amare e rispettare la pasta!" She was telling me that I must learn how to love and respect the pasta. I adored them both.

For the most part, many celebrities and Beverly Hills residents were gracious. Rosemary Clooney would come to the pizza section and say, "Hey Paul, whad'ya got today?" After showing her the various pizzas for the day, she would have me cut an entire slab up into squares. She loved the pizza bianca the best. I adored Rosie, and we developed a nice rapport.

One evening, Dino hosted a party for the French and Italian athletic teams that were part of the 1984 Summer Olympics in Los Angeles. Dino also invited many celebrity guests. Among them were Arnold Schwarzenegger, Armand Assante, Christie Brinkley, Barbie Benton, Drew Barrymore (who was only a little girl at the time), Michael Jackson, and many others.

Over time, as fun as it was, the novelty began to wear off. The resentment I was developing with L.A., in general, was getting stronger. Each night they dumped out barrels and barrels of food—good, fresh, unspoiled and untouched food from the gastronomia, bags and bags of bread, as well as day old fruit. It was starting to irk me and something felt "off." It made me sad, especially since L.A. was plagued with so many homeless.

In the meantime, if Michael Jackson wanted the most expensive chocolates, we were told to give them to him at no charge. It made no sense to me. In fact, it irritated me to the degree that I could no longer hide it. I asked my manager, Patrick, if it would be possible to at least take the bags of bread to the mission soup kitchen in downtown L.A. Fortunately, Patrick agreed to let me and for a few weeks, I was able to do so.

One day shortly after I arrived to work, he pulled me aside.

"That bread you're taking at the end of the day; you have to stop. We can't do it anymore, sorry."

"Why, Patrick? It only goes in the garbage and we're feeding so many people."

"Because I said so, that's why." After a moment he shrugged and said, "It would be unfair to other groups who knock on our door who we reject. It's not right to give to one group and not another. Before you know it we'll have all these charities knocking on our door and Dino doesn't want that." *So what?* I thought. *There is so much abundance here!*

There was something wrong with this picture and over time I was so disgusted with the waste that I went to the garbage pail that had no trash in it yet, but a full tray of steaming salmon lay across it waiting to be dumped. I just couldn't bear to see an entire tray of untouched gourmet food being tossed, so I took a piece.

I decided to be ethical and after removing it from the trash, I paid for it. Rather than register the food with my usual 30% discount, I gave myself a 50% discount since it was on top of the garbage. As I was preparing to leave, my immediate supervisor, Carol, who I adored, asked me to come into the office. She seemed very nervous.

After I sat, backpack in tow, I said, "What's cookin'?"

She proceeded to hand me the package of fish I had put inside my backpack. Evidently, when I was unaware, someone went into my bag and took it out.

"Did you take that fish from the garbage can?"

"Wait, what? Yes, yes, I did. It was about to be dumped . . . but I paid for it, Carol."

She started to get choked up and said, "You know I love you and it kills me to do this . . . but you should have given yourself a 30% discount, not a 50% discount."

"But Carol, it was on top of the dumpster." With that, she started to cry.

"I have no choice, but I have to terminate you. I am so sorry, Paul.

I have no choice . . . I have no choice. You know I love." *Something else was going on here.*

I told her it was all right and I started to comfort her rather than the other way around! It was clear that she knew it was all bullshit. Rumor had it that she was instructed to cut back on employees and they were looking for any excuse to let go of people—from walking in 10 minutes late to missing a staff meeting (the reason John was terminated the following week). So much for the DDL Foodshow and the lure of Beverly Hills—you can keep it!

I returned to Actorfone. I continued chanting and my spiritual quest became my priority. Again, the big questions haunted me— who am I? Where am I going? What is this all about? What is truly important in this world? Have I lived before? What is it like when we crossover? These questions became my focus and I was vocal about them wherever I went. John, Rochelle and I spent hours turning these questions over.

My spiritual search started to change me. Something was rapidly shifting within me. My world was being colored by my spiritual path. The experience at DDL put a bad taste in my mouth, and I found Actorfone to be sleazy. I once again experienced that deep well within. I rested in the intense darkness of something much greater than myself that carried me from my deepest recesses. I intuitively felt that all I needed to do was remain prayerful and wait. I knew there was a better way, but it had to come to me when the time was right. I also chanted, prayed, and meditated for the next acting role to come along . . . and that it did.

In March of 1985, I was sent to Columbia Pictures to see Judy Taylor from Fenton/Feinberg Casting to audition for one of Alan Arkin's triplet sons in the film, *Big Trouble*. Judy and I hit it off right away, and I had "that feeling" one gets when you know a part is yours. I looked like I could play Alan's son and the question was finding two more guys who looked like me to make triplets. If I was the prototype, I had to be patient while Judy matched two other guys to play my brothers. Judy had success and Stephen Alterman, Jerry Pavlon, and I were signed by Columbia Pictures to play the Hoffman triplets in *Big Trouble*.

The film's writer, Andrew Bergman, had also written the hit film *The In-Laws*, and *Big Trouble* was written as a second film for the successful comedic pairing of Alan Arkin and Peter Falk. The script was hysterical and many of the original *In-Laws* cast members were signed for the project, including Charles Durning and Richard Libertini. *Big Trouble* would also star Robert Stack, Beverly D'Angelo, and Valerie Curtin. It was clearly going to be a sure-fire hit and a major motion picture.

The film is about an insurance salesman (Alan Arkin) who has musical genius triplets (I was the piano player), all of whom were accepted to Yale. The problem was finding the funds to pay for the tuition. When Arkin has no luck in requesting the money from his boss (Robert Stack), he resorts on a plot to embezzle money with two shysters (Peter Falk and Beverly D'Angelo). Valerie Curtin, who I loved and admired as the dizzy waitress Vera from the film *Alice Doesn't Live Here Anymore*, played our mother.

I had three full weeks of work ahead of me and my first day on the set was an exciting one. I was met by Judy, who introduced me to a few people before she departed. I was shown to my trailer and prepared for the first day's shoot inside the "family home." The first shot would be with Valerie and Alan as the triplets prepared to leave for school. When I arrived to the set, however, the energy was off—something wasn't right. It felt quiet and foreboding. Where was our director, Andrew Bergman?

Since the film was already in production and the triplet scenes were being shot last, I had no idea that Andrew Bergman had walked off the film. He was replaced by Peter Falk's friend, John Cassavetes. Supposedly, Bergman was hitting heads with Peter Falk and when he couldn't take it anymore, he washed his hands of the project. While I was honored to have the infamous John Cassavetes as a director, I wondered how we were going to fare with timed comedy since John was known for a lot of avant-garde and improvisational film work (*A Woman Under the Influence, Gloria, Love Streams*).

As I approached the lawn of the house to have wardrobe look me over, I was instantly taken aback. I heard shouting.

"What the hell are you doing, Valerie? *What are you doing?* This is not a fucking soap opera Valerie. It's a fucking comedy." John was evidently screaming at Valerie Curtin.

"I'll try it again," she humbly replied.

I instantly became uncomfortable with what I was hearing. What was going on and why was Cassavetes screaming like that? How can anyone play comedy in that type of scenario? I walked away from wardrobe and sat on the lawn next to Beverly D'Angelo.

Beverly and I looked at each other as we heard Alan Arkin shout, "Just tell me what you want John. Tell me what you want and I'll do it! I don't know what you are looking for here. Just tell me what you want!"

Oh boy, I thought! I looked at Beverly and asked what the hell was going on? She stared at me straight faced and said, "We have a new director. His name is Allen Funt" (Allen Funt was the director of the television show, *Candid Camera*). We both laughed, but John made me nervous. He was a man who I deeply respected and had his own vision and way of doing things. Some of the crew had even mentioned that some of the stars wanted to pull themselves from the picture.

John, unfortunately, was not well at the time. He had cirrhosis of the liver. There were many times when I would watch him sitting on his director's chair hunched over and looking like he was nodding out from his medication—similar to Charlie. His stomach was enlarged, and he did not look healthy. He looked like he needed to be home and resting but maybe, I thought, work is keeping him alive. He was a very nice man and I enjoyed watching him work. They said he was a genius, and I trusted that. My scenes went well and I was happy that I was not on the receiving end of any rants.

The studio assigned each of the "triplets" with a music tutor, prior to shooting. Since I was the piano playing triplet, a small piano was sent to my Studio City apartment, and my tutor visited twice a week. We were to play the first movement of Mozart's "Eine Kleine Nachtmusik" and Hayden's, "Trio No. 15." The emphasis was on making sure our hands were in the right places should the camera close up on the playing. I also thought it would be nice to bond with my brothers so I had them over for dinner a few times and we practiced as a trio.

When we shot the scene where we would be playing the Mozart piece, between takes, I was fooling around. I stood up and pretended I was playing the piano like a rock star. Peter Falk saw me and thought it was hysterical.

"John, John, you gotta come here and see this." Cassavetes came over smiling with a half burned cigarette dangling from his lips.

"Do it again, Paul." I was dismayed because I really didn't know what I did, I was just having some fun and being silly—something I do organically with little or no thought.

"You want me to rock out on the piano?" I said

"Yea, exactly what you did," Peter replied.

I stood up and started to play the piano like I was auditioning for a rock bank rather than Yale. John laughed and said, "Let's keep that. Do that when we shoot, Paul, okay?" *Wait, what?*

I was very disappointed. I had inhabited the mindset of a young musician hungry to get to Yale as a concert pianist, and they wanted me to act silly. Steve and Jerry didn't have to be silly, only I did.

I took the direction, but with apprehension. I thought it was stupid. I decided to lessen the "silly" bit when we started shooting and, fortunately, no one said anything. In the final cut, you can see my shoulders bobbing as if I was playing "Blue Suede Shoes" rather than Mozart—but I didn't stand up. If I was famous, I would have pushed back like some stars do, but I didn't. I did not want to be another casualty on a set with so many apparent issues.

After we were done shooting, and editing began, the studio decided they could not afford any more time and money to try and salvage what they deemed to be a mess and, ultimately, a loss. The film was finally released in May of 1986 to try to recoup some of the financial loss. It had a limited run at selected theaters and opened to terrible reviews. The film lived up to its title, *Big Trouble*. It was supposed to be a big film break for me but, unfortunately, that did not happen. It was also Cassavetes' last film. Everyone was disappointed, including Cassavetes. Over the years, however, it has gained the reputation of being a cult classic.

The best part of the experience was getting to know Valerie Curtin (such a sweet, nurturing woman), Beverly D'Angelo (hysterical), Robert Stack—who, when he spoke with me, would look me in the eye, smile and hug me like a son, and of course, Alan Arkin who told me on the last day of shooting, "Working with you is a real gift. You give me so much to work with as an actor, and I just wanted to say thank you." Could a young actor possibly ask for anything more?

While I was filming *Big Trouble*, an unfortunate incident happened at the studio that upset and frightened me. Demi Moore, who had become a friend, began working at Columbia on the film *Saint Elmo's Fire* at the same time I was shooting *Big Trouble*. Rochelle was appearing in a play at a small theater in Van Nuys, and we decided to meet up at the theater after shooting to support Rochelle.

After the show, we had a few beers and Demi was showing us her new Kawasaki motorcycle. I said, "Demi, you have to give me a ride on this thing."

"Hop on," she said.

I jumped behind her on the bike and held on tight to her waist. The both of us had been drinking and we both had beer bottles in our hands, and no helmets. Demi was very free-spirited and could be a real dare-devil, so I was a little concerned about the ride. I abandoned myself to her and closed my eyes as we flew through streets of Van Nuys—my face buried in her back as she picked up speed. Afterward, heart pounding, we went back to the theater and then finished our evening at a local bar.

The next morning on set, one of the crew members asked me how I was and what I had done the previous night. I told him that I met up with some friends at a theatre and that afterward Demi took me on a joy ride on her motorcycle, followed by a good time at the bar. It was simple enough and the end of the conversation.

At about 8:00 PM that same night, my phone rang. It was Demi.

"Paul, who did you speak with at the studio today regarding last night?"

"Hi . . . what do you mean?" Demi can be very intimidating, and I got very nervous because of her tone.

"Do you have any idea how much trouble I got into today?"

At this point, my heart began to pound. I hate confrontation of any kind and this felt uncomfortable.

"Demi, what do you mean you got into trouble today?"

"I am being watched right now because of drinking, and someone who you spoke to evidently started sharing about me and it spread like wildfire throughout the studio. I want to know the name of the person you told."

"First of all, I had no idea that you were in any sort of trouble or that you were being watched, so I apologize for that. You know I would never intentionally hurt you!"

"I know that but just give me the name of the person."

I did not want to provide the name of the person because what if, in fact, he was innocent about it too and meant no harm? The guy had three kids and I didn't want to see him fired. Demi had a tendency of being irrational—especially if she was drinking—and I wanted to play it safe.

"Whoever you told shouldn't have said anything to anyone. And you need to know something . . . if you say something about me in New York at 3:00 PM, I'll hear about it in L.A. by 6:00 PM the same day—everything gets back to me. Please, tell me his name."

"I'm sorry, Demi . . . but I feel like I just can't."

"Okay, thanks a lot." She hung up the phone.

My heart was pounding, and she scared me. I tried to calm myself down. I hated this. Hollywood could be so nasty.

About half an hour later, my phone rang again. It was Demi.

"Look, I'm sorry that I got so upset. I didn't mean to. You're a good guy, and I know you would never do anything malicious to hurt me."

"Never—of course not!"

"Just give me the name of the guy." *Here we go again!*

"I'm sorry, Demi, but I won't." Again, she hung up. Ten minutes later, the phone rang again.

"Hi, Paul?" It was a man's voice this time.

"Yes?"

"Hi, it's Jon Cryer." Jon and Demi had been an item at the time, however temporary.

"Hi Jon, how are you? Are you calling about the Demi incident at the studio today? Did Demi ask you to call me?"

"Actually, yes. She's pretty upset. Would you do me a favor and just repeat the story one more time?"

And then I thought I heard a "click"—it was a sound that I was used to from my answering machine when I wanted to record a conversation—answering machines could do that in those days. While I cannot say for certain that I was being recorded, it was unnerving and I was starting to get paranoid. I tried to stay cool, calm and collected this time and I carefully repeated the story, telling the truth.

"What was the name of the guy?"

"I didn't give you the name of the guy, Jon. And I must admit I can't deal with this anymore. I have lines to memorize for tomorrow and I have to be at the studio at the crack of dawn. I am so sorry that this happened, a lesson learned, but I won't hurt another person. Please tell my friend that I am sorry. I feel awful."

I hung up the phone and feeling complete angst, I believed in my heart of hearts that I had done the right thing, regardless of the outcome. By today's standards, and looking back with a more mature mindset, if Demi would have said that crew members need to learn to remain silent and that he may not have been fired but would only get reprimanded because those kinds of rumors are harmful, then it would have been a different scenario.

Demi was one of the nicest people I have ever met. She was very loving, kind, and even bought a car for Rochelle after her old car died. I adored her. Evidently, and in retrospect, Demi was battling her own demons at the time—but that didn't take away from how special she was to me. There was a certain vulnerability underneath the party girl exterior and she always appreciated my support and kind words to her.

After a few weeks, and my consistent messages of apology, we began to speak again. She once called me to come to her home when she was lying ill in bed. She lay there under a thin sheet. When I sat on her bed, she turned to me and took my hand.

"I know that you are a spiritual guy. You're very sweet and my mother loves you too."

She wiped away her tears and I wondered what had happened to have her in such a sad state.

"I have faith too, you know," she said matter-of-factly, as if I doubted her.

"I know you do, Demi. Your good heart couldn't possibly live within a bad spirit. You are fighting demons, that's all. And I will always be there for you."

She then broke my heart by pointing to her heart and saying, "God lives right here."

It was sad. I wanted to hold her in my arms and make everything okay for her, but I know I couldn't. I felt like I was with a female version of Charlie and the rescuer in me was alive and well at that moment.

Demi's assistant was due at the house, and after she fell asleep, I left and went home.

I will always have a special place in my heart for Demi. I am so proud of the woman and mother she has become—and her long-standing sobriety. Our prayers worked. Even though we are no longer in touch, I still wish her every happiness in the world—and her mom, Virginia, who I also adored, a restful repose.

The mean side of what show business can do to someone was becoming more and more evident. Hollywood was not about getting a role and concentrating on good work, it was a rat race, a competitive, back-stabbing, "anything to get ahead" business, and I was quickly losing interest. It was a lifestyle—and whether you were shooting or not, it was easy to fall into "the ugly." I was too young and too immature to know how to navigate it all. I began to go deep inside again, as I had done with Charlie when I was frightened or in panic mode.

Amid the darkness around me, I began to sincerely pray to God to show me the way. It was all starting to appear as folly. The novelty of Buddhism, chanting, Beverly Hills, parties, and "celebrity" was wearing off fast. It felt God-less, and I sensed an underlying evil to it all. There was no room for God amidst the demi-gods. Was I willing to go down that road? Is this what I really wanted? Was I strong enough to separate work from lifestyle? Was it possible? I began to hunger for the stability of home. I wanted to be around "normal" people who lived simple lives. I was starting to feel like it was no longer for me.

I remembered Jack Hexum and thought I would give him a call; tell him I was in town and maybe resume my friendship with him. At the very least, I thought he could steer me in the right direction. I tried calling him a few times but only got his answering machine. In those days there was no caller ID, so you never knew who was on the other line.

Finally, one night I tried again. He answered the phone and shouted, "WHAT?" into the receiver! Yikes! I was stunned. He sounded pissed off as if this was one call too many. I said, "Um . . . hey Jack, it's Paul . . . Paul LaGreca . . . from Closter . . . from the Red and Tan number 20 bus to New York."

There was a pause. "Oh shit, oh wow," he said, "Paul?! How are you?! Paul from the bus? I apologize about the way I answered, but they don't leave me alone!"

"It's okay, I understand, and I am sure you are always busy."

"You have no idea," he said. "They can drive you crazy. Enough of that, tell me about yourself and what you are doing."

We shared about my arrival, my success, the studios, and what we had both been up to. He was happy to hear from me because I represented home to him. We promised each other that we would meet up for lunch or dinner. He sounded tired and edgy—I had never heard him like that. It was also a few years since our last conversation, and people can change. I was disappointed and sad for him. Jack made me ask myself if I wanted to be in the same boat!

We never did meet up. A few weeks after I touched base with him, while watching the evening news, the headlines read that Jack had accidentally shot himself in the head while goofing around on his new

TV series, *Cover-up*. He suffered from brain hemorrhaging and died later in the day. He was making believe that he "couldn't take it anymore" while waiting on the set and put the gun to his head and pulled the trigger. He, evidently, forgot that there were blanks in it. The Jack I knew was a fun and sweet guy. He was probably being silly just to make someone laugh, as he had done with me the day he sang "Happy Birthday" to me at Farrell's ice-cream parlor.

Jack's death deeply affected me and made me sad beyond words. We were two Jersey boys trying to make good in Hollywood and now his story ended in tragedy. It was only a few years earlier that we commuted together and shared our dreams of success. To this day, whenever I pass his house in Tenafly, I offer up a prayer for him. I hope Jack knows that.

While Jack's life shifted to the great beyond, mine was about to shift and to take a major turn. April Lerman, an actress I knew from Universal, played Leila as a series regular on the TV series *Charles in Charge*. I had also known April indirectly years earlier in New York when she was doing *Really Rosie* on Broadway and the National Tour of *Annie*. We both ran in the same New York "show biz kids" circles. April also had success as "Duffy" in the film version of *Annie*.

April invited me to join her at 20th Century Fox for a gathering of studio people, celebrities, producers, and other industry folk for a UNICEF charity promotion. It was the kind of event where you'd watch a video on the charity, write a check, have some champagne, kibitz, and network.

We arrived at the studio, went to the theater, and took our seats in the over-sized screening room. The lights went out and I was feeling very disengaged. I was very tired that night and not in the mood for much. I sunk in my seat.

The UNICEF film started and like a magnet to my heart, I was riveted. I watched on the screen crying children, half-naked, starving, in the dirt, distended stomachs, and diseased skin. I saw mothers trying to breastfeed with milk-less breasts and watched their tears. I was frozen in my seat. I felt immobile and my eyes welled up with tears. Like the Grinch, I felt my heart swell to 10 times its size until I thought it would burst.

At that moment, I experienced an epiphany similar to what I experienced in my father's arms at Saint Frances de Chantal all those years earlier. I had an intense moment of self-realization; a part of who I am woke up—a part I'd forgotten about and abandoned. I felt the presence of God and I was completely overcome. My mind was racing, and I wanted to be alone to process what I was feeling. What had happened and where was all this coming from?

I thought back to when I was a little boy at Saint Mary's. The students were sitting on the library floor as we listened attentively to the guest missionary speaker talk about the poor. Standing to the left and right of us in the small library were teachers and parents who had come to hear the missionary speaker. I sat on my hands as he spoke. He showed us pictures of the poor, of the starving, and children in desperate need throughout the world. His words filled my heart, and I was overcome with a great desire to serve God—to be a light for those most in need.

The missionary's words touched me so deeply that I was compelled to interrupt him. I jumped to my feet and told him that I loved the poor so much that I wanted to die for them. Everyone was still—a few parents and some of the nuns in the room looked at each other and I heard giggling, while my friends looked at me like I was crazy. I suppose my outburst was endearing to some of the nuns and adults present, but I knew what I was feeling in my heart. It was a strong conviction—a conviction that would stir in my heart over and over again and never leave me.

A supernatural "beam of light" came off that 20th Century Fox movie screen and made a clear line right into my heart. I was struck with pure love and a desire to serve. I was surrounded by God—God within me, God around me and my heart on fire. I wanted to cry with joy, and I also wanted to love and be with those children. I wanted to go to them.

The film ended and I closed my eyes. I silently thought, *Sweet Jesus, here you are my Lord, hiding in the recesses of my heart. How kind of you to show your face, my true love, my Lord, my All. You are a jealous lover and there can be no one but you. That is why you preserve me, save me for your own. Oh Lord, I love you. Enlighten my heart and show me the way that I might serve you in these children.*

The experience also acted as an instant catalyst against everything I was experiencing in Hollywood. For the first time in a long while I saw myself as self-indulgent and I inwardly experienced all the "Hollywood-isms" that I'd developed over the years. I accepted my newfound awareness and felt compelled to bring it all to a close. I felt God and every atom of my body wanted to stay in Him, and with Him.

When the lights came back on April turned to me as I sat motionless.

"Are you crying?" she asked.

"Yea, I get very touched by that sort of stuff." I tried to play it down since I knew a nice Jewish girl from Brooklyn might not fully understand.

"You are so funny!" she replied.

Since April was a "name star" in town, she began to get pulled by many people who knew her. As soon as she did, I darted to the lobby area to find the evening's coordinator—Valerie Harper ("Rhoda")—who was heading up the program. I approached her and thanked her for such an outstanding presentation.

"Valerie, what can I do? I want to do more than just write a check tonight. What opportunities are there for me, right now?"

She smiled at me and was quite lovely.

"Look, you're young. You just got to Hollywood, right? You're doing well—stay in your classes, keep studying, don't do anything crazy. Down the road there will be opportunities for you. If you're here to be an actor, be an actor and learn your craft."

I wouldn't accept that answer. It sounded like a brush off. Maybe she didn't get it. It was not what I wanted to hear. I wanted her to put me on a plane for Africa.

"There has to be something more that I can do for the poor, though. Why should I wait to do something when there is such a great need?"

"Okay, look," she said, "Dennis Weaver and I have a great organization right here in town called L.I.F.E.—it stands for Love Is Feeding Everyone. Why don't you call this number in the morning and tell them I sent you. Maybe you can volunteer with us. We ask people who are shopping at supermarkets to remember the hungry in Los Angeles by buying an extra can of soup or tuna. It helps fill the food banks and you'd be helping the hungry right here in Los Angeles. It's a great place to start."

"Okay," I smiled, "that sounds great. I'm in! Thank you so much."

I felt at peace and knew that she was right. I had to start somewhere. She gave me a hug and went on to the next person. I felt a type of serenity that I hadn't felt in a long time. At that moment, I felt that I wanted God more than I wanted success as an actor.

My logical mind tried to figure out what was happening. Amid this newfound serenity, I had an inner knowing that this was "God-stuff." I was inspired. Something had happened—something pivotal—and I wasn't sure how it was going to express itself. I wasn't sure what it was or what it meant, but I was going along for the ride to see where this would lead.

I called the LIFE office the following morning and began to volunteer the following weekend. It felt good to do something for others and not always focus on myself. I met a group of new and amazing friends who also introduced me to volunteer work at City of Hope—a hospital for cancer patients. I was enjoying this new piece of my life; enjoying it so much that it began to interfere with my acting career.

In the winter of 1985, I was sent to M-G-M to audition for the television series, *Fame*. *Fame*—my very first audition in New York five years earlier. I was asked to read for the role of Irving Abromowitz, the best friend of character Dwight Mendenhall, perfectly played by David Greenlee.

Abromowitz was a sincere, warm, young drummer who was committed to his Jewish faith. The dialogue accurately reflected the spiritual commitment I had to my own spirituality, so in some ways my work was done. When it aired, I was told by friends that it was typecasting. I am a firm believer that when a role resonates with the actor, it is because there are aspects of the character alive and well in the actor. Casting directors are looking for a connection to the role with little or no acting—an organic connection that embodies the character—that is what makes art real. Truth!

I was not particularly enamored by the *Fame* set. I found it to be cold and hierarchical. Perhaps it was because there were so many musical theater types which, in general, I have always found to be needier than dramatic actors. I was perceived as the new kid on the block and a few people made it known to me that I was on the bottom of the totem pole. This is a common dynamic for anyone guest starring on a television show. An actor must know their place. You are not there to make best friends with the series regulars or to elbow your way into the cast. The guest star should be present, pleasant and prepared to work when called on set—nothing more, nothing less.

I did have the opportunity to see Cindy Gibb again—the actress who was in the Ron Santo(s) scene with me on *Search for Tomorrow*.

Cindy was a regular on the show and was as lovely as ever. I also enjoyed the company of Nia Peeples, Gene Anthony Ray, and Carlo Imperato.

Carlo calmed me down during one scene. For whatever reason, I couldn't get the scene right and our director was getting agitated. It was late on a Friday night and everyone wanted to get home. The last thing they wanted was some guest actor holding up the crew. Carlo looked me in the eyes, grabbed my shoulders and told me to breathe and calm down.

"Don't let him get to you. We've all been through this. Just look at me in the eyes and stay focused and we'll get the shot, okay?"

"Okay. Thank you." I took a deep breath and trusted Carlo.

After that, we got the shot, but I know it was because of Carlo. He put me at ease. Sometimes God sends His angels. The most delightful person for me on the *Fame* set was Valerie Landsburg, who played Doris. She was intelligent, mature, and refined, and together we shared about spiritual truths.

The best part about being on *Fame* was being on the M-G-M lot—the home of *The Wizard of Oz* and the Hollywood I dreamed of as a boy. During breaks, David Greenlee would show me around. We ate in the infamous M-G-M commissary, and he even took me to sound stage 23 where yellow bricks from the yellow brick road were still piled at a back wall. As I had these magical experiences at M-G-M, I couldn't help but wonder if they were all a manifestation of my fantasy life and my determination to succeed from childhood. Again, was it all a coincidence? *Fame* brought me full circle from my first audition in 1980 to the present.

After *Fame*, I was starting to get tired, exhausted in fact, and I felt that I was losing steam. I wanted and needed my family. Life in Los Angeles started to feel uglier and uglier. Even though I was doing quite well, I learned that it was also not the heaven I thought it would be. It was not bliss. I was growing up and getting a reality check. There was a lot to deal with. I found Los Angeles to be superficial, shallow and, in general, many people I met were out for themselves. Where was the heaven I sought? Was I living some illusory reality that made me believe that self-realization was my success as an actor?

I learned that my volunteer work at the City of Hope and LIFE could make a difference in the lives of others and have a positive impact on the world by being an ambassador of peace. The joy of giving seemed, over time, to replace the self-aggrandizing world of show business. I began to feel a consistent peace in my heart—the same way I had experienced God as a young boy. I decided to resume my faith as a practicing Catholic and registered at my local parish, Saint Charles Borromeo in North Hollywood.

I stopped chanting and chose to leave Nichiren Shoshu Buddhism. It started to feel like a cult. If I missed certain events, they would call me to ask me where I was and why I missed the event. Sometimes, they even showed up at my door to question my practice. It felt creepy.

The icing on the cake was at a big event in Santa Monica. While we were seated to listen to the president of NSA, I decided to go outdoors for some fresh air since I was not feeling well. I went to the exit where NSA security guards were stationed. They inquired as to where I was going while the NSA president gave his speech. I said I was going out for fresh air. They promptly told me that I could not and to return to my seat.

That was the straw that broke the camel's back. I complied with their request, but I was done. The members behaved as if they were brain-washed. I saw it clearly for the first time. I was told that my desire to leave was just negativity from past lives and if I could just get past my issues, I would receive many spiritual benefits and I would defeat it. *Seriously? How about kissing my ass?* When I make up my mind about something, especially when I feel threatened, no one and nothing stands in my way. *Get out of my way!*

My love affair with Hollywood was coming to an abrupt halt. Jack was dead, relationships were shallow, the sexual obsession ever present in show business repulsed me, and my last few acting jobs were riddled with negativity. I loved acting, but the industry was turning me off. Perhaps I was simply growing up.

One morning in early November 1985, while in the shower, I looked up to the skylight in my bathroom. The rays of the sun shone through and I felt like I was showering outdoors. Suddenly, a very strong impulse rang through me. It felt like a voice, but it wasn't. It said, "Go home!" It was out of the blue. I listened to the silence while the shower beat on my skin. I stood still as I positioned myself in the sunshine that poured through the ceiling. And then, in the recesses of my heart, I realized that my time in Los Angeles was over. I accomplished what I needed to do. I no longer felt like I had to be a performer to feel like a whole human being. I no longer needed applause. Something within me was satisfied. Something seemed to have shifted.

Yes, I thought, *go home*. I stood under the shower and let the water wash over me cleansing me in my new birth. I smiled and was filled with so much happiness that I started to cry. I phoned Flo later in the morning and told her about my experience. She was not pleased.

"Baby, don't do it. You know if you leave Paul that your career will dry up out here—out of sight, out of mind."

"I don't know what it is Flo, but I honestly feel that I am supposed to go now. Something is finished."

"Paul, if you leave Los Angeles, you will be sabotaging your career. You have built up a wonderful momentum and you're about to throw out the baby with the bathwater."

Nothing Flo was telling me mattered. My mind was made up and I wanted to be with my family in simpler and humbler surroundings. Since it was November, I knew that if I acted quickly, I could ship everything home and be back in time for Christmas.

"I've been working on trying to get you seen as a series regular on the new series *Fast Times at Ridgemont High*. There's interest there, babe."

"Flo, thank you! Thank you for always looking out for me and for everything you've done. You will never know how much you mean to me. I love you like a mother and I would never do anything to hurt you. I just know that I have to go." The last thing I cared about at that moment was auditioning for *Fast Times at Ridgemont High*.

"I love you, kiddo and I only want what's best for you. But please, can you just think about it a little longer? We can talk more about it tomorrow."

"Thanks Flo, I will."

I hung up the phone, looked around my small studio apartment, and knew that I could get everything shipped home, purchase a plane ticket and sell my car before Christmas. I immediately focused on my escape plan.

I had been acting for five straight years since graduating high school—with a year and a half in Los Angeles. I had been on TV, appeared in several films, I was requested by casting directors and had a reputation at the studios, and I made a few good friends for life. The hunger to be acknowledged had passed. My inner sparkle and innocence had waned. I also allowed myself to dip my toes into dark waters: I smoked pot, I did cocaine if it was available, I drank, I cursed like a truck driver, and I lost my purity of heart—although the one thing Hollywood didn't take from me was my virginity. I noticed that I, too, was becoming competitive and greedy. Continue to hang around something long enough and you become a part of it.

One thing Los Angeles did give me was the freedom to explore my spirituality. I delved into the big questions through books, seminars and with friends. I was leaving with a restored sense of God in my life. There were no mistakes. I believe it all unfolded exactly as God wanted it to—each job, each step of the way, each incident.

Los Angeles was not heaven—no sir. I wanted to do more for others. I learned that nothing could fill me with more joy than helping my fellow man. It was the joy I felt with the sisters from Saint Mary's, it was the same joy of being alone in the church, it was the joy of being still and KNOWING that He is God. A new road lay before me. I was young and knew that if I was making a mistake, I could always return. I began to pack and ship my possessions.

My boxes, my bedroom, and my family were waiting for me when I walked through the back door of my home in Closter, New Jersey on the evening of December 19, 1985. I felt safe and loved as I ran into my parent's arms that night. I was happy and at peace. I was home.

Contemplating life and seeking answers to bigger questions.

Chapter Fourteen

———

Finding Mother

I returned to the butcher shop to work full time for my Dad. He permitted me to take off if I had an audition in the city. The staff at the time was me, Dad and Eddie. My other brothers were either married or embarking on careers of their own: John was an extremely successful salesman, Tom was practicing law as a corporate attorney, and Jamie was studying accounting at Pace University. Only Eddie chose to follow in Dad's footsteps and remained a butcher.

While working full time at the shop, I voraciously read spiritual and religious books during slow times. I continued my spiritual studies and I was hungry for God. I no longer read fiction. I had a thirst that was so powerful and deep that I wanted to fall in the blackness of the abyss that was at the core of my being—an abyss that was God's love. I had changed since I left Hollywood. 1980 through 1985 brought me to a spiritual place I would have never anticipated . . . and I wouldn't have changed it for the world.

My father, at the time, was a volunteer at the Society of the Missionaries of Charity Sisters in the South Bronx. Dad used to bring carloads of meat and food that he and his cousin Gaspar would purchase and donate to the sisters for their soup kitchen which fed a few hundred men and women daily. It was my understanding that Mother Teresa had recently come to the Bronx to establish another branch of the Missionaries of Charity—the priest branch.

The charism of the Society of the Missionaries of Charity was to satiate the thirst of Christ on the cross who cried, "I thirst." They would do this by seeing Christ in the "distressing disguise of the poorest of the poor," and serving them.

The MC Sisters had two branches—active and contemplative, as did the MC Brothers, and now there was the newly founded MC Fathers. The crucified hands of Jesus on the cross would represent the active sisters and brothers who did the "hands-on" work with the poor. The crucified feet would represent the contemplative branches—who pray for the active branches and the poor they serve through ongoing contemplative prayer. The heart, where Jesus was pierced with a lance and that overflowed with water and blood, would represent the MC Fathers, who would bring the outpouring of the Sacraments to the branches of sisters and brothers and most importantly, to the poor. It sounded beautiful and perfect to me.

My father recommended that I read the book "Mother Teresa: Her People and Her Work" by Desmond Doig. There was something about Mother Teresa that captivated me. I wanted to know more about her and her work. I felt the spirit of Christ in her work and knew, based upon what I read, that she was most likely a living saint. There was something mystical at work in the life of Mother Teresa. The more I read about her, the more my heart seemed to catch on fire, not so much to do the work, but more of a yearning and desire for God. Mother made me want to love God more. I wanted to be with God, to merge with God, and to enter into His mystery. I did not understand what I was experiencing or what any of it meant. I needed to explore and understand what was going on internally. One day, I decided to join my father to meet the sisters while making his delivery. I felt compelled to meet them.

Pop and I unloaded the station wagon. A few of the sisters looked at us in silence and smiled as we silently carried cases of meat into the soup kitchen basement. When we were through, one of the sisters asked my Dad to knock on the convent door before we left because they had to something to give to him. My father adored the sisters and I could see why. After they would say something to him, he would say under his breath, "beddu, beddu"—Sicilian, for beautiful.

The sisters were gracious, pious, peaceful, lovely, and warm. As complete renunciates, they surrendered their families and all their possessions to follow Christ in the most radical way. It was profound and appalling, but I was riveted.

We rang the convent doorbell and one of the sisters came down the stairway to let us in. She was Caucasian but spoke with a heavy Indian accent; an almost "affected" accent.

"Hello Jack, so good to see you."

"Hello Sister, how are you?" My father let out his usual chuckle and like a schoolboy rubbed his right hand against the side of his pants.

"Very good, Jack, very good. Sister Priscilla wanted me to give this to you." My father took the envelope, as he often ran errands for the sisters.

"And who is this, Jack?"

"Oh, Sister, this is my son, Paul. He is an actor and just moved back to New York from California." At this point, I was enamored with this angelic sister and I was all smiles. My father told me afterward that I was glowing.

"Hello Paul, so good to meet you. An actor, my goodness! I can see the resemblance between you and Poppa. And are you returning to California, Paul, or will you remain?"

"No, no Sister I am not returning. I am working as an actor here in New York instead and will be in the city. I also work for my Dad in his butcher shop."

"Oh, I see. Very good. I'm sure Poppa can use you. Well Paul, if you are interested, we are short on volunteers in our summer camp for our children here in the projects. Perhaps with your acting skills you can come up with some good ideas and help us out, yes?" I was flabbergasted and did not know what to say.

"Um . . . sure Sister, I can see what I can do."

"That would be wonderful, Paul. God will bless you, thank you so much. You can get our number from Poppa and maybe you can give us a call next week for more information."

"Okay, Sister. Sounds good—thank you."

"God bless you and thank you, Jack."

"Okay, see you soon, Sister," my father replied.

After we left, I felt inspired and loved what I witnessed. These sisters worked in silence and labored for the poor. Their heart was in their work and their devotion to Christ was everything. I was so impressed and deeply moved. I felt alive there and when I left, I experienced the dichotomy of how everything "in the world" paled against the magnificence of heavenly sacrifice. It called to me and everything in me wanted to know more. I was thirsting too!

I purchased another book called, "Mother Teresa: Contemplative in the Heart of the World" by Brother Angelo Devananda. Brother Angelo was a member of the MC Brothers, and I found out later that he was instructed very clearly by Mother not to publish this book. It contained portions of her personal letters, as well as portions of the Missionaries of Charity Constitution which were not public but were for the Society alone. Nevertheless, I read the book and it inspired me beyond words. I had a chance to peak into the lives of the sisters and brothers.

For the first time in many years, I wondered if God could be calling me to become a priest. The idea frightened me because it seemed very real and at the same time it filled me with excitement, anticipation, and above all, peace. There was a joy in contemplating giving my life to God. Once and for all, I would be married—married to the Christ who called me as a child.

I reflected on my life's journey, my experiences in front of the cross at Saint Frances de Chantal, learning the power of prayer during Charlie's illness, the sisters at Saint Mary's, my alone time with God in churches, my disdain of all that was fake and pretentious in Hollywood, and the fact that I was still a virgin meant that I could give God my sexuality as a gift. If I were a priest, I could give God all that I am, all that I feel, all my affections—everything. I knew it would be a difficult road, but my life would be an oblation of love to Him.

Why did I decide to come home after having that epiphany in the shower on Aqua Vista Street? Why was it so effortless to pack up and return home within a month? Was all this God's Will? Was this God's plan for me from the start?

"Oh Lord," I prayed, "Show me the way." If I was going to give myself to Christ as a priest or a brother, the Missionaries of Charity resonated with me in a way nothing else in my life had until this point. I wanted to be holy.

"The vocation," Mother said, "was not to work for the poor, the vocation was first to belong only all to Jesus." The vocation expresses itself through the vows of poverty, chastity, and obedience, and a fourth special vow of wholehearted and free service to the poorest of the poor. This is how the vocation would express itself—to be Jesus' first, and then serve Him in the poor wherever I was sent. Those words! My heart was on fire.

On the acting front, nothing much transpired in New York and the irritations I felt with show business in Los Angeles followed me to New York. The "pollution" of Hollywood stayed with me and the notion of entering religious life felt pure, clean, and far more appealing.

I decided to contact the MC Fathers in the Bronx to inquire about their next "Come and See" experience. A Come and See is a two-week visit to a community where a candidate experiences the daily routine and lifestyle of the order. The visit helps the candidate to discern if they are being called to that particular congregation. Coincidentally, there was a Come and See planned for May, so the timing was perfect. I would attend the weekend, and then work summer camp for the sisters in June and July. If the visit prompted me to apply, and if I was accepted, then I would enter the Society on the Feast of the Assumption of Mary, August 15, 1986.

While I discerned if I had a vocation, I also began to volunteer in the soup kitchen and was present and ready to do whatever the sisters needed of me—to be a Missionary of Charity—but one temporarily living in the world.

It was during my Come and See experience that I met Mother Teresa for the first time. The Missionaries of Charity Sisters were opening a house for the dying in Washington, DC. The Bishop of Washington, D.C. had given Mother the home particularly for AIDS patients who were in their final stages and had nowhere to die with dignity. The home would also serve as the Tertianship for the sisters.

The MC Fathers had been asked to drive down to Washington DC to assist with cleaning the home and to make preparations for the Bishop. Mother was there to assist with the opening of the new home, "A Gift of Peace," as it was accurately named. I was so fortunate to be on Come and See at this time. I looked at the coincidence (God-incidence) as a great gift of grace.

I anticipated our arrival with great joy—not only to be a part of opening this new home, but also to meet Mother. I'd read so much about her work and life; I felt that I knew her. I felt blessed and knew that Jesus was smiling upon me.

After four plus hours of driving to Washington, DC from New York, we arrived at the big house on Otis Street. It was at the top of a hill with a long driveway, and I thought it would be a wonderful place for people with nowhere to go to die with dignity.

When we entered the house, Mother was in the foyer. She came forward to greet us with a big smile. Here we were—one of the first groups of men that would be at the ground level of the newly established MC Fathers. My first impression of Mother was that she appeared as if she could be anyone's grandmother. She was slightly hunched over and barefoot as she approached us. She seemed overjoyed that there were vocations entering the latest branch of the Society. She took it as a clear sign that this was God's will.

I tried so hard not to appear "star struck." After all my time in Hollywood working and meeting celebrities, this was the one celebrity that made me gush. I tried to remain cool, calm, and collected, but I couldn't help it, I beamed with joy to be in the presence of a living Saint.

All the brothers and Father Eugene made a circle around Mother, and Father asked us to sing her a song. We proceeded to sing "City of God" and when we were finished, Mother addressed us, welcomed us and came to greet each of us personally. She looked very well rested and full of joy. She took each of our hands and held them as she asked us questions, such as "Where are you from?" or "What is your name, Brother?"

When she got to me, I was smiling from ear to ear and so was she. She stared at me intently and I felt as if she was looking right through me. She lowered her eyes as she held my hands and said, "What is your name Brother?"

"Hi Mother, I'm Paul . . . Paul LaGreca . . . I am here on Come and See."

"Paul! Very good, very good—we need a Saint Paul in the Society," she said as she laughed.

She continued to look at me and said, "But I know you from somewhere. We've met before."

"No Mother, I don't think so. This is the first time I've met you."

She replied, "Are you sure?"

I chuckled and said, "Pretty sure." She was so humble—not even suspecting that anyone would forget the first time they would meet her.

She smiled, squeezed my hands and moved on the next person. The other guys were all staring at me and Father Eugene was smiling. Afterward, some commented, "What was that about?" But all I could say was I didn't know. She met my father a year earlier in the Bronx and maybe she was connecting us. But, on some crazy level, I felt that I had connected with Mother. Being near Mother, and later working with her, caused me to want to please Jesus more and more—to be a good son of the Church.

When we finally settled in, we began our work in the house. Mother Teresa joined us and began washing the windows in the room to the right of the foyer. She scrubbed and moved with the rest of us—in silence. We tried to curtail our desire to celebrate and share since it was time for work, and we fell into silence as we scoured each room.

The sisters were happy to have many men to assist with the housekeeping. Mother approached me with a dirty bucket of water and kindly asked me to dump it and refill it with clean water. This time she wasn't smiling—it was work time, so I knew I had to be quick and on the ball.

Mother Teresa, while saintly, did not walk on a white cloud throwing rose pedals—she could be tough. She knew when it was time to laugh and when it was time to work. Work time meant scrubbing the floors for Jesus, to partake in the humble works for the greater glory of

God. I obeyed and wanted nothing more than to spend the rest of my life as a Missionary of Charity. I loved the hard labor, the sacrifices, the offering of my life to God for love of souls. Besides the work, there was so much joy and camaraderie with these men and women from all over the world who were giving their lives to God. The house was filled with sisters and brothers from every continent. I felt that I was in heaven. I wanted so much to be a part of it all.

My Come and See experience confirmed my desire to enter the Society, but I knew the hardest part of entering was going to be saying goodbye to family and friends. The Missionaries of Charity live their Rule very similar to pre-Vatican II standards for religious life. The complete surrender of self to God included being sent to any part of the world at any given notice with limited communication with parents and friends. I loved my family and friends, but I wanted God more. I was ready, willing, and able to make that complete sacrifice of myself to God and to the poor.

I settled my worldly affairs, phoned my friends in California who thought I had lost my mind, said goodbye to Flo Joseph, and courageously prepared for my entrance date into the Society. From that point forward, I would be only all for Jesus. I knew the learning curve would be a big one, but I had to try. I was only a child in God's eyes, and I knew I would please Him through this effort. I had nothing to lose but everything to gain—especially the hope of heaven—the only thing my soul hungered for. Perhaps this would finally be what I was searching for.

Brother Paul and Sister Dolores at A Gift of Peace, Washington, D.C.

Chapter Fifteen

——

The Aspirant

The homeless person can be challenging and a source of growth for one striving for perfection in the religious life. In soup kitchens, they will sometimes fling the soup back to you and tell you it's not hot enough, or rudely say, "get me more," or tell you "the soup sucks," or even yet, call a sister a bad name. This is the reality. Many people have romantic notions of helping the poor, but it is not the reality. It can certainly be that way at times, but not for the most part.

The challenge for me in the Aspirancy was to remain loving and kind, and not allow my own pride to get in the way of seeing Jesus in the distressing disguise of the poor. It was my responsibility to remain focused and to love each and every one of them. This was our life. It was not about handing them the soup—that was the easy part—rather it was to love them despite their hardships and shortcomings.

A real lesson came to me one morning when a tall African-American homeless man called Sister Angelina to the door at our Bronx soup kitchen. Sister Angelina was an American sister from Pennsylvania. I had a special place in my heart for her and always found her to be so devoted. Sister was sweeping and put down her broom to turn to him. The man pointed his finger in her face and shouted, "I AM MAD AT YOU." He startled us all but Sister knew him by name so he must have been a regular.

"Why, Darius? Why are you mad at me?"

He continued shouting, "You have passed me by the past few times I have been here. You haven't greeted me or spoken to me like you usually do and you act like I don't even exist. It is intentional and I am upset with you. I can't even look at you."

As I listened to the exchange, my heart went out to Sister Angelina and I wanted to say, *hey, back up buddy. What gives you the right?* I was appalled by his gall.

When he stopped his rant, Sister Angelina tenderly looked him in the eyes, paused, and took his hand.

"Oh, dear Darius, dear Darius, you are right. I *have* ignored you, haven't I? I am so sorry for doing so. Will you forgive me?"

Her humility and sincerity flabbergasted me. Darius bashfully lowered his head and turned into a ten-year-old boy. With a sheepish half smile, eyes to the ground, he said "Okay, Sister. I forgive you."

"Have a beautiful day, Darius. You and your intentions will be in my prayers in a very special way."

He left looking happy, and Sister watched him and waved as he headed for the door. While initially appearing hostile, it was perfectly diffused by love, mercy, and compassion. The sisters and the homeless began to teach me—I had so much to learn.

As we worked alongside each other day by day, I began to bond with the many of the sisters and brothers. We were a beautiful international community from every continent, working side by side to lift a piece of our suffering fellow man, all for the greater glory of God. The inspiration we experienced at times was otherworldly with a type of joy that can only be experienced by living our surrendered lives. It felt like heaven. I was so happy and so at peace to know that this was where God led me—that this was where He wanted me. He saved me, he preserved my sexuality for Him, and He taught me that there could be nothing greater than to serve others. The joy of the Society and service to the poor was everything I was seeking. It was when I returned to our convent that my anxiety would rise.

I was very "gun-shy" around Father Eugene. He was a disciplinarian and very strict in terms of formation. In religious life, it is critical that those being formed by their superiors surrender their wills so that God can form them through and with the superior. What comes from the mouth of the superior should be deemed as the holy will of God. Obedience and surrender are essential virtues to be formed. For some, the vow of poverty is a real challenge and for others, chastity, but for most obedience is deemed the most difficult by far. When young people enter religious life, they are challenged with relinquishing their wills and blindly obeying, but in time and through much practice, they learn to get better at it. This is one of the reasons why so many leave during the formation period—they are challenged by the Evangelical Counsels of poverty, chastity and obedience. I, for one, due to my exuberant nature, was challenged by obedience and keeping my rebellious nature at bay.

I spent the greater part of my life protecting myself. I shielded myself behind the china cabinet as a boy as a means of survival, later in life in my bedroom in Closter, and when I arrived in Hollywood, my apartment became a safe harbor. I learned to pour myself into books and music to escape. But now, for the first time, I was not permitted to have my own private place. There was no such thing as taking a walk by myself—you always had to have, not one, but two community members with you. This would help alleviate any desire for gossip among only two.

We were not allowed to take naps on free time, so being alone in the bedroom was off limits. The primary purpose of the bedrooms was for sleep. Our superiors kept a close eye on us to ensure that we were being formed in the same manner as the sisters and wanted to ensure that there was no scandalous behavior in our house.

I understood these rules and I embraced them. I entered knowing full well what I was getting myself into. I was encountering the difficulty of blindly obeying Father Eugene, as both the Master of Postulants and the Master of Aspirants. He let nothing pass.

If we noticed a fellow brother breaking the Rule when Father Eugene was not present, it was our duty and obligation to inform Father Eugene what we had observed or heard. In the world I had just come from, we called it a "snitch"—in traditional religious life, it is called "justice"—provided the brother reported what he saw in a spirit of charity out of concern for his brother.

In my first few months as an MC, I was called into Father Eugene's office often. As with all the men, he was trying to mold me into a good MC and to bring to my attention anything that was against the Rule. Unfortunately, I tended to be very silly. I have a sense of humor that does not stop. I find humor in everything. It is a gift but can also be a curse. My humor was the first thing Father Eugene tried to reel in.

I was given the assignment of setting up the altar before Mass, not necessarily the Sacristan, but small things like lighting the candles. One cold morning, with the lights of the chapel still dim, I walked onto the altar. I looked out at my brothers sitting on the floor in prayer and immediately smiled. First recipe for disaster—an actor spots his audience. I should have held my head down and practiced custody of the eyes as I had been taught. I made the forbidden eye contact while we were still in the Grand Silence and fought back laughter. I looked at Brother Raul who could make me laugh just by looking at him. He had a ridiculous fear of Father Eugene, which amused me in and of itself.

I removed a burnt-out candle from its holder and was trying to replace it. For some reason, the new candle would not properly set. I decided to take the entire candle holder (about 5 feet tall) into the sacristy to fix it. Wrong move! The glass holder slid off the top of the stand and smashed onto the altar. Instead of demonstrating remorse for my error (which I was), I started to laugh out of embarrassment. At that point, I heard the guys trying to contain themselves as they fought laughter. I received help cleaning up the broken glass, but it cost me a tap on the shoulder and a visit to Father Eugene's office where I was reprimanded for being careless, breaking the silence and for remaining unfocused. He was not wrong.

As time went on and we became more and more immersed in the Rule, I wanted to come out of myself and have breathing time—a time when I could let loose. There was no opportunity for it, so making eye contact with any of my brothers during the Grand Silence could, more times than not, send me into hysterics. In plain English, I was immature, but also a "creative"—an actor, a dancer, and a singer, and I looked for ways to act out. I needed an outlet.

Sometimes, when I returned from the soup kitchen for lunch and was sharing about our experiences, I would automatically start imitating the person I was speaking about. I just did not think about it. I am on autopilot when it comes to imitating others. I explain it as "people passing through me." I have an uncanny gift of picking up every nuance. Sometimes I don't even know I am doing it. The brothers would roar with laughter during some of my imitations and I could see Father Eugene fighting back a smile, but I could also tell that he wanted the conversation to stay on a straight and holy path and not veer off into un-charitable talk or slander. Once the guys started laughing, that was fuel for my fire, and I would go on a roll. When Father Eugene tapped his glass with his spoon we were to revert into complete silence. We would all stand, pray our thanks, and in silence all head to the kitchen to do the dishes.

Often, I would see the guys still smiling from my mini-comedy routines when we reverted to silence. Father Eugene did not want us to get lax, but always to remain focused on Christ. Fun was good, but it was important to reel it back in. I had great difficulty shifting—going from standup comedian to a contemplative brother at the tap of a glass. It seemed to me that the other guys were great at it, but not me. It took a lot of time for me and it was a concerted effort. Father Eugene would call me in his office twice, sometimes three times a week, to discuss my infractions against the Rule, but I must admit, nothing was ever done intentionally. I had to remain focused, but I struggled.

One evening I was on the roof hanging my clothes to dry on the clothesline. With no one around, I used it as an opportunity to sing as loud as I could—it was my way of letting it all out. I heard the bells ring summoning me for meals. But, by the sound of the bells, I knew that it was the second set of bells, which meant each brother should be in their final standing position at the dinner table. We did not begin until everyone was gathered, and I knew I was late. I must have missed the first set of bells when I was singing! I ran like a madman down the convent stairs to the refectory.

I flew down three long flights of stairs. My sandaled feet made a loud clip-clapping sound as I descended (more trouble, I thought). I passed the statue of Saint Teresa the Little Flower on the second-floor landing as I continued to descend and did not even try to control my panicked noise. I knew I would be spoken to again. I was a twenty-five-year-old-man feeling like I was a ten-year-old child. I ran and ran for what seemed like an eternity. It felt like I was in a scene from "The Birds" when Tippi Hedron was trying to escape an attack. I heard the deafening silence as I loudly clumped my way into the refectory and saw that everyone was waiting for me.

I ran to my place panting loudly and said, "Sorry" (another infraction—I broke silence). Father Eugene gave me a long, hard stare. Some of my brothers had their heads down trying to contain their smiles, and others were visibly annoyed by me. Then, Father began to say grace.

I was mad at myself and I prayed that I would "luck out"; *if I play my cards right and smile a lot during dinner, I might get away with it.* I wanted this to work and to grow in holiness but instead, I was starting to feel more and more like the misfit child from Hollywood, who, some friends claimed, was just playing another role, only this time as a religious. It wasn't true. I gave up everything to be there and I wanted to do well.

As I dried the dishes that evening with the other brothers, I felt a tap on my shoulder. It was Father Eugene. He had an exasperated look on his face and cornered me in the kitchen hallway. He adjusted his sweater over his shoulders and looked sad and disappointed.

"Paul, why were you late again? When a seminarian exhibits such undisciplined behavior, then we need to evaluate the vocation, eh? To be a good and true Missionary of Charity, we must try to please Jesus, even in the little things. Being on time is how Jesus is asking you to please him at that moment. Do you understand? Remaining faithful to the Holy Rule is THE way we please Jesus most. Please come to my office after dinner to further discuss."

I could not believe that I was being spoken to again. I felt so guilty. The prior week I had two incidents that got me into trouble—both over music. Father Brian, the Novice Master, heard me singing "La Vie En Rose" in our library during house duties while he was trying to conduct a meeting with the Novices. Right after the meeting it was mentioned to Father Eugene who later asked me why I was singing "like a French chanteuse" in the library while I was supposed to be cleaning in silence? The truth was—I thought no one was downstairs and I was disobedient by singing, rather than praying while I worked.

The second incident occurred before Mass while we were in the Grand Silence. Father Eugene tapped me on the shoulder during morning meditation and summoned me out of the chapel and into the hallway. Brother Ramon, a novice, who was assigned to music that week, was ill. Father asked me to play the guitar in his place and make song selections for Mass. I went into a complete panic since I only knew a few chords on the guitar, but Father Eugene liked my voice and thought I could pull it off. It was 5:30 in the morning and my voice wasn't even warmed up.

My hands were shaking as I quickly ran through our music book and picked the only songs I thought I might be able to play with limited chords. The first song was "All Good Gifts." Easy, I thought. I knew the song from the Broadway play, *Godspell*, but I had no idea that it was originally a hymn and was structured differently from the Broadway tune. I only knew it as a Broadway song, but I figured since it was in our book, it had been rehearsed and the brothers would know it.

When prayers started, I was shaking like a leaf and could not even pray. I began the song and started singing, "We plow the fields and scatter the good seed on the land . . ." After the first and second lines of the song, voices started falling off and no one sang with me—I was alone with this one—solo—nada from the boys. My panic started to rise. Why weren't they singing? Rather than allow myself to fall down the ever-impending black hole of anxiety and fear, I said to myself, *If I am in trouble, so be it—you might as well finish the song. I felt the blood rush to my face as I continued.*

Not only was no one singing, but there was a key change in the song that makes it higher, so you must sing louder in order to hit the notes and finish. I surrendered to my error and thought I would finish it bravely, regardless of the outcome. I was totally humiliated. I was also upset because no one was even trying. I was angrier with Michael because I knew he was familiar with the song and even he was not singing! I looked up at him across the aisle and he stood there with his hands in prayer, his head bent, and his eyes downcast on the floor. Either they were laughing at my faux pas, or they just couldn't sing it.

Immediately after Mass I stayed on the floor of the chapel begging and praying God that I would not get into trouble. Within seconds of my prayer, I felt the infamous tap on my right shoulder and Father Eugene's finger motioning me back to the hallway.

"Yes, Father?"

"Why did you select a song that no one knew?"

"Father, I honestly thought they knew it since it was in the hymnal." The guys were all looking at me as they filed out of the chapel to house duties.

"Yes, but we never rehearsed that song in choir practice. You made an assumption. Furthermore, you sang it as if you were on Broadway. Were you intentionally trying to single yourself out?"

"What? No Father . . . I . . ."

"We don't sing songs this way in the Missionaries of Charity," he interrupted. "I am serious Paul; I do not want this to ever happen again. I really don't know what else to say to you."

"Yes, Father. I am so sorry. It wasn't intentional. Please forgive me."

"Can't you ever take instruction without always trying to explain yourself? When you can be admonished and not respond, then we know we are making real progress. Pride. This is something we all need to work on, eh?"

"Yes, Father. Thank you." I couldn't win. Nothing I said was right.

I went about the rest of my day in silence feeling sad and stupid, but I accepted it as a lesson in humility. Later in the morning, Brother Raul came up to me with his strong Spanish accent and said, "This morning in chapel, you sound like you were on a Broadway stage. I want so hard to laugh but then I said, Father Eugene will see me laugh and then . . ." (He made a motion across his throat as if he was slitting his throat).

"I said to myself, LaGreca is a crazy man—what song is dat?"

He then pushed up his thick bottle glasses, looked up to the ceiling, put his hand over his mouth and broke into hysterics while walking away.

Unfortunately, according to family and friends, I can be very funny at times without me even knowing it. I am sometimes very serious but will say or do something that will leave others laughing—this can be very irritating and frustrating when I am trying to be serious. I usually do not know what I do that others find so amusing. It made me nervous as an MC because I did not want to attract Father Eugene's attention.

Such was the case one evening during the Grand Silence when I saw a huge roach crawling up the wall of the bedroom hallway. I was disgusted and since it was dark in the hallway with no one around, I slowly slipped my sandal off. I approached it carefully and then hit it as hard as I could. It fell off the wall leaving a huge streak of blood. It was still alive and trying to get away on the floor. I felt bad that it was suffering and decided to hit it with my sandal so it would die and not run away.

The halls echoed as I hit it and when I looked up, I saw Brother Ray behind me with his head down, facing the opposite wall and not moving. His head remained toward the wall as I noticed he was trying to contain laughter. He saw me do the bloody deed. Because we were in the Grand Silence, I could not explain myself but when I turned around to walk away, staring at me with his office door wide open was Father Eugene. His arms were folded, his sweater was over his shoulder and he told me to get into his office. Another scolding.

This is how it was for me. Many brothers intentionally stayed away from me because they were afraid I would get them into trouble with Father Eugene, but some were resentful and saw me as a nuisance to the MC Fathers. They did not see me taking it seriously enough and it bothered them. But it wasn't true—I truly and honestly wanted to be a good MC. When I am happy and alive with joy, I come out of my skin—that is just the way it is for me.

———

The more serious problems began for me in about my third or fourth month into the Aspirancy. When the cold weather began to kick in, on top of the grueling routine, I began to suffer from severe exhaustion. Cold weather can knock me out even after being awake for only an hour or two. I always said if I were an animal, I would be one that hibernates in the winter. When I am tired, I am often glib, overly sensitive, and say what is on my mind.

A bad incident happened one cold evening during Recreation. Recreation time in religious life is a time to share, to laugh, and to spend fraternal time in common. It is supposed to be a fun and nice time to relax and share with your brothers, but one still needs to be mindful of what is shared. Amid my exhaustion from our daily routine and the cold, I did not want to be around my brothers and would have preferred to be alone in the chapel, but we were obligated to attend. While I sat there with a half-smile and trying my best to be social and charitable, my ear went to a conversation a few of the brothers were having off to the side. One of them said, "Oh and that Shirley MacLaine, she is a crazy nut. She is an instrument of the Devil."

Having come to the Society directly from Hollywood with an understanding of how spirituality is expressed in Los Angeles and other parts of the world, the statement went right under my skin. It sounded judgmental, cruel, and something an immature, inexperienced, and uneducated person would say. There was zero eloquence in the statement.

"Wait a second," I chimed in, "Who are you or anyone else to judge her journey? The woman had experiences and she chose to share about them in a memoir. It's *her* story. What does her spiritual path have to do with *you*?" It sounded angrier than I intended.

Everyone stopped speaking and stared at me. I did not care. His comment was arrogant and uncharitable. I was starting to get a bad taste in my mouth with the "everyone needs to be a Catholic in order to be saved" belief system that I was starting to hear more and more of as I integrated into the community.

They were dumbfounded by my strong and brash response and someone else said "Don't tell me you actually believe that garbage she writes about! *DO YOU?*"

"It's not whether one believes it or not. It's a matter of letting her journey take her where it will. My spiritual journey took me to the Missionaries of Charity, and I did not always walk a devout Catholic path. What I am saying is we need to be careful in what we say and how we say it. Doesn't even Mother herself give Hindus a Hindu funeral and Buddhists a Buddhist funeral? Mother never discriminates against anybody."

"Sorry Brother, but that is not what we are here to study and do. We are here to be Catholic priests and we adhere to the teachings and Magisterium of the Church. This other new age garbage is all a diversion from the truth."

"Who the hell is talking about disobedience to the Magisterium? Let me ask you something, *did you read her book?*"

"No, of course not! Did you?"

"As a matter of fact, I did, and I loved it." Deafening silence. This turned into an all-out confrontation and no Superiors were present to witness it.

I continued, "Do you not believe that the spirit of God can manifest itself outside the walls of the Catholic Church? *Seriously?* So what you're saying is no one in the world can know God and be saved unless they are a Catholic, right? Is that what you're saying? The Buddhist woman in some remote village in China who shares her one bag of rice with her poor neighbors is not living the spirit of Christ because she is not a Catholic? Is that what you are saying? Because I have news for you my dear brother, that Buddhist woman is more worthy of the kingdom of heaven because of her act of charity, *NOT* knowing Jesus, than someone who is studying Theology for the priesthood and does not know sincere charity. We have to be careful we do not become modern day Pharisees."

They stared at me like deer in headlights. I was shaking and trying to get a hold of myself. I attempted to add a compassionate tone to my voice to bring the conversation back to where it needed to be. It was all of them against me.

I smiled, "Don't you want to know what other people believe who you will encounter out there someday? Isn't it healthy for us to have good discourse on other religions and philosophies? Why are you all so frightened of anything that differs from our faith? I'm not saying you must subscribe to it; I am not saying you should believe it or accept it . . . what I am saying is to listen and learn and meet people where they are so that our hearts remain open . . . and when our hearts are open, we can love better." Silence.

Their mouths were agape as if I had pulled a gun on them. One of the newer brothers said, "Let me ask you a question. Why are you even here?" and before I could respond the bell rang indicating the Grand Silence. The conversation had to stop in its tracks—the Rule. We lowered our heads and headed to chapel for Night Prayer. My heart was pounding in my chest. I was full of disappointment, anger, guilt, and fear. I felt very alone and took the question to heart, *why am I even here?*

I was hurt by the last comment and I realized that I was arguing with a nineteen-year-old child. Matthew, who made the comment, was young and did not have my worldly experiences. He did not have a drug addicted brother, he was not forced to grow up ahead of his time, and he never left the state of South Dakota.

I thought: *how could anyone be so pompous and self-righteous to think that God didn't express Himself in all lands and places?* But, to be clear, that does not mean that the fullness of His expression did not come through Christ—which I and all good Christians were supposed to believe. We believed the fullness of God's expression comes through Christ as expressed through His Church.

Was it my job or anyone else's to say Shirley MacLaine was heading to hell in a handbasket? Was I going to hell because I was once a practicing Buddhist, which, incidentally, led me right back to my Catholic roots? The entire conversation put a bad taste in my mouth. I disdained the pomposity.

I felt that many of these young men, as well-intentioned as they were, had not experienced enough of life. I found their responses to be immature and scary, considering the people we were going to encounter in India, Africa, Asia, and South America. Something in my heart told me not to be too harsh on them and not to respond with a similar arrogance, but to listen with compassion and understanding. I had been given a great gift through my many experiences and I had to find a way to forgive them.

When I lived in Los Angeles, I explored my life fully. I was also glad that I had the capacity to "meet people where they were." I did not want to verbally attack the belief systems of the poor we served while on apostolate, but to smile and listen—not condescendingly— but to genuinely accept that this was where he or she was in their spiritual journey. Mother never forced us to shove religion down anyone's throat, so I was unsure where all this "we're right and they're wrong" nonsense was coming from. I was very turned off. For the first time, I wanted to run to Father Eugene's office and say, "thanks, but no thanks."

The incident made me think of a young African-American woman I had met in Lincoln Hospital the prior week. She said to me when I entered her room, "No, no, no . . . you with the cross turn around right now. I don't want to hear what you have to say. I'm a Muslim and I don't eat pork."

"Okay," I said, "That's cool. I try not to eat pork either, and my Dad's a butcher." She paused.

"I'm only here to say hello, to offer a smile, and to let you know I am praying you have a speedy recovery."

"Well, I don't trust you. And besides, how can you even be a Christian? How can someone be born in December and a few months later die at 33? It makes no sense, and this is what you people believe?"

I smiled to myself at her sweet teenage innocence and found her to be amusing. As off as she was in her date and time assessment, I continued to listen and speak to her with all the love I could muster—as hard as it may have been. The brother that I was with wanted us to move on because he found her to be rude and disrespectful.

"Brother," I whispered, "No. Be still. And, get ready. Not everyone is a Christian. Some will attack us. It's not a nice world out there. Not everyone will love us. Did they love Jesus?" Our meeting with our young Muslim sister was brief, but ended cordially.

As I prayed that evening, I took a deep breath. I was not sure if there would be repercussions for what transpired at Recreation, but I toughed it up and braved it. I was too tired to think about it, but I started to wonder for the first time if this was where I belonged. I was there for almost three full months and I sensed a rift between me and some of the guys. I needed to share and process with someone about what was happening. I felt alone and isolated.

My father raised my siblings and me to ask questions—the truly important spiritual questions, to study other religions and philosophies, and to confirm my own belief system by having spiritual knowledge. The reality of the ultra-conservative and rigid mindset of the Missionaries of Charity appeared at times to be a type of fire and brimstone. There was no speculation. You were a child who was handed a Rule book that you were to blindly obey, and you were not to question anything. We were there to believe what we were taught, direct questions to your Superior, and move on. In modern religious lingo, they call this type of formation, infantilizing.

I wondered to myself, *If I study for my B.A. in Philosophy over the next four years, followed by my M.A. in Theology for the following two and followed by two years of Divinity studies, how in the hell am I supposed to survive this? As theologians we are to think and ask questions! How could I become a theologian if I could not think and question? Was I studying to be a theologian or a robot?*

The next day I felt more rested and put the incident out of my head. I had to eat, sleep, drink, pray, and work with these guys, and I did not want to be ganged up on because of Shirley MacLaine (who they were fixated on). I did decide after Morning Prayer to speak with Father Eugene about my vocation. I had to admit and own that for the first time; perhaps I was not being called to be an MC. The joie de vivre I had when I entered was turning into a mild depression and I started to experience great highs and then great lows—one day happy and full of joy, and the next day sad beyond words. I needed space and I was starting to resent having these guys on me 24/7. I was starting to feel trapped. I was suffocating. Even my work with the poor suffered because I was not putting my heart into the work as I should. I was more focused on the guys around me and who would go running to Father Eugene to report me for something. I worried about what I said, and how I said it. What I did or did not do and on and on. *What could I have done better?* I was falling into a bad case of scruples.

I began to eventually enter a rebellious mindset, and I looked for ways to escape. I went from angry to sad to rebel. The conversation at Recreation was the straw that broke the camel's back. I began to long for my family and friends—I had a support system in Los Angeles that was open and loving. I longed for open people.

I was a successful actor and a mini celebrity in my own right. I loved my acting career and gave it up to follow Christ. My agent warned me that if I abandoned my career, it would be sabotage. *Was the Missionaries of Charity the path to make me more like Jesus, or was my acting career my way of reflecting Jesus to the world?*

The joy of performing—from dancing with Kim and Grant at the Academy of the Dance to the New York stage, and from making movies and being discovered at Universal Studios had dissipated. Where did it all go? It was time to think and reassess. I also had no idea what that conversation at Recreation would cost me. The army was preparing to battle the guy who sang like he was on Broadway and had sympathy for Shirley MacLaine.

Mother Teresa blessing us in the chapel.

Chapter Sixteen

Internal and External Battles

"Paul," Father Eugene began, "You are here to be a Missionary of Charity. You are not here to receive affirmation, applause, or whatever else the Evil One whispers in our ear to discourage us. Your life is a gift to God, and He knows the Life we live is not easy. God has called you here and you have said 'yes.' Just because the going gets a little tough, it doesn't mean you run. No, it means that you offer it up to God for love of souls. It means that you bear your trials; you suffer in a spirit of patience and humility, as difficult as it may be. Even the greatest Saints had to walk through the same trials that you pose to me today. Keep persevering, Paul. Don't let the Devil get the better of you. Do you understand? There is no reason to leave. Don't let Satan win."

I sighed and looked up at him. He said all the right things and my doubts lifted. After a ten second pause I said, "Okay, Father. Okay. I will continue to try."

And try, I did. Over the next week into November, I persevered, and Father was right, it passed. The subject of the intense talk on Shirley MacLaine, reincarnation, and new age metaphysics had not come up. I was hoping it would be gone forever and that I could get on with remaining focused and becoming a good MC. The brothers hadn't brought it up either.

Father Joseph and Father Eugene announced that Mother was planning to come through the Bronx on her way to South America. We were to have one-on-one time with Mother, so we were all very excited. Father Eugene made it clear that the house was to be scoured and we should prepare a song to sing for Mother when she came through the doors. I began to feel like I was part of Von Trapp Family Singers.

At the time there were three fully-professed MC priests (Joseph, Eugene, and Brian), two novices, three Postulants, and seven Aspirants (my classmates). I was happy that Mother was coming and that I was going to have an opportunity to speak with her.

The morning she arrived, we sang our song and then were instructed to promptly head to the chapel where we would remain in prayer while each of us met with Mother one-on-one. I was looking forward to speaking to her about my vocation. I decided to let the Holy Spirit take over. It would make no sense to try and plan a conversation.

Father Eugene tapped me on the shoulder as I knelt in prayer in the chapel. He said nothing but gave me his usual stare and indicated with his index finger to come forward. I knew it was my turn to sit and converse with Mother. I was led to the small room off the chapel. I entered feeling slightly intimidated and found her sitting demurely at the side of the table with her hands in her lap. I shut the door firmly behind me. I bowed my head, folded my hands in greeting to her and bowed to her before sitting next to her (our custom of greeting was Indian namaskar).

Mother looked tiny. Who would have thought that this petite woman could make such an impact in the world? She sat with a type of silent resolve—and it was that resolve in its most basic form that made her appear so holy. She smiled at me, but she looked very tired and I felt some guilt being with her—as if I was taking a little piece of her. I knew she had better things to do than to have us meet with her individually.

"Hello Mother, I'm Brother Paul." I wasn't sure if she'd remember me from Come and See when I met her in Washington, DC.

"Hello, Brother Paul, yes, yes, very good, very good, of course," she smiled.

I brought my MC Prayer book with me which she immediately took from me and inscribed, "God Bless You, Mother." She looked up at me with her deep and sullen eyes. Her smile was gone, and I felt God's presence in her soul.

"Are you happy and at peace here at the MC Fathers, Brother?"

"Yes, Mother, I never thought I could be so happy." *Lie.*

"Good, good."

"Mother, I want you to know that even though I am happy, I also struggle here. Is it supposed to be like this? Sometimes, I am just not sure if I have a vocation to the Society."

She looked me in the eye with a faraway look and said, "You *do* have a vocation here. God has already called you to serve Him and you have said yes, and so you are here. You have been called by name to belong only all to Him. No matter what struggles you endure, Brother, let them be only all for Jesus. Remember what Mother says, if they should take you and cut you up in many pieces, all those pieces will only belong to Him. No one can separate you from the love of Christ." I'd heard her say this before. Mother had a small list of sayings she repeated frequently.

"I understand."

"Saint Paul loved Jesus so much, so much. You have to be like Saint Paul." She smiled again.

"Yes, I do want to be holy. I want to be a saint."

"Of course, of course. Look at Saint Paul; he had such a conversion . . . such a conversion."

"Yes, he did Mother, and you know, I did too." I wanted so badly to tell her about my experiences in Los Angeles and how I came full circle.

"You see that!" She responded like a parent with a child. I was endeared and enamored by her sweetness.

Mother then proceeded to write a note for me to give to my parents. It said:

"Dear Parents of Br. Paul. Thank you for giving your son to God and the Society. He is a real gift to us all. God Bless You. M. Teresa."

I was so grateful for that note and I knew my parents would be thrilled. But the meeting felt incomplete, seconds were ticking away, and I knew I wanted to go deeper with her, but I didn't know what that "deepness" was. I felt like I was losing my chance.

Mother then took a miraculous medal out of her pocket, she kissed it and handed it to me and said, "Never let go of Jesus," and then emphasized, "Through Mary."

I surrendered to the fact that we needed to cut off the conversation, and that I would not have the chance to speak further. I was grateful for the time we had.

"Please pray for me, Mother."

"Yes. Mother prays for all of you and you must pray for Mother."

"Thank you, Mother."

"God Bless You."

"And God bless you."

I rose from my chair with a sense of peace but also melancholy. I wanted to stay with Mother. I didn't want to leave her. She reinforced the desire to stay. Knowing that I couldn't be with her all the time, but that I could be close to her by doing the holy will of God as an MC, gave me peace. She restored my desire to persevere and I, once again, felt like I was part of the MC Fathers. The other minutia seemed silly, irrelevant, and fell away. It was the love that we shared that was most important. It erased the negativity. Love changes everything.

When Mother was done meeting with all the men, she came into chapel for prayer, and sat behind me on the floor. We turned to our prayer books and sang.

Sweet Lord, Thy thirst for souls, I satiate, with my burning love all for Thee. My chalice will be filled with love, sacrifices made all for Thee. Evermore, I will quench Thy Thirst Lord . . . evermore; I will quench Thy thirst Lord for souls. In union with Mary our Queen, I will quench Thy thirst.

Mother had a slight vocal wobble in her voice. She was childlike. I harmonized and together we lifted our voices to God in thanksgiving and for the gift of each other in this world.

I was truly grateful for the moment, for the opportunity, for the graces. I loved my vocation again; I loved the Society—my MC sisters and brothers—and I loved Mother. I felt that I could have spent hours with her talking about everything from spiritual thoughts to Calcutta. Her presence and my time with her inspired me to persevere with the things that please God—to let my light shine and to be an instrument of His love.

A few weeks after Mother left, while still in deep thought from our meeting, Father Eugene summoned the community to the third-floor library. We were missing Brother Ricardo, but Father started to speak anyway. I received my first real shock. Father Eugene informed us that Ricardo had chosen to leave the Aspirancy and return to La Paz, Bolivia.

"Fellas, this is the first time for some of you when one in your group has chosen to leave. Ricardo had his reasons and we must pray for him. At this time, Ricardo thought it would be best to return to his family. This will not be the last time one of you will leave. When someone goes, as difficult as it may be, you must learn to keep the focus on your own vocation. The best thing to do is to pray for Ricardo and for his needs and intentions."

In actuality, it didn't surprise me. Ricardo started disappearing from apostolate and chapel, claiming to be sick. He also spoke no English and was learning it amidst an already tedious Aspirancy schedule. Whenever you asked him a question, he always responded with "could be." The poor guy. *Hey Ricardo, how is that book you're reading?* He would shake his head and say, "could be." *Brother Ricardo, did you see Father Eugene downstairs?* Could be. *Ricardo, what time did Father say to meet for confessions?* Could be. It was a little annoying, but also very sweet. I loved Ricardo. After he left the next morning, I never saw him again. In the secret of my heart, I was glad he was going to be with his momma and poppa again. If God was calling him, he would be a good priest with his people in La Paz. *God bless you dear Ricardo, wherever you are.*

Someone leaving the community can be a very upsetting thing. It jolts you. It is shocking, sad, and somewhat scandalous. It can also raise questions as to your own vocation. Ricardo's leaving shook me up. If he couldn't handle it, could I? Was I wasting my time? My talk with Mother went right out the window. The Good Lord knew that I struggled every day, but struggle was part of it. It was through struggle that we grew in faith and stretched ourselves to grow in holiness. The question always comes down to: What is an authentic struggle where one remains? At what point do you have to realize that this, in fact, may not be where God is calling you?

The attrition rate is very high in the Missionaries of Charity for the simple reason that it is a very hard life to live. It is strict and demanding, and only a handful from each class perseveres to the end. Many vocations from third world countries do very well as MCs because they are used to the great sacrifice that is demanded of them. They do not know the material wealth and the freedom that we have in the west, and so they have less to miss.

When I was on Come and See, two of the brothers who were Postulants were no longer there on the day I entered, so I was somewhat familiar with that empty feeling of missing a brother you'd gotten close with.

Chris Shaw was a very powerful force for me. He was from Boston and from the first day of my Come and See, he radiated Christ. He was warm beyond words and had a wise sensibility about him. When you spoke with him, he would squint his handsome Irish eyes and listen intently giving you 100 percent of himself. He was respectful and so full of kindness that I said to myself, "If this is the kind of person I can become, then sign me up." You can only imagine how I felt when I entered and found out that Chris had left. I was devastated.

Juan Carlos, on the other hand, was from Mexico. He was insanely funny and brought so much humor to the Come and See candidates. He behaved a little flamboyant (so I knew Father Eugene must have been on his case). As we would walk to the van for our apostolate in the morning, he would pretend he was on a conga line and dance his way to the van. And one time when Father Eugene asked us to pick a Saint to portray for a play we were going to perform for the Contemplative Sisters, he said in a very strong Mexican accent, as he crossed both arms across his chest, "Please, let me be Joan of Arc, so I can burn at the stake." I could not help but laugh out loud, and I could see Father Eugene struggling to compose his laughter.

Coming from Hollywood with all those "over the top" people, I thought he was a riot. On the day I left my Come and See, as I was walking down the walkway, Father Eugene was at the front door waving goodbye but right above him two flights up and out of his view, was Juan Carlos, waving a white hanky out the window and shouting, "Please have a cocktail for me . . . go dancing. Dance, baby, dance!" He did not know Father was listening and I could not turn around and show him that I was laughing. I bit my lower lip and walked out of the gate. I couldn't wait to return knowing that we would be brothers forever, but I never saw him again. Juan Carlos left a few weeks before I entered. He returned to Mexico due to a visa issue, but when the Fathers went to pick him up at the airport, he never came off the plane. I was sad to learn this after my entrance day.

Unfortunately, attrition is a part of "the life." A long formation is beneficial to someone discerning his or her vocation. The life of a religious is not for everyone. Poverty, chastity, and obedience can be very challenging to live day-in and day-out. A strong prayer life helps and guides the soul to the desired virtues deeply rooted in Christ, but sometimes God calls some to the married or single life. Not everyone has the capacity to make the required sacrifices for a lifetime—some learn this right away, while others leave after profession. It is a life against nature. An MC sister, priest, or brother could be sent to any MC house in any part of the world on a moment's notice, so the vocation needs to be solid, mature, and deeply rooted in God.

Some of the sisters and brothers were saintly in their approach, and I knew I needed to emulate them. Here I was in the United States, my country, and feeling pain over missing family and friends who could visit me on the first Sunday of each month. Around me were sisters, priests, and brothers from Italy, Ireland, India, England, Germany, France, Brazil, and Bolivia, and each day they persevered beautifully—they never knew when they would see their families again. Seldom did their pain show. By the end of November 1986, I wondered if I, too, could remain. Ricardo's departure opened Pandora's Box, and it took away my peace.

Finally, the week after Ricardo left, I went to Father Eugene. "Father, I hate to tell you this, but the feeling of wanting to leave has returned. I just have a gnawing feeling that I do not belong here. I feel creatively stifled and I am not sure if I have the stamina to continue."

"Did you share any of this with Mother when you sat with her?" I recapped my conversation with Mother, and he said very matter-of-factly, "Then it is clear, isn't it, Paul? You are being tempted yet again. This is the third time you have asked about leaving and I wonder what it is about you that the Devil wants so badly? Some of the greatest Saints have struggled with these issues. Keep praying, Paul. Run the race, fight the good fight. Don't let anyone who leaves the Society prey on your weaknesses and your ability to give and to love. You are stronger than that and as your spiritual father I encourage you. Go and plead with Our Lady, our dear Mother in heaven. She will guide you."

At moments like these, I loved Father Eugene. He had to be tough with us and form us into solid priests, but deep down he was a gentle and loving soul who probably struggled with his own demons. I genuinely loved him—even writing these words after many, many years, my eyes well with tears thinking about him. I wanted to hug him in gratitude which was against our Rule. I began to realize how badly I needed affection. I wanted to share with someone, I needed to be heard . . . I wanted a long bear hug. I wanted to feel loved.

I left his office and felt much better having let the steam out of the kettle. I also beat myself up because I was so weak; I wanted to appear strong and solid. Perhaps, I thought, God allows this to happen to humble us so that we can learn true humility and surrender to Him. I learned that we can do nothing on our own; God had to be in the driver's seat at all times.

I wondered if the other brothers struggled as much as I did. I know Michael did. I was still close with him and we tried our best to practice detachment from each other. We broke the Rule and shared alone only when we absolutely had to for the sake of retaining our vocations. We couldn't always run to Father Eugene for everything and some things are best shared with a brother—not with Father Eugene. If not for Michael, I would have had no one else to turn to. If we went to any of the other priests, the chances were good that Father Eugene would be informed.

At the same time, poor Father Eugene was under an incredible amount of pressure. Not only was he the Aspirancy and Postulant Master, but his brother was living in Manhattan and had gone into full blown AIDS. His brother, Timmy, was gay and had no family nearby except Father Eugene. Father wanted to ensure that his brother was cared for and would die with dignity—and hopefully return to the Church. Also, our Superior General, Father Joseph, had malaria and was often ill in bed, leaving Father Eugene to run the house.

This kind of pressure would exhaust any normal human being and Father Eugene was no exception. As time went on, he became more and more curt, and his patience was minimal. Minor infractions against the Rule often became big in his eyes, and everyone walked on eggshells and feared getting in trouble. By this time, I tried to develop a tougher skin and learn how to navigate Father Eugene. Once I know my players and how they operate, I can work well around them. *Thank you, Hollywood!*

Father Eugene used his brother's illness as training for his Aspirants. Timmy became a part of our apostolate, and because I had a career in show business, Father asked me if I would accept a new assignment caring for his brother. Timmy had been an aspiring actor at one point, but basically ended up abandoning his career. He was a loving, sweet, maternal type, and worked in New York restaurants. He also socialized with Broadway's elite, so it was a good match.

My duties included cleaning his house, cooking, or helping him in any way he needed for the few hours I visited. It was also important that I speak to him about God's love and mercy. I was honored that Father Eugene asked me and took it as a great compliment. Since we do not travel alone, Brother Andre was assigned with me. Father Eugene felt that because Timmy had been in show business, he would be able to relate to me.

Andre and I took the D train to Manhattan from Kingsbridge. I had to contain my excitement but as soon as we stepped onto the streets of Manhattan, I let out a big sigh of relief and said out loud, "Hello, Manhattan! It feels so good to be here." Andre smiled without commenting but my heart was racing. I was home and in my stomping grounds. I missed it all! I wanted to visit Phil Black's, run into friends, have a bagel with a smear of cream cheese, and see what shows were playing on the Broadway billboards. I secretly relished this grace God had given me and we proceeded to Hell's Kitchen; Timmy's apartment was on 9th Avenue and 51st Street.

Timmy and I hit it off instantly. It was as if we had been friends for years. He was very "show biz"—and his lingo opened the door I was trying to contain as a religious. He started calling me "hunny," as we show people like to do. We spoke about what was happening on Broadway, his friends Chita (Rivera) and Liza (Minnelli); we looked at photo albums and on and on. We were friends from the get-go. Andre did not add much to the conversation, since it was a world beyond him, but he did smile at our excitement. While I conversed with Timmy, Andre would assume the humble tasks of clearing mouse traps, cleaning Timmy's stove, and sweeping.

Timmy was ill and emaciated, but still able to get around the apartment. Father Eugene wanted him to go to the AIDS shelter the MCs opened in Greenwich Village named, "Gift of Love," but Timmy refused to. He felt that he still had friends and somewhat of a social life and was not in need of nuns caring for him until death.

In addition to cleaning, we also picked up small amounts of groceries for him at D'Agostino's, and basically provided him with a fun home visit. He shared stories with me of Father Eugene when he was young. I found him to be charming and grew very close to Timmy.

At times, however, he would push the envelope and say, "Why are you even pursuing this priesthood thing? It's not who you are. The one in the kitchen cleaning was made to become a nun, but not you, hunny—you still have life in you." His words rattled me and he hit me in my weak spot.

"Tim, I know what you mean, but I think our creative energy is God energy. Isn't it all the same thing? I believe whether one chooses to pray in a seminary or to pray on a stage by touching hearts through a good performance, it's very similar. An actor does for an audience member what they sometimes cannot do for themselves. I think God has called me to something different and I'm happy."

"Whatever you say baby, but one thing I can tell you, when my mother comes to town and sees what Eugene looks like, she's gonna have a fit. He has gotten too skinny." He pulled out his photo album and showed me a picture of Father Eugene with a woman in his younger days. He had been a successful doctor.

As usual, I bid my dear friend a fond adieu and with a closing prayer, Andre and I headed back to our home in Highbridge.

That evening at dinner, Father Eugene said, "And how is Timmy faring, Paul?"

"He is doing well Father. He is great, so funny; I never realized how hysterical he is. We really enjoy each other's company. Today he showed me an old photograph of you in your younger days . . . a full set of hair . . . and . . ." I continued, and as I did, I felt that what was coming out of my mouth was getting me in trouble. It was too late to back-pedal and inwardly I felt myself going into slow motion, but the words were out, and I was toast!

Father Eugene's face went red. I am not sure what I said exactly that triggered his anger. I also wasn't sure if it was Tim that would be in trouble or me, but he was mad and could barely contain the steam in his kettle.

"Have you been talking to him about Jesus?" he asked an hour later in his office.

I stumbled for a second because Jesus had not been the main topic of our meetings.

"Uh . . . yea Father . . . at times, yes, but not all the time."

"At times?"

"Yes." He folded his arms and stared at me.

"And what do you talk about in all the in-between times?"

"We speak about show business, things that make him happy, his friends, new restaurants . . ." Wrong, wrong, wrong.

He looked as if I told him I put a school on fire. His eyes widened.

"Oh, Paul. How disappointing. I trusted you. I trusted you to go and inspire my brother." My heart sunk and I felt like the biggest failure in the world. I let Timmy down and Father Eugene.

"Father, I am so sorry. I thought that by being a friend to him and listening to him, no matter what he wanted to share about, that I was doing God's Will."

"Yes, but it is also your responsibility as a seminarian to bring God into the conversation."

"I did, though, Father, I did. Truly. I tried so many times, but he wasn't receptive. I was giving it time." Father wasn't hearing it. He looked down at this lap.

"This confirms what I had heard from Andre, who has already come to me. He told me that you are not fully adhering to what was asked of you." Father Eugene was exasperated, and I felt that he was over-reacting.

"I have no more to say here. I need to think about this conversation. You are excused now."

I got up from my chair feeling guilty and frightened. I did not fully understand what just went down between my superior and me. One thing I knew for sure, I was not the type of person to shove God or Jesus down anyone's throat. Timmy and I had become friends and we understood each other. I knew from experience that introducing someone into a deeper relationship with God takes time. It is not forced or shoved, and Mother would be the first to tell us that (each morning we prayed, "Not by my words, but by my example . . .")

I believed that by developing a friendship with Timmy he would eventually see that my life in Christ could be a joy filled one. He would continue to pray with me and Andre and slowly God would kindle his heart and perhaps even ask to have Confession before he passed on. He respected my boundaries and even though he asked me why I was there—a very normal question given my exuberant nature—he never persisted or made me truly uncomfortable. Perhaps I was wrong. Maybe my approach was all wrong.

I began to wonder if perhaps Father Eugene was upset with the fact that I saw into his own past by being shown the photo—a past that was personal and that he did not want shared with the men who were in his care. I was praying and hoping that Father Eugene would not call his brother and scold him. He seemed so happy with our visits.

I was not as upset with Father Eugene as I was with Andre. He had gone to Father and shared that I was not living up to the expectation of our apostolate with Timmy. Of course, he delivered the news in "a spirit of charity," but I do not believe that. Andre appeared to be jealous of me. He was extremely insecure, and the two of us had a natural rub from the start.

He had reported me a month earlier when we were assigned to kitchen duty together. We were two men with no cooking experience and were expected to come up with meals from donated scraps. My "takeover" attitude and my desire to get the job done had been perceived as "pushy and bossy," and he told Father Eugene that he could not get along with me in the kitchen.

Father Eugene had suggested that I might want to consider, in a spirit of charity, conceding to Andre and letting him take over, no matter what I thought would be the next best thing to do in the kitchen. I was to fill my heart with kindness and love and be mindful of not being condescending to Andre, but allow him to take over in a spirit of humility. It was an opportunity for spiritual growth and perhaps Father Eugene was correct. It just angered me that Andre ran to Father Eugene to inform him that my conversations with Timmy were not always about Jesus or returning to the Church.

Andre resented my Hollywood past based on some of his off-handed comments ("The cameras aren't rolling right now" or "Is that face you just made a TV look?") or perhaps it was plain jealousy. Who knows? It was fine, though. I knew that with prayer, time, and forgiveness things would be better, but I was so hurt to think that he would report me to Father Eugene without at least making some suggestions about Timmy to me first. I did not believe that Andre reported me to Father Eugene in a spirit of charity. I think it was done in a spirit of resentment. It made me start to question the validity in the "reporting things to your superior rule" because many brothers took it out of context. Was it in place for the purpose of control? Otherwise, it made no sense to me.

The morning after my meeting with Father Eugene, I was again summoned to his office. With very little emotion he said, "You are to join Michael and begin work with the mentally disabled at Lincoln

Hospital. Sister Maureen will explain the apostolate when you arrive. I have assigned another brother to join Andre with the home visits to Timmy."

I felt like a complete failure, but I knew I had to accept it. Disappointments were a part of the life. If I was not going to accept these exercises in spiritual growth and learn from them, it would be better if I just left. I braved through it, however, and dealt with it.

At lunch the same day, Andre made a point of telling me that Timmy asked for me and sent me his regards. I looked at Father Eugene and he smiled—not maliciously—but with compassion and kindness in his eyes—as if to say, "I know it is a sacrifice, but it is all for the best." As much as I wanted to be angry with Father Eugene, I loved him very much. I do not believe for one second that the pain he caused some of us was ever intentionally malicious. He wanted what he thought was best for us.

Meanwhile, on the floor for the mentally handicapped, a male patient stripped when he saw me and jumped on my back while I was playing the guitar and singing with the patients. It took three nurses to get him off me. I was with Brother Michael, who was so mortified that he spent the rest of the day with his back against the wall so he wouldn't be jumped.

We also met Norma, who was about nineteen years old. She begged me and Michael to call her mother for her and to tell her she loved her and that she would be home soon. She didn't have a dime to give us for the phone call, but she gave us her phone number. I loved Norma—she was very dear, and I was happy to help. As I was leaving, I promised the head nurse that I would phone Norma's mother for her. The nurse looked at me and said, "Call Norma's mother? What? Who asked you to do that? Norma?"

I smiled and said, "Yes."

"She's taking you for a ride, Brother. She tried knocking her mother off a few weeks ago." Michael looked like he needed smelling salts, and dramatically put his hand over his mouth and backed up against the wall. At that point, I just wanted to get the hell out of there. I was exhausted and felt like I would soon be admitted myself. At home, Father Eugene's pressures surmounted—and so did ours!

"Visiting Sunday" - the joy of seeing Mom and Dad
and the pain of watching them leave.

Chapter Seventeen

Things That Make You Scream

In the Catholic Church, on what is referred to as a "feast day," such as the Annunciation, or Christmas week, the title of "solemnity" is given to the day. It is a day, even if it falls on a weekday, that is deemed like a Sunday; Sundays are always solemnities. This meant the rules lessened somewhat in the house, and we had the opportunity to let our hair down. We could speak at meals and have treats, such as coffee (instead of tea) with breakfast, and peanut butter and various jams (instead of the traditional oil with salt and pepper dip). On one such solemnity I was very at peace and happy.

At breakfast, I took a piece of bread and spread peanut butter. I then proceeded to place some grape jelly on it. I poured some coffee and began to enjoy my breakfast, laughing, smiling, and joking with my brothers. I was truly happy. The brother serving us placed a new type of jam on the table so rather than spreading more grape jelly, I tried the new orange marmalade. I commented and said, "Wow. This is delicious."

At that moment, I looked up and saw Father Eugene's face and thought to myself, *oh crud.* I knew I crossed some type of line, but I wasn't sure what I had done wrong. It was likely that my comment about the marmalade tasting good was simply made in poor form. I proceeded to finish my breakfast and tried to put it out of my mind.

As we proceeded to the kitchen to wash dishes, I felt a tap on my shoulder and was motioned into the hallway by Father Eugene. I braced myself and tightened my gut.

"Yes, Father?"

"Are you aware of why I looked at you at breakfast?"

"No Father, I'm not. What did I do?"

"You added two types of jam to your bread."

"Yes, I did. I guess one jam would have enough?"

"We want to be mindful of virtue, Paul. It's a type of gluttony. I know it might sound silly but we need to be mindful of what and how we eat. Yes, one type of jam on the bread would have sufficed." In the greater scheme of striving for virtue, what he said made sense but I was getting more and more exhausted by it all and I wanted to scream.

I took a deep breath and with everything I could muster, I said, "Yes Father, I see. I never looked at it that way. I'm sorry. Thank you. I promise that it won't happen again."

He pulled back and seemed to appreciate the fact that I acquiesced to his admonishment. I know I must have turned beet red in embarrassment and went back to the kitchen trying to process what just happened and knew that I would have to confess gluttony on the following Friday in Confession. When I entered the kitchen, I made eye contact with Michael. He looked at me with a half smirk and knew I must have gotten in trouble for something.

The week before, I was irate with Father Eugene because Michael was getting ill from some of the food we ate. Father Eugene, in more words or less, told him that if he could not handle the dietary standards of being a Missionary of Charity, then he should leave and go to the Dominicans who would be more than happy to accommodate his dietary needs. When Father was angry, he always suggested alternate congregations—which I gather was supposed to act as a threat.

I received the old "alternate congregation" threat once when we were gathered for tea after our 1:00 PM siesta. I gave a yawn which came out too loud and feared Father Eugene's wrath. He looked at me, however, and grinned—almost laughed. I relaxed.

"Paulito, did you not get enough sleep?" Whenever he called me Paulito it usually meant he was in a good mood, and I was in good standing, so I did not think I would be in trouble by saying, "Oh no Father, I'm fine. I just think I need a little sugar to pick myself up. I'm actually craving ice-cream for some reason."

Everyone hesitated and looked up at me. My classmates knew I meant nothing by it, but the Novices who were far more advanced along the road to becoming full-fledged MCs knew Father Eugene would disapprove of the comment by the look on his face. Father Eugene wasted no time and said, "The Carmelites, I believe, serve a lovely dessert each evening after dinner. I'm sure they would love to have you. There are probably all kinds of ice-cream with a variety of flavors."

I kept my mouth shut and looked down. I was embarrassed. Just moments ago things had been going so nicely and I blew it again. I started to feel as if I couldn't win. If I spoke, I said the wrong thing; if I was quiet, it was *why aren't you sharing with your brothers?* If I was being funny it was, *why are you trying to make yourself the center of attention?*; if I needed alone time, it was, *why are you isolating?* It was starting to drive me crazy and being a creative guy, the suffocation worsened. I am certain he felt the necessity to break me down so that God could build me up, but truly all it was doing was making me angry. The "rebel boy" in me just wanted to stand up, tell him to shove it, and walk out the door.

I was exhausted beyond words. I felt deprived of sleep from our daily routine and life. *If I could only get some extra sleep*, I thought, *I wouldn't be so sensitive, and I could deal with everything better.* I needed time alone and I needed to think—just think with no one around me. Quite frankly, the desire to leave reared its head again. I could no longer see myself living this way for the rest of my life. I wanted to draw, daydream, stare at the trees in the woods, sit by the ocean, have a cup of coffee with Mommy and not worry about everything I said, to hug Daddy and rest my head on his meat-stained flannel shirt, smell my yard after an August rain, lay on my bed at home and just think—nothing more, nothing less. I knew my days were numbered.

Mother made another surprise visit to the Bronx after coming from Nicaragua, where she was asked to open a new house. We had Mass with her at the MC Sisters' convent and then afterward she received us, the Aspirants, into the Society—even though we had already been there four months. It was more of a formality to be received by Mother. We were nearing our Postulancy and there was no guarantee when we would see Mother again. It was like a rite of induction. She had also given Father Eugene permission to remove six months off the normal time in the Postulancy—that would mean a year and a half of Postulancy instead of two years—that was huge. I could only surmise that they wanted to make priests out of us sooner rather than later.

I looked into Mother's eyes with joy as she took my hands in hers. I was on my knees in the chapel as she stood over me. I held her hands tightly and sent her the vibrations of a loving son. She was getting old and looked very tired, but she always had time for her children—the fathers, sisters and brothers, and, of course, the poor.

Mother smiled back at me and said, "Brother Paul, accept this rosary as a sign of your entrance into the Society in the name of the Father and of the Son and of the Holy Spirit." Father Eugene watched standing in a corner with a look of satisfaction and joy on his face. I was elated and thrilled to be one of Mother's sons. I decided again to forge forward and keep "fighting the good fight," as Father Eugene had suggested. She kept my vocation alive.

Mother went on to the next man until she had finished giving each of the Aspirants their special Missionaries of Charity rosary beads, and these rosaries were special indeed. They were made by leprosy victims from the MC leprosy colony in India and the beads were seeds from Indian banyan trees.

I kissed my rosary beads and quickly placed them in my right-hand pocket, ever to be my comfort and strength—not only were they made by the poor, but Mother handed them to me. I couldn't wait until the Postulancy when I would receive the next visible sign of my life as an MC—a cross over my heart. Hopefully, I thought, Mother would be in town at that time as well.

After Mother gave us our rosaries, we headed over to the soup kitchen to serve the men for Thanksgiving. Mother and Sister Frederick, a senior sister from Malta, came to work and greet the men and women in the shelter. It was lovely and a beautiful day. After we cleaned the soup kitchen, we stayed with the sisters until later in the afternoon, and together as a community we watched the film, *Mother Teresa*—a film produced by Ann and Jan Petrie that had just been released theatrically about Mother and the Missionaries of Charity.

Mother hated any kind of publicity and how the Petrie sisters convinced her was beyond me, but the film was beautiful and touched the heart of what it meant to be an MC—the formation, the work, the labor, the fraternity, the poor, and how we satiated the thirst of Christ on the cross.

The Society was not for everyone. It was a very specific call. It originated in India where sacrifice was a natural part of everyone's life. No one craved or wanted what they did not know. I knew there would be suffering, but I did not know to what extent. Even though I wanted to run for the hills, I had the fortitude and patience to give it my best shot or as my father would say, "the old college try"—and that I did.

I had years and years of practice as a child in dealing with painful situations, so it was ingrained into who I was. Living with a drug addict brother, understanding self-preservation (without consciously understanding what I was doing), and realizing I was very different from my siblings created a strong survival instinct within me. I had to learn how to laugh in the face of adversity, or I was never going to make it as an MC . . . or in life, in general.

December came and with it came visiting Sunday. I needed the comfort of my family and on this one Sunday in particular, many came to visit. I was not sure how thrilled Father Eugene was to see so many people show up so he gave us one of the larger rooms in the front parlor; otherwise we would have taken over the refectory. I was nervous about that visit and wondered if he would say something to me about so many family members showing up. It was so important for me to be in the loving arms of my parents at that time. *This was real love*, I thought. This! What I had with them—that unconditional love that knows no end and has no boundaries. I understood what Mother meant when she said, "For love to be real, it must hurt." My heart was in two pieces the entire time my parents visited. I wanted to leave with them, and it was so difficult to fake it for them. I wanted them to think I was happy and not to worry. I was fine before they arrived, but each time something reminded me of the life I left behind and what it meant to be *truly* happy, it reminded me that I wanted to leave.

On that particular Sunday, my Mom brought a large pot of tomato sauce, a tray of lasagna and meatballs. She made it for the brothers as a gift. When I handed it to Father Eugene, he placed it with the other donated goods. I thanked my mother up and down for her generosity and my heart was so heavy. She wanted everyone to get excited and say, "Mrs. LaGreca made us Italian food! Wow! That is awesome." She would then feel like she made an impact by doing something nice and making us happy. Unfortunately, we were not permitted to comment—but she didn't know that.

When my family left, they were so happy, and it took everything in me not to break down. The dichotomy of the love I felt with my family and the "love" I felt with the MC Fathers were two different things. The Fathers was rooted in suffering and sacrifice. I was very, very tired and no longer felt I had the strength to bear the routine. I wanted the kind of charity my family offered.

The next day, Father told us that all the donated food was sent to the soup kitchen and only selected items would be retained for the house. I had a hunch he would send my mother's food away and my feeling was confirmed the next day. I wanted to believe he did it for love of the poor, but at times I was not sure what his motives were. I suppose he was trying to make us humble.

On Christmas Eve, my feelings were solidified when we got to call our families to wish them a Merry Christmas. It was my first Christmas without my family. When it was my turn to call home, I dialed my home number, but the phone was busy. Rather than hold up the line, I got on the back of the line again. When Father saw me, he asked me what I was doing. I said that the phone was busy, and I didn't want to hold up the line.

I watched him think for a moment, and then he turned to me and said, "Accept it as God's Will that He does not intend for you to speak with them tonight." He then dismissed me from the line. I would not be calling home. He also added, "Besides, your family is local and comes to visit every visiting Sunday. Imagine how some of your other brother's feel whose families are far away?"

I was shocked, hurt, and couldn't take it anymore. I was at my wits end and felt like I was being punished for having a loving family that happened to be local.

After Christmas, at our monthly renewal of permissions meeting, Father Eugene looked tired and irritated. He gave me his hard stare, so I felt something bad was coming.

"Paul, I received a disturbing phone call. One of the parents, who will remain nameless, informed me that you have openly shared with your brothers that you have issues with the Catholic Church and that you believe in reincarnation and subscribe to the new age philosophy. I was told you were pontificating about Shirley MacLaine. Can you explain this?" *WHAT?!*

For the first time, I lost it! I saw red and wondered who the idiot was that shared this with their parents. Who was the parent who had the audacity to call Father Eugene?

I raised my voice for the first time. "Oh Father, *YOU HAVE GOT TO BE KIDDING ME?* What is wrong with these guys? And these people? Do you all live under a rock? Who called you?"

"How dare you! I don't owe you any explanations, rather you owe me one."

"As seminarians and men studying philosophy for the priesthood, we conversed one evening at Recreation about various religions and forms of spirituality—some of which I studied in the past. It was not anti-Catholic at all, rather I tried to present an educated dialogue into things we should be aware of in a world filled with spiritual diversity. It was nothing more, I can assure you. Pontificating?"

"First of all, I make the decisions as to what dialogue on spirituality we have and when. Secondly, these men had every right to be annoyed with you. They are here to be Catholic priests and didn't want to hear you proselytize about your spiritual discoveries. No one is interested in your Buddhist past. Additionally, I have made it very clear that the past is the past and should not be discussed with anyone."

"Well, if we can't be open and discuss these things with each other, I cannot see how any of these guys can reach out to people in strange lands. Not everyone is Catholic. These men live in insular worlds when it comes to what is out there."

"I'm only going to tell you this one more time; it is my job to form these men, *not you*. You must assure me that you have let go of these beliefs and that you will not instigate a debate again." *Yea, whatever.*

At this point, I just wanted to leave. I had enough of him, the place, and the big babies who cried to Daddy. It was all stupid and a reflection of such a fear-based and overly orthodox mindset that it was making me sick. I was a traditional seminarian for sure, but I was open to dialogue about other belief systems. I was kind, and I celebrated people for who and what they are. What happened to the words TOLERANCE, and CHARITY? How about non-judgment? I wondered if Father Eugene was going to scold the other guys for being judgmental. If I was being accused of shoving an unwanted mindset down their throats I would have deserved to be admonished. Clearly, they did not know how to cope with anything that was different.

"Yes, I assure you of this and I won't speak of it again." I patronized him.

After that meeting, I fell into a very deep depression. I was not sure if I wanted to recite my promises to enter the Postulancy on January 11, 1987. I developed a deep-rooted resentment. I prostrated myself in the chapel when no one was in there and handed Jesus my cares and worries. Fortunately, the chapel was the only place you were permitted if you were not with another brother. I remained in the dark and stared at the altar.

Why, Oh Lord, have you called me here, only to have me fail? What is it that you want of me God? I am so alone, so afraid. Please come to me and give me peace and consolation. Please Father. I gave up my acting career to be here. I feel so lost, so alone. I want to be holy. Is it me, Lord? Am I hard-hearted? Will I ever learn humility? Or is it my superiors? Is it their lack of experience at being superiors? Are they troubled too? How do I survive this Lord and make it work? Have mercy on me, O Lord, have mercy on me.

I decided to put on my best face, but I was only going through the day-to-day motions. I was hoping and praying that God would send me inspiration so that I could persevere in my vocation. It wasn't all Father Eugene, the guys and the house. It was me, as well. Perhaps this is not where God wanted me, and I only needed to be here to learn certain lessons. Maybe I had to undo some of the self-seeking behaviors that took root when I was in Hollywood.

As hard as I tried, I did start to break the rules. I broke the Grand Silence when I needed to share, and my prayers began to feel empty, dry, and meaningless. I fell into severe desolation and rebellion. I could not stop thinking about leaving once again, and I made up my mind to go. This had to stop. I wanted to rest, and I needed sleep.

I once again asked Father Eugene if I could meet with him in early January to share about leaving the community. I felt stifled, I was suffocating, and I could not take it anymore. I needed a creative outlet and I needed to be alone.

"Can't you see, Paul? It is so clear to me that the Devil is tempting you right before your entrance into the Postulancy. You are one week away, and Satan will do everything in his power to remove you." *Here we go again.*

"In all honesty Father, I am not sure how entering the Postulancy will change the way I feel."

"I am telling you, I have seen this before; it is the Devil. He is tempting you to leave us. For some reason he wants you out of here. Again, I emphasize that you should remain and enter the Postulancy. Laugh in the Devil's face."

I asked if I could pray about it, and he said yes but not to wait too long to get back to him. And, off I went once again, to pray and discern God's will. Was I being called to this constant roller-coaster of ups and downs? When does one know when it's finally time to throw in the towel? I put our meeting out of my mind but prayed to God to give me a sign whether I belonged there. It was all so exhausting.

Lost, lonely, and depressed.

Chapter Eighteen

Defeated

The soup kitchen apostolate became my favorite, primarily because I was friendly with so many of the sisters and they brought me needed peace and consolation. Since I entered, one of the sisters in my group, Sister Janice, had been sent home. It was decided that she had no vocation as an MC and that perhaps she would flourish elsewhere. Once again, she vaporized, no goodbye, no phone number, nothing. It made me sad because I loved her energy and the joy she brought to the poor. I will never forget the two of us leading 60 day-camp children through the streets of the South Bronx singing "Hooray for God."

Sister Pascal, a French sister from Lyon, who I had also known from summer camp, was professed and waiting to enter Tertianship prior to final vows. I would often catch her watching me from afar and when we made eye contact, she seemed far away, sad, and lonely. I caught on to her stares and tried to speak to her. I found her captivating.

"Sister, I know I have no right to ask you this, but are you okay?"

In a very thick French accent she replied, "Paul, please pray for me. I am praying for you too."

"Thank you, Sister, that means a lot to me. But I am concerned about you. If you don't mind my saying so, you look like there is something disturbing you."

"I am thinking to leave, Paul. And if I do, will you promise to remain in touch with me?"

"Wait, what? Oh, Sister you can't leave, you can't abandon your vocation. You are about to enter Tertianship."

"No one knows Paul, and I'm sorry to have to burden you with this. Please forgive me. You have always been so kind to me, and I know that I can trust you."

"When would you leave?"

"Mother is coming to town and . . ." Sister Pascal had no time to finish since another sister was approaching and we both feared being reported to our Superiors for speaking in private.

In January 1987, the six Aspirants preparing to enter the Postulancy were about to begin our studies at Saint John's University in Queens, New York. I was thrilled because I love academia and have a hunger for knowledge. We were about to commence our studies as first year seminarians.

It was announced the following day at the Bronx and Harlem soup kitchens that we would no longer be there to assist, but the newly entered class of Aspirants would take over. Most of the sisters smiled, nodded and genuinely wished us the best of luck as we embarked on the next step to priesthood. They were so proud of us—priests in the making.

A few of the sisters, however, got teary eyed and one, Sister Jabamala, made a bit of a scene telling us how much she would miss our presence and how much our help meant to her. She cried and said, "Please come back soon."

That evening Father Eugene called the Aspirants into the third-floor library and went into a tirade. He was angry, and visibly upset.

"I received a phone call from a few of the sister superiors. What is this I hear about sisters being attached to some of you? A few sisters were upset at the announcement of your going to University?! What has happened? I want to know right now what kind of conversations you had with them and why they would react like this! Mother has made it very clear, *VERY CLEAR*, that the brothers and sisters should be very mindful of their time together so as not to be attached. This is how vows are broken by careless and mindless comments here and there, a wink of the eye; all of it that eventually leads us down the wrong path. The Devil will use anything and everything in his power to bring you down. The day you no longer believe that, is the day you need to pack your bags and go."

The sexual undertones and innuendos of Father Eugene's admonishment felt creepy. As he spoke, I kept thinking—*for the love of God, we are human beings!* A sister got upset, so what? It happens. Mother herself said we were born to love and to be loved. I never witnessed anything overtly sexual during my time with the MCs and I was spiritually fed by being around the sisters, and now, with the onset of studies, that lifeline was cut off from me.

In the eyes of the world, what Father Eugene was sharing would seem wacky, but if I forced myself into the mindset of the superiors who showed concern, I understood. I didn't like it, but I understood their perspective. It was not uncommon for priests and nuns to fall in love.

Father Eugene and Father Joseph were clear and adamant that there would be no scandal in or out of our house. There would be "no cracked doors" that would allow Satan to shove his foot in—everything was nipped in the bud the minute it was spotted.

I learned over time that some of the other brothers (and sisters) walked on eggshells and were in fear most of the time. We all tried our best to persevere. I knew that this was all a part of formation and I had to be strong and solid in my faith to handle it.

I decided not to ask to leave again and made a conscious decision to continue. I promptly informed Father Eugene that I would like to be installed into the Postulancy and to begin my studies at Saint John's University. He was thrilled with my decision and told me he was proud that I shared what was on my mind. "God must have wonderful plans for you, Paulito."

The limited notes I have in my MC notebook, states, "My month of desolation has ended. I have come out feeling renewed with great joy and happiness with new insights into myself. Praise be the name of Jesus Christ. Struggles are learning experiences and we need them. I am happy . . . imagine! A Postulant! Take Lord and receive all my liberty, my memory, understanding, my entire will—give me only your love and your grace—for that is enough for me."

On January 11, 1987, we recited the official formula into the Postulancy and received the MC cross which was pinned over our hearts. It was to be pinned each morning for the rest of our lives.

Our schooling began immediately. I hoped that this new adventure, which would take precedence over the apostolate with the poor, would help me and ground me. I could not wait to sink into the books.

After breakfast, the other Postulants and I piled into the MC van and headed for Saint John's University. We were to retain silence in the van after saying one rosary. Upon arrival at the University, we were instructed to mortify ourselves by keeping our eyes down. Father Eugene explained that there are some who have a sexual appetite for men studying for the priesthood. We were shown where the chapel was and were to stay close to each other—no one person would ever be permitted to be off by himself. If a brother had a class alone, he was to regroup with his brothers as soon as possible.

Father Eugene enrolled me in five courses for a total of 15 credits: English, Spanish, The Fulfillment of Man, The History of Medieval

Philosophy and Theology: The Liturgy after Vatican II. I had brothers in all my classes, except English, which meant that after class I had to meet up immediately.

The University world was exciting to me. I wanted to learn. Something woke up in me. It was exciting to discuss ideas, ask questions, interact with other people, speak with the Professors—I loved every minute of it. Even more exciting was visiting the amazing library. I loved walking up and down the rows of books. Books! I relished running my hands along rows of binding. I felt at home and alive at school and I knew it would be a wonderful experience.

My first large group lecture for the course The Liturgy after Vatican II was with Dr. Julia Upton, a Sister of Mercy. She did not wear a religious habit but wore a small cross on the lapel of her blouse. She deemed herself a Sister, naturally, but also a professional woman, and wanted to be addressed as such. Some of the other brothers in the class felt scandalized by her, primarily because she was not in a religious habit, and secondly because she clearly presented the more progressive ideas in the Church. It may not have necessarily been my style either, but I immensely respected her and was open to her human experience.

The Vincentian Fathers who ran Saint John's University were also progressive. To them, orders like the Missionaries of Charity, were archaic and did not help the Church move forward. My brothers warned me to stay prayerful, be attentive, and to only do what I was asked to do. My brothers reeked of conservative orthodoxy and what they were professing was just as extreme as what the progressives were teaching. It was all too ridiculous and creating unrest in me.

During Professor Upton's lectures, Isaac would turn to me with his face aghast at what she was saying. She scandalized him to the umpteenth degree, but each time he turned to look at me, I turned away. I refused to make eye contact; I found her to be very interesting. *She may not be like an MC, but wasn't she entitled to express her spirituality in her own way?* She was presenting the reality of the Church as it is today and I felt that my brothers and I, no matter how much we may have disagreed with her, should learn the state of the Church. Education is powerful to me. Learn the facts! The Church has a large umbrella and I felt there was room for diverse thinking—to each his own is a wonderful thing!

One of her lectures included a guest speaker, Father Damian, a Vincentian, who gave a talk on women in the Church and proceeded to speak about women's ordination to priesthood. He asked the auditorium, "How many of you think Julia would make a good priest?" Half the hands went up around us and I thought my brothers were going to faint. I thought that Father's talk was somewhat manipulative and quite frankly, Saint John's had a large population of non-Catholics, as well as young, non-practicing Catholics who could give two hoots, so it wasn't like he was asking the question to the fervent of prayer.

Something wonderful but challenging happened at St. John's. I was able to breathe fresh air again. I felt somewhat liberated in those hallways. I found quiet places to think alone without the confines of being watched. The atmosphere was an experience to be lived, but I could only participate within the capacity to which I was permitted. It felt like I was living in a stuffed closet and was only allowed a few hours a day to go outside for fresh air. It was amazing. I loved it there.

In the classes, the guys continued to annoy me with their combative dialogue with professors or other students—all in a spirit of charity, of course. They were defending the faith whenever they felt an untruth was being taught or expounded, which, in all honesty, I respected. They were very courageous. I usually kept my mouth shut, but these guys would not let some things go. There were times, however, when they sounded plain, downright judgmental and it was starting to turn my stomach in a way it hadn't before.

At home, it was worse. In our poverty and limited possessions, we had one typewriter, and we had to share it. We could only study in the designated time periods of our routine, which were extremely limited, and there was no way, as a new student, that I could absorb some of the lessons. My hunger to learn began to supersede my hunger to be a Missionary of Charity, but my love for God never wavered. I was getting angry. *Why even bother sending us to school if we couldn't maximize our potential?* It made no sense to me and I could no longer buy into the notion of simply doing what you're told. The formation model felt condescending and non-collaborative.

Father Eugene told us that the important thing was not to worry about getting A's, just do what you can, and do well; the vocation is to be a Missionary of Charity, not a scholar. He was right, I suppose. School should have been secondary—but for me it wasn't—and therein was a clear indication that I had no calling to be an MC. I wanted to love God and give my life to him, but I knew deep in my heart that it was only a matter of time before I left—and this time there would be no thinking about it. It wasn't *if* I would leave, but *when*.

One of the saddest moments of my life came when we were driving back from school one afternoon. I was depressed and feeling trapped. I sat in the last row of the van with my head against the window as I watched the cars on the Cross Bronx Expressway drive by me. Suddenly, riding alongside our van was my father in his meat truck. My heart leapt out of my skin. If I would have stretched my hand out of the window, I could have touched him—that's how close he was to me. I went into a state of shock and shouted, "Hey. It's my father. It's my Dad." I started banging the window hoping he would see me if only for an instant, but he drove past us and never saw me.

I placed my forehead on the window and tried to fight the tears. It felt like I was kidnapped, and my rescuer had driven by and missed me. The brothers all looked at me because of my outburst. No one reacted. No one said anything. They all looked like a bunch of cold, brain-washed zombies. It was a moment of clarity. It was so unnatural. I had to get out.

The next day at the University, we parked in our usual spot and began our walk towards our first classes. Technically, we were still in silence.

Just then, walking out of a room was my friend Miriam who I had not seen since before I entered—the Miriam who told Jack Hexum "it's my friend's birthday" at Farrell's Ice Cream Parlor many years earlier. I knew she was going to law school, but I did not know it was at St. John's.

I let out a scream, "MIRIAM," and I ran away from the guys and right to her. I hugged her, kissed her and we were both so excited to see each other. The guys quickly approached, and I introduced them to Miriam and gave them a brief history of our friendship. They politely nodded, smiled and then waited to the side. At that point, I could give a shit about what they thought.

I asked Miriam what building she studied in and when the guys had their heads turned, I gave her a wide-eyed stare and quick head shake so that she would know something was not right. She said she is in the law café every day from 11:00 AM -12:00 noon. I whispered that I would meet up with her; there was so much to share.

Miriam was an oasis in a desert. I kissed her goodbye and ran off to join the guys, both of us knowing that we would speak again. My heart leapt with joy and I counted the minutes until I could get away from the guys and get to her. I did not care. It was over in my heart. I crossed an invisible line.

I snuck to the law café in my free time and met up with Miriam.

"Paul, I am so happy to see you. Oh my God! It was weird when you called me. I was like, *is that Paul?*" We both laughed.

"You look like you lost a lot of weight though. What's going on? Is everything okay?"

I began to recount my experiences from beginning to end, soup to nuts, and told her I had to get out of there.

"I don't blame you. Oh my God, Paul. It sounds kind of insane. Don't stay any longer. I think you should continue with your studies, but I'd get out of that house if I were you."

How I needed Miriam! I wanted to stay with her and not leave her side. She made me so happy and gave me the peace I needed. I felt authentic love with her. After speaking with Miriam, and subsequently meeting with her on whatever free time I had, I chose to leave. I was breaking rules all over the place and my list of sins against the Rule grew exponentially.

Coincidentally, the brother who had left after my Come and See, Chris (from Boston) was also continuing his studies at Saint John's. He was living with one of the MC lay helpers who assisted him after he left. I thought I was never going to see him again, but my heart skipped a beat when we all ran into him. As MCs we were instructed to be cautious outside of our own. Once someone leaves, they should be avoided. It was always important to concern yourself with your vocation and protect it from outside influences. We were warned by Father Eugene that we might see Chris, but secretly, I couldn't wait. I loved Chris and so did everyone who got to know him. I was so happy.

Chris and I made eye contact and he began to chat with the group. I kept the conversation alive and well. I did not care how the others behaved but it was too uncharitable to walk by someone we once called a brother and then ignore him—Rule or no Rule. It was mean, rude, stupid, and mostly, un-Christ-like.

I gave Chris a big bear hug and whispered that I wanted to meet up with him. He told me his schedule, so I knew where to find him and I did. I told him everything that was happening in the house and what I was going through. He looked at me with his typical concerned, loving eyes and said in his strong Boston accent, "Pollie, it's not good for you there. Ya gotta get out. "

We were conversing out in the open on a small hill and anyone could see us. Unlike Miriam, he knew the drill. He was only staying with the MC lay helper until he finished his school year. "Come on, follow me. Let's get out of here for a few minutes."

I was breaking the rules again, but it felt liberating and wonderful to run to his car with him. I got in the passenger seat and we went for a spin while he told me what had happened while he was there and why he left. He still had his beautiful faith, but he had demons to walk through since leaving. I knew that if I left, I would have much to deal with. Chris was damaged, angry, and trying to process his experience. I was so grateful to be with him. I wanted to wrap my arms around him and embrace him for as long as he needed, or for as long as I needed. I truly believe that God sent Miriam and Chris to me—my two Irish buds—to give me the strength I needed to leave once and for all. My mind was made up.

I was cornered by Father Eugene on the evening of February 1, 1987. He wanted to speak with me. He recounted that someone had reported seeing me with Miriam and he wanted an explanation. I told him the entire story of my long-lost friend and how happy I was to see her. He was not thrilled with how I told him the story. There was no more fear or trepidation in my voice. I was in the driver's seat.

When I was finished, I took a deep breath and said, "And Father, I do want to leave. I would like to go as soon as possible. I am grateful for my time here, but I do not think I can live this life anymore. It is not my love for God, Jesus, or Our Lady that I walk away from, but I can't live the MC life. I will return home and possibly begin a search for another order."

"I have told you time and time again that it is temptation. It is the Devil that is trying to get you out of here and . . ."

"No Father," I interrupted, "It is not the Devil. Mother said, 'God speaks to us in the silence of our hearts' and my heart is telling me that I cannot stay any longer. Please bless my decision before I end up leaving on bad terms. This is the fifth or sixth time I have come to you and in all honesty, I can say that I have tried."

He slammed his hand down on his desk and said, "You are obstinate and so full of pride, Paul. Couldn't you try one more time, for Our Lady?"

"No Father I can't try for Our Lady, or for you. I want to go home. *I want to go home.*"

After a long pause, and a silence that seemed like ten minutes, he looked at me defeated. "Okay, but the only thing I ask is that you go about the routine normally and tell no one. I don't want the house upset. I will find the right time for you to go and then you will leave straight away."

"Okay," I said with a sigh of relief. "I can do that."

"That's all then."

"Thank you, Father. Thank you. I will never forget my time here. I love you all."

I felt free and I wanted to jump up and down! It felt great to know that I wouldn't have to worry about the small stuff anymore—scrupulously looking for sins I commit, asking permissions, trying to get along with everyone, trying to be perfect, being snitched on. Yes, it felt good not to try to be perfect for once. I just wanted to be me.

I sat in the chapel during Recreation and, as requested, did not tell anyone. I prayed to God to make sure I was making the right decision and that if it wasn't, to give me a sign, but it felt right. All I could think about was seeing my mother and father soon.

Before retiring for the night, a note had been placed under my door by Father Eugene summoning me to his office. I was in my pajamas and felt stupid and exposed.

I gently knocked and hoped he hadn't changed his mind or wanted to further convince me to stay. I heard a very gentle, "Come in." He was reading the newspaper at his desk and did not look up from it.

"I changed my mind," he said nonchalantly as he flipped pages. "I don't want you to wait," he said as he continued to read. "You should leave in the morning, first thing." He looked up. "After breakfast go to the chapel and meet me there and you will be on your way." His delivery was emotionless and cold. I was glad that he was sending me on my way, but I had nothing left in me. I was a confused mess and didn't even know who I was anymore. I wanted my parents. I wanted to fall asleep in my bed with the sound of my sisters talking in their bedrooms.

I stared at him and finally, I said, "Okay, thank you, Father." For whatever reason, he wanted me out of there as soon as possible. Fine, I thought. I figured he loved me, he was hurt and did not want me to go.

The following morning was business as usual although I was getting more and more nervous. I had not been out of the convent walls as a civilian since the summer, and I had become another person in a six-month period. I would no longer be protected on subways by wearing my cross and by being with my other brothers. I would be alone.

I did what I was instructed to do after breakfast and stayed in the chapel. I was kneeling in deep prayer and begged God to quickly intervene if my leaving was not what he wanted. Suddenly, I started to feel guilty and full of dread but at the same time I could not imagine myself staying another day. It was a double-edged sword. It was a crazy dynamic.

After the brothers left for University, Father came to the chapel to fetch me and we walked down the side stairs to the door. I had my MC bag with me containing my one change of clothes and my bible. Father Eugene handed me back an envelope of cash I had given him when I entered. It is customary to save monetary donations until profession so that if anyone should leave, they should have their money back to start their new life. I thought that was very kind.

Father Eugene looked me in the eye and put both hands on my shoulders. He was smiling but it looked like he wanted to cry. His eyes became glassy and his face was illuminated in love. I was trying to cough back tears as I looked at him.

"You've been a joy in our community, Paul, and a gift to all who know you. You have been a ray of sunshine and I think the most difficult thing for me is how I am going to tell the fellas that a very strong light has left us. Like me, I think they will be very sad."

I was very touched by Father Eugene's words and I kept coughing back tears. I said, "Oh Father that is so kind of you. If the Rule permitted me to take a rest to catch up with myself or even just to sleep, I think that might help. I just need to rest. I can't go on."

He smiled broadly, threw his head back in laughter and kindly said, "My goodness, can you imagine how unfair that would be to the brothers if we allowed you to go home and rest and then come back?"

And with that he gave me a strong and long hug—the embrace I hungered for—and I felt his love and fatherly care. At the end of the day, when all the formation is said and done, this was the real Father Eugene. He was no ogre; he was a beautiful man of God, with a lot of pressure trying to run a house. He was doing his best. He played devil's advocate very well in trying to retain seminarians.

I asked for his blessing and got on my knees. He blessed me and when I stood, he handed me a token for the train. I hesitated to open the door and I wanted to burst into tears. I felt so torn, so confused. My heart was so full. I turned around and looked at him. He was smiling with so much love in his heart and I felt like I was hurting him.

"Be well, Paulito," he whispered, "And don't be a stranger."

"I won't Father. I promise. Thank you for everything. Thank you."

On February 2, 1987, I closed the door to the seminary and took the side walkway to the front gate for the last time. I was trembling as I lifted the latch to the gate and closed it behind me. I looked back to take it all in one last time—the upstairs window where Juan Carlos cried out that I should go dancing, our little garden on the right where we grew our own vegetables, the side of our beautiful chapel, and the front walkway that Mother Teresa took to our front door each time she visited. I took a deep breath and said thank you to God.

I began to cry. My hands started to shake. I kept saying to myself, *don't panic, you'll be alright.* Don't panic. I tried to compose myself without falling apart but I couldn't. I began to cry hysterically and stopped to cry against an apartment building. I tried to compose myself and rushed to catch the D train to Port Authority. Tears were rolling down my face. I wanted to get home as soon as possible so that

I could see my parents. They had no idea I was coming home. Something opened up in me and I became frenzied and uncontrolled.

While my heart wanted nothing more than to leave less than 12 hours earlier, my heart was now full of love for the Society, Father Eugene and my brothers. I could not cope with the guilt. Guilt. Guilt. Guilt. This was not ordinary guilt, but debilitating guilt. I was in a state of complete panic as I headed home.

I remembered a similar walk home when I was a little boy freezing at Ruckmond Pond. I was panicked then too but I learned to rely on God. My spirit was shattered, and I felt lost and alone. I could not think straight. I prayed to God for the strength to carry me—and He did. I could not do it alone. I had only to trust.

I transferred from the A train at 176th Street Port Authority to catch the Red and Tan number 20 bus to Closter. I would now be home in 30 minutes.

After I disembarked the bus, I walked down High Street, the block I lived on, with my one bag and my head low. I wanted no one to see me so I picked up speed. When I saw my house, I started to run until I reached the walkway to the front door. I stood on my porch and looked around taking it all in. It was a surreal experience and felt like I was dreaming—not because I was happy, but because I was not in my right mind.

I looked at the porch, which needed to be swept, covered with leftover autumn leaves. The chipped gray paint of the wooden floors hadn't been scraped and painted over. I placed my hand on the small black mailbox next to the front door—the same mailbox that brought news from Hollywood studios when I was a boy, my World Explorer membership kits, and the acceptance letter from the MCs. I wondered if this is how Sister Janice felt when she was sent home, or even Ricardo. I took a deep breath and rang the doorbell. Seconds later my father answered the door.

"Daddy?" I threw my arms around him and started to cry. I placed my face on his shoulder and held him close to me. I smelled his shirt, his skin and wanted him to hold me like I was a little boy again. I wouldn't let him go.

"Paulie! Oh, for heaven's sake, what are you doing here? What's wrong? What happened?"

"I left, Dad. I couldn't do it anymore. I just couldn't do it. I'm sorry."

"It's all right, poppa, you're home. Don't worry."

My mother heard my voice from the kitchen and when she saw me, she screamed, "Paulie!" She ran down the hallway in her apron and started hugging and kissing me.

"It's okay," my mother said heavy-heartedly. I could tell she was trying not to cry as she smothered me with kisses. She required no explanation. "Don't worry dolly; you're home now."

They were confused, but I was too distraught to speak. Everything I held back came forward as if a floodgate had opened.

"Come in, come . . . have a cup of coffee and talk to us."

They were speaking but their voices were drowning out. I was caught in the reverie of their love—a love that I was hungering for. There are no words to describe how happy I was to see them. And yet . . . and yet . . . while I was grateful to see them, there was another underlying layer. I had lived a life immersed in God and now I chose to leave and come home. The guilt had reached its apex when I walked into the house.

My head was spinning with questions. *Had my heart been on fire all along for God at the MCs and I just didn't know it? Could it be that I couldn't see the forest for the trees? Oh my God, I am home, but I am so sorry if I am offending you! Was Father Eugene right? Did the Evil One get me?* And on and on went my thoughts until I thought my head would explode.

Yes, I was happy to see my parents and my body was home, but I realized within the first hour that my heart was lost, and my mind was nowhere to be found.

Daddy, me, Gloria and the twins, Debbie and Mary—the warmth and safety of home.

Chapter Nineteen

Home

I went to my bedroom and looked around. It was filled with the remainder of things I had not given away. Prior to entering, my wardrobe had been donated to the poor, and the journals I held close to my heart since childhood had been burned as an offering to God, but my bookshelves were still lined with books and records. I started to go through them one by one. The guilt of leaving was so overbearing that I felt determined to eliminate anything that hinted of worldliness or "evil." I was having a mini nervous breakdown.

I became frantic and went from shelf to shelf pulling off records and books. I paused for crying jags that I could not control. I collapsed on the floor and curled into a ball and stayed there crying until I fell asleep. My parents thought I would be happy to be home, but the guilt of leaving was intolerable—I could not cope. I then started feeling guilty about making them feel bad.

Each day I made a new pile of things to toss. I loaded large garbage bags full of cassette tapes, videos, books, records, and anything that didn't have God attached to it. My parents watched me with pain in their eyes as if I'd gone mad—and in some ways, I had. They were at a loss and there was nothing they could do. They had an innate understanding that I was undergoing a process, but they could offer me no consolation, as hard as they tried. The impact of the Missionaries of Charity on my psyche was intense and it wasn't until recently that it subsided.

Going into the refrigerator was also an overwhelming experience—*all that food*—every shelf filled to the brim. Lights were on in rooms with no one in them *(waste!)* and water flowed abundantly when it shouldn't be running. No one prayed before meals and if we prayed grace as a family, it was too fast. *Dear God*, I thought, *save me, save me from all this. What have I done, O Lord?! What have I done? I have made a grave error. Help me, Help me.*

I was weak and not eating and my parents continued to worry. My father told me years later that there was a sadness and heaviness in the air that was worse than the day Charlie died. Everyone walked on eggshells around me for fear of triggering me. I was in a complete fog. I would go to the attic storage closet, sit on the floor and cry out loud so no one could hear me. Much of my time was spent in prayer at Saint Mary's church across the street.

I also started to obsess about the sisters and brothers and wondered what they were saying about me. I wondered if they hated me or if anyone missed me. I mentally continued living the routine with them. Each time I passed a clock and saw the time, I knew where they were in the daily schedule. I tried to live it with them even though I was not there. I was experiencing intense withdrawal and separation anxiety. I knew I needed help.

Since I was enrolled at Saint John's in the winter semester, it would have been foolish to drop out of my studies. School was keeping me sane and I wanted to continue. Books and learning were to become an important part of my recovery. I also knew that I would see the guys. I hung onto the hope that they would embrace me and assist me in easing my conscience. Out of respect to the MC Fathers, my father had the semester tuition transferred to his name so that he could pay for my first semester of college.

My first day alone on campus was a traumatic experience. When I parked the loaner car my father provided, his old green station wagon, I got out and the first thing I saw was the guys from afar. I ran to them and put on my best face. When they saw me, they all smiled and greeted me, but no one said much. It was extremely superficial, and I could have been anyone. Some looked at me sympathetically and others were stoned faced as if I was now in the enemy camp.

Brother Clark, however, did tell me that he was sad that I was no longer in the house and that when Father Eugene shared my departure, he told the guys that "sunshine" has left our community. I was very touched and surprised to hear that. He beamed as he told me as if he were handing me a gift.

No one said much after that. It was awkward and I was not about to explain my decision or what occurred. I think most of them knew that I was not a fit in the Society. I was mentally frail and psychologically holding on to them, fearful of breaking down and justifying them to say, *"Just look at Paul. Do you see how he broke down? See, this is why no one should leave."* As polite as they were to me, it felt distant. They were following the Rule.

I was able to make eye contact with Michael who told me with his eyes that we would speak later. That was all I needed—a tiny spark of affirmation. Since I was in most of their classes, I knew I had to play nice in the sandbox. I had to do my best to get through the semester and bite the bullet considering my suffering. I did what I had to do.

The good thing about returning to the University was that it kept me occupied and helped to acclimate back into a routine.

Later in the day, Michael pulled me aside when no one was around and handed me a letter. He told me to read it later, but he also filled me in and said that Father Eugene reminded the guys that they should be mindful of what they shared with me (as they would with any MC who left).

We were taught that when someone leaves the Society, they should be respected but caution must always be made. The "glamorization" of leaving and returning to the world could tempt others to follow in suit and the vocation must always be protected. My religious life experience seemed to mirror what one experiences when leaving a cult, as much as it bothers me to have to admit that after all these years.

Michael's letter was a sweet recognition of our friendship. He wrote about how difficult it would have been if both of us remained, since we were such good friends and always in trouble. One of us had to be the "sacrificial lamb" and leave for the other to remain. He looked at me as that lamb and promised to pray for me forever. Michael was truly a brother, although I did not believe one word of that letter. In my heart of hearts, and with all the struggles he endured (worse than mine), I knew it would only be a matter of time before he left as well.

Recognizing my mental state, I realized that I needed to share and process my experiences. I decided to speak with Dr. Julia Upton, my professor from the lecture hall—the "progressive and dangerous" nun. Sister Julia seemed like a very viable option because I knew she would objectively listen to a troubled student. She was not a fan of the pre-Vatican II religious model, so I felt she would appreciate what I had to share and offer insights.

I went to the lectern after my next class with her to inform her

that I left the MCs and that I chose, on my own, to finish the semester
I had begun.

"So please, don't associate me with them. I am on my own now."

She was immediately sympathetic. "Are you okay?"

"No, I am not okay. I feel lost, sad, guilty, and emotional . . . I
don't know . . . I can go on and on, but I am really struggling." She saw
that I wanted to cry as my voice started to crack.

She invited me to come and speak with her the next day; the
woman who was criticized by my brothers demonstrated kindness,
empathy, and charity.

I poured out my heart to her and I cried trying to explain what I
had experienced over the past year. She listened attentively and shared
some of her own feelings ensuring me that I was not crazy, but processing and actually grieving. She assured me that others have gone
through the same thing after leaving religious life and did suggest I
see an on-site counselor at the University. She understood the need to
process guilt.

Most especially, I was constantly worried that I was committing
a sin if anything negative came out of my mouth about the Society. It
was drilled into us that whatever happens in the Society should remain
proprietary. We must never publicly share how MCs live their lives
because not everyone would have the grace to understand our Rule,
our choices to enter, and why we wanted to live a more austere life.
I did not disagree with this notion, but I still needed to share and
process.

I promptly met with a counselor who suggested that what I
described was "cult-like" and that only time would heal me if I consistently process and journey through the experience with a professional.
I was very open to that but again, fearful of what I was sharing. I did
not want to bring any scandal to the MCs.

A week after I left, my father's brother, my Uncle Frank, had a massive heart attack and passed away. His wife, my Aunt Betty, was legally blind and there was no one to look after her. Coincidentally, she lived in Whitestone, Queens and was minutes away from Saint John's. I volunteered to move in with Aunt Betty and stay with her while I commuted to Saint John's. My plan was to finish the semester and then attend a local college back home in New Jersey. I was enjoying university and wanted my B.A. At the same time, I could be a missionary in my own way and still serve the poor—in this case, my Aunt Betty who was in need.

Sister Julia and I developed a very nice friendship. I began to see that her spirituality and the way it expressed itself was just different. She solidified my notion that the more "progressive" sisters, brothers, and priests had a place within the vast umbrella of the Church. I knew and she knew, however, that on the flip side of the coin, there were progressives who thought orders like the MCs were archaic in nature. We were a few decades past Vatican II and the majority of the orders in the Church no longer lived within the context of the former model. A good representation of how we lived our lives as MCs can be seen in the outstanding Australian mini-series, *The Brides of Christ*, or the Audrey Hepburn film, *The Nun's Story*. No exaggeration—these films contain the closest depiction of my experience.

The more austere orders of the Church basically felt that progressivism "let the world" into their convents and a process of secularization had occurred, thereby watering down the total sacrifice men and women made in giving their entire self to God. I do not entirely disagree with this notion. The more progressive groups, in addition to no longer wearing the religious habit, sometimes lived in apartments rather than community. They did not adhere to a strict and regimented Rule that guided their every step. They socialized, went to films and restaurants, and basically lived secular lives. Mother used to tell us that the vocation was to belong to Jesus first within the walls of our MC houses and that "when there were no more poor to serve, we would be contemplatives."

Sister Julia was very kind, and I wanted the MCs to know. When I shared what she had done for me they seemed appalled that I would even consult her. I shared that she invited me to her final profession which would be held in the university chapel. They asked me if I was going, and I snapped back with, "You bet! I wouldn't miss it for the world."

At the end of March 1987, I learned that when some of the sisters asked about me, Father Eugene told them that he "dismissed" me because I had trouble with Catholicism (back to Shirley MacLaine again)! After I asked to leave five times because I was stifled, exhausted and could not live the MC life, this is what the sisters were being told. My sorrow and guilt turned to anger, but there was nothing I could do. I took the high road and let him say whatever he wanted. I tried to switch my perception of his wrongful sharing—believing that he was hurt because I left.

I also learned that surrounding myself with the MCs at University or in the soup kitchen on the weekends, was not healthy for me. I needed to make a clean break from them. I needed the semester to end so that I could get on with my life. Sadly, a few weeks after I left, some of my other former classmates started to leave.

Two weeks after I left, Michael bid the MCs a fond adieu—so much for the sacrificial lamb note. He returned to his parents' home in Scranton. Andrew left shortly after and returned to Steubenville, Ohio. Boy, was it good to speak to Michael on the phone! We processed our feelings together. It was a time of healing without rules, snitching, scolding, and whatever else stood in the way of developing the friendship that existed between us.

I was sad that the others left because I did want them to succeed but I also think a part of me felt validated. I did not feel like I was alone and crazy. I even felt guilty when others left because I feared that I may have said or done something that caused them to leave. Perhaps that was natural considering how we were trained, but of course, it was not healthy thinking. I had power over no one. Others had learned that "the life" was too difficult over the long term, as I had.

Still being attached to the sisters, I did not stop volunteering at the soup kitchen. It was always a joy to be reminded of why we were there—to serve Jesus in the distressing disguise of the poor. Doing the work itself and living the life of an MC inside the Society were two different things.

I finished my first semester of college and earned 2 A's, 2 B's and one B+. I made the honor roll. The most important thing was that I was away from the guys. The blocks in the road to healing were clearing. By the end of May, I was starting to relax and breathe again, and may I dare to say, even feel happy. I started to spend a lot of time with my high school pal Joan and it felt great.

Joan was a big part of my high school years; it felt like we were soul mates. She was, and always will be, a great light in my life. Joan was encouraging, supportive, loving, and helped me to see the value in who I was as a person. She was, and is, the epitome of a best friend. Each Friday and Saturday night we would go out. Joan helped me to buy new clothes and afterward, we ended the night with a fun dinner and some drinks. I started to feel great about myself again—I even managed to gain some weight back.

I was about to turn 25; it felt surreal. The first 25 years of my life were packed with eclectic experiences. I'd abandoned my career, which now seemed like a distant memory, and I left religious life. I did not know where I was heading exactly, and I needed time to sort it all out. I decided to keep taking courses towards a degree and to get a part-time job. Since I began my academic career as a Philosophy major, I figured it would be best if I retained it. If, in the future, I chose to return to religious life, the necessary philosophy degree would be in place, and secondly, at twenty-five years old, it was important to complete a degree, rather than switching majors and postponing completion.

I secured a job at a local retail store and prepared to take general courses at our local community college. At the start of 1988, my brother John had a receptionist's position open at his company in Valley Cottage, New York, which I gladly accepted. I continued to study and work. At the end of each day, however, I still found myself with confusing thoughts and feelings—school, the MCs, depression, Hollywood, and more guilt. As hard as I tried to be holy in the world, it was challenging.

Joan recommended that I speak with a therapist she knew; Dr. Lillian Raeff, a practicing Catholic. I figured that it might not be a bad idea to speak with a professional who also understood Catholicism. But it was a catch 22 for me—find a therapist who is not Catholic and they will think the entire experience was nuts; find someone who is a conservative Catholic, and they reinforce the same attitudes I was looking to escape. But I chose the latter because I needed someone who innately understood the experience.

Dr. Raeff and I hit it off right away. She was not judgmental, and she helped me sort out and process my transition back into the world post religious life. At the same time, my childhood friend Wendie shared that she had been attending meetings for people who grew up with addiction in the home. She observed that a lot of my behavioral patterns reflected classic symptoms of living with addiction. She suggested that in addition to, or instead of therapy, I may want to try attending these specific and pointed meetings with her so that I could begin to confront the demons that haunted me, as well as find healing from the MC experience.

Wendie explained that many people who grow up with addiction in the family feel the need to take care of everyone but themselves. They ignore their own needs with an over-developed sense of responsibility; they people please, fear authority, can be addicted to excitement, frightened by angry people and personal criticism, avoid confrontation, judge themselves harshly, have low self-esteem, isolate, are afraid to show their feelings, and on and on. I was amazed because it sounded like me. I fit almost every bullet point in the described mold, and I decided to join Wendie at a meeting to see if it resonated with me. It also made sense to me why Wendie and I related so well in our youth.

The meetings proved to be very powerful and beneficial. I related to everyone who shared. I loved the kindness that was shown to me, and a new sense of hope was restored. I tried to focus on the behavioral characteristics so that I could pay attention to flaws within myself and begin to do the work of becoming whole again. It felt right and good and I loved the beautiful, creative, interesting, and spiritual people I was meeting.

I also began driving up to Boston for weekend trips to see Chris, who had returned home after his last semester at Saint John's. Chris and I had a very deep and intimate friendship that was rooted in spirituality. He would tell me repeatedly that when I was with him, I was safe and to never feel judged.

My relationship with Chris felt as if we came to this earth together to learn and experience similar things. It was deeply rooted in our love for God, the poor, and for serving humanity. Chris embarked on a nursing career and has been a healer ever since.

My trips to Boston and the acceptance that Chris offered began to give me freedom and happiness. It started to feel good to be back in the world and to come into my own. I continued to work for my brother John and attend meetings as I explored who I was and what I was supposed to do. One thing was for certain, I was damaged goods and the challenge for me was being able to stand on my own two feet, to get out from behind the china cabinet and to make a life for myself. It was time to bring personal healing to the next level and to embrace the notion that light always shines brighter through broken glass.

Mom and Dad took me to the Bahamas after I was back on my feet again.

Chapter Twenty

Learnings

I pondered daily on what God wanted for me and what I wanted for myself. Didn't God create me with gifts to use and share with others? Was I supposed to continue to sacrifice everything and still become a religious but in a different order? Or was it both?

While the intellectual part of my life was stimulated at school, the psychological challenges were being addressed, and my physical health was restoring, I decided it was time to address the spiritual. I did not want to reject God or the Church because of my experiences.

I went to visit Father Richard Nielsen, a priest I knew who was associated and friendly with the MCs. He was an old priest and a very holy man. He was one of those silent and wise owl types—quick to listen and slow to respond. I phoned Father Nielsen and he invited me to his parish on Park Avenue in Manhattan. He was from Scotland and had a very thick accent. He knew me well from hearing my confessions and I know that he genuinely cared about me.

"Ahhh, Paul!! Yes, yes . . . Paul." He said contemplatively as he sat across from me, eyes closed and downward in his book-filled office.

"How very sad I was to hear of your departure, my dear Paul. But we don't know what the Lord has planned for us, do we?"

"No Father, we don't. I believe the old saying that when one door closes another one opens."

"Ah, so true Paul, so true. It is our job and duty to remain ever faithful to our dear Lord—to abandon ourselves daily and to allow him to use us as He wills. Do you agree?"

"Of course, Father and I guess that is why I am here." I hesitated. "How do we know when we've made the right decision? Looking back over the past year, I often wonder, should I have stayed no matter how bad or how miserable I felt? When is enough, enough?"

"My dear Paul, you are a breath of fresh air in our turbulent world. God will use you anywhere he puts you. You have a great capacity to love and you give hope to others—never lose that, my dear son. Your problem, Paul, is that you are seeking heaven on earth—something which we will never attain until we are with Our Lord." His statement hit me like a ton of bricks!

"Wow, I can't believe you just said that. I think that is what I've been longing for my whole life—heaven. How right you are, Father."

"Heaven, my dear Paul, is not of this world. Here in the valley of tears we learn to move forward with God ever at our side, hoping that one day we can rest in his eternal glory. But in the meantime, we must deal with this world and this life, which can be bitter at times. But I say to you, accept what God gives you and where he has planted you, and there you will find him deep within the recesses of your heart. Think on our beloved Saints, Paul—how they faced such adversity in this world knowing that one day they would earn their just reward."

Father Richard reminded me of Mother's words as well, "They can take you and cut you up into many pieces, but still each and every piece will belong to God. No one can separate you from his love." And that would ring true whether you were in a seminary or living in the far reaches of China.

I left Father Richard with a newfound hope. Has my journey for the past 25 years been nothing more than a search for heaven on earth? Was Sister Lorraine right all those years ago when she said: "I am hungry for God and will be never be satisfied in this world?" Was I jumping from one thing to the next because I was struggling to find the bliss I desperately wanted—a bliss not attainable in this life? Had God instilled His love into my heart as a boy to carry me through the rough times I would encounter? And while He gave me a deep-rooted faith, had the years since Charlie's death only been my way of processing 16 years of living with an addict? So many questions!

How sweet and tender Father Richard was with me—not just a priest, but a true Father. He made me see and understand that I needed to do nothing more than sit still wherever God planted me and to let the roots of his love live within me, and no matter where I am and no matter what I do, nothing can shake my innermost peace. Perhaps healing, as they said in my meetings, was an "inside job"; a notion that aligned with Father Richard's wise words.

As I walked to the subway after leaving Father Richard, I reflected on where and how God has had a hand in my life. How had He manifested Himself to me in my life and what is my real vocation?

Yes, I thought, God has spoken to me in very intimate ways throughout my life. He is within and I have only to trust and no longer run to find and pursue something that will never be reached on this earth.

In retrospect, God tapped the heart of a little boy in his father's arms who stared at the cross on the altar and connected in a profound way to the Crucified—that moment of intensity—that was God's gift to me. He said, "I am yours and you are mine. I have claimed you for my own."

The ten-year-old child who rocked his mother in his arms as she sobbed when her drug addict son was pulled by the cops down two flights of stairs—that was God manifesting in an instrument called Paul. This was the boy God loved—this child who was given a great capacity to love—that deep love that is within—*within*.

The little boy who hid behind a china cabinet and in closets, clutching statues of the Blessed Virgin Mary to make the shouting go away—this was the boy who learned the power of prayer and how to go within—*that deep well within*.

The ability to sing, dance, and make people happy—this was the mission—to bring God's joy to a troubled world. And it didn't have to be grandiose—the gifts had only to express themselves wherever God placed me. It was in the present moment. Here. Today. Now! *Within*.

And one day God says, so you want to experience what it is to be a professional actor? I will do that for you. He sends me to Hollywood, and I gain success in theater, film, and television. And just when I am heading for bigger things, God says, *"Oh no, little one—look at this UNICEF film—do you see my people? Who will feed them?"* My heart went on fire and I had no choice but to say, "YES, yes, here I am Lord; I have come to do your will." I returned home to a haven of love I left behind, remembering the real purpose of life—not fame and success, but love.

How then did I take it to the next level, this hunger for heaven, this hunger for God, this hunger for love? I find a living Saint who says, *come and see our life*. I think that even there I have found my bliss, but I haven't. What I find instead is the gift of lessons—deep spiritual lessons prepared for me by God alone—the lessons in saintly virtues that will be instilled in me for the rest of my life, no matter where I go or what I do; humility, sacrifice, courage, long-suffering, kindness, charity.

I left the MCs because I still had not found heaven. When the storm passes, the soul can see the many gifts given by God because the blinders have been lifted—I see! I was blind, but now I see. I know what God has given me. I know that wherever I am, no matter the circumstance, God is at work.

Most importantly, I learned that many of my decisions after Charlie's death, including Hollywood and the need for recognition, were my way of processing Charlie. The addict isn't the only victim of their disease. Many damaged people are left in their wake. But healing was possible. I no longer had to run to find heaven. I could process it all safely with the help of friends and God.

I am reminded of a poster my sister Jacqueline once had on her bedroom wall. As a youngster, I would read it and re-read trying to grasp its meaning but now I understand: *Peace does not dwell from outward things, but within the soul.*

I know, most importantly, that I have been given the task to touch hearts, and that God is ever present—even amidst suffering. In times of trial, it is God who remains close to me, but it is human nature to reject Him. He stands and waits for each of his little ones to return and call upon Him. Each and every person on the earth has their trials—some are evident, and some are not, but it is indeed these trials that are designed to bring us to the deepest parts of ourselves.

I learned that the ultimate goal any of us can have is to discover the divine light within; there is nothing more. The world, our situations, the people we meet, our jobs are all characters in one big cloudy dream that will one day pass. The only thing that is real is love.

Saint Maximilian Kolbe sacrificed his life for a fellow prisoner in Auschwitz because his light was so bright within, it wasn't sacrifice, it was pure love. It was God within that made him so self-actualized that nothing mattered. He was able to say to the Nazis', "Save this man who has a family and has a chance to live, let me die in his place." They placed him in a cell and tried to starve him to death but the only sound the S.S. could hear were his prayers. They finally gave him a lethal injection. He belonged only to God.

How grateful I am that in the infancy of my spirituality, I learned these things and made these discoveries. We need to bloom where we are planted, as the saying goes. I no longer need to feel guilty about getting on with my own life. I need only to be an instrument of goodness, wherever God places me. I have only to listen to that small still voice within, day by day. It is my duty to share the gifts God has given me and to try my best to be a beacon of hope. Very simply, all I ever have to be is what God made me.

Where the road leads, I shall follow (taken at Gethsemani Abbey, Kentucky).

Epilogue

I finally made peace with Charlie, only I was not the initiator. Charlie knocked on my door almost twenty years after his death. I had a very intense experience on a hot summer night in August, 1997. In the middle of a very deep sleep, I jolted awake. I looked at my alarm clock on the dresser, which registered 3:00 AM on the dot. I stood up in the darkness and rubbed my eyes and slowly went to my bedroom door.

As I walked to the door, I realized that I was not in my bedroom. I was baffled and thought I had fallen asleep at a friend's house. I looked around. There was dead silence and I saw that I was standing in the attic of 347 High Street, the house in Closter where I grew up. I then realized that I was dreaming, and yet I wasn't. I was awake and what I was experiencing was as real as real could be. I literally pinched myself to wake up, but I didn't. I was alert and could see and feel my feet and hands as I walked to the center of the attic from the top of the stair landing. I even noticed the different décor in the attic from the new owners of the house and in a sense; I felt that I was haunting it. I tried to be quiet so they wouldn't hear me and wake up, but I wondered how I got there.

Suddenly, the floor began to vibrate. The darkness was somewhat illumined by a greenish-yellow color, or rather a vibration of some kind that filled the floor and back wall from where I stood. It felt like the light was alive and just kept vibrating. I was in a complete state of shock but in an instant, I felt something coming forward from the light.

It was Charlie! He did not come to where I stood, but remained in the light staring at me. He looked young again with dark curly black hair and a youthful face. As he stood in the light, he was very serious. He looked at me sadly and said, "Paulie, please stop saying bad things about me. You're holding me back. I love you." I was so happy to see him, and completely overwhelmed at the same time. My eyes welled with tears and with a heart full of love I said, "And I love you too, Charlie. I will stop. I am so sorry." He descended backward into the light and I watched him disappear.

As soon as he was out of sight, I jolted in my sleep and sat up. I looked at my alarm clock and it registered at 3:10 AM. I don't know what happened that night, but I do not think it was a dream. I believe my brother visited me, and we had a spiritual reconciliation. I had the impression that he was in some type of afterlife, but it didn't feel like the best place. My instincts told me that he was "learning" and going through something. He needed my love, support, forgiveness, and prayers. I will never forget that night.

I have also reconciled with Father Eugene. In the late 1990s, I received a letter from him explaining what he was going through at the time I was an Aspirant. His letter reflected on the seminarians in his care, and the pressure he had been under. He told me he was particularly hard on me and apologized. That letter meant the world to me. I never disliked Father Eugene, and I could only imagine what he must have been going through. I truly love him, and I am so grateful for everything he taught me. He will always have a special place in my heart.

I went for a two-week visit to the MC Father's house in Rome in the year 2000 (they have grown and expanded globally, and now have seven houses). Together, Father Eugene and I chatted, laughed, and reminisced about old times. I even went to work and uprooted old trees with him in their garden. It felt so incredibly good to be "home" and working with Father. My heart was full of love as we worked together. I couldn't help choking back tears. I wish Father Eugene and all the Missionaries of Charity every good thing that God has to offer. I will always be an MC in my heart and as Mother once said to another brother, "Once you are an MC, even if you leave, you will always be an MC."

She also said when she started the MC Fathers, and I paraphrase, "Many of you will leave and many of you will suffer—it is natural—but because of your sacrifices and suffering you are a critical part of the foundation of this new branch, even if you should go." I am glad to know I am still an MC. Thank you, Mother.

My classmates at the Missionaries of Charity are now scattered throughout the world—some have become fully professed MCs and some have left for other religious orders or the diocesan priesthood. I do not get to see them, but on occasion, there is a good word that is passed on from one to another.

If I could only begin to tell you what I have gone through in the years that followed my 25th birthday in 1987, it could fill another volume. The lessons I've learned in life have stayed with me through thick and thin. Like anyone else, life has its ups and downs.

If someone has faith, it doesn't mean they live a perfect life. It is really quite the opposite. Having faith means you have the strength to ride the wildest storms, to hang on in the face of adversity, to recognize the good days and bad days, and to go forward regardless of how bad things could become. We can spread joy and try to be a beacon of light to others, but it does not mean you are exempt from suffering.

I gave priesthood one more shot, believe it or not, and entered a diocesan seminary in the year 2000. The political system of the diocesan priesthood was not for me. I chose to return home. This time I had no guilt and knew I made the right decision to continue my life as a lay-person and not pursue priesthood.

I graduated Summa Cum Laude from Saint Thomas Aquinas College in Sparkill, New York with a degree in Philosophy and Religion, and later my Masters degree in Theology from Seton Hall University in South Orange, New Jersey. I was recruited upon graduation by a top Wall Street investment firm and embarked on a successful business career.

My healing from Charlie continues and I must constantly keep myself in check to make certain I do not repeat unhealthy behaviors. Recovery, whether you are an addict, or someone who has lived with an addict, is a daily process. Sometimes I simply forget to take care of myself, and when tending to my own needs, I have to remind myself that I am not being selfish and that there is no need to feel guilty. I have an unhealthy obligation to take the weight of the world on my shoulders. This became physically evident in 2008 when it was discovered I had an Abdominal Aortic Aneurysm. The years of abdominal angst caught up with me and I required emergency surgery. Emotionally, intellectually, spiritually, and physically, humpty was being put back together again.

My siblings and I are all still very close. If I add up the number of my siblings, their spouses, their children, their children's spouses and their children's children, we now total 97—all because Mom and

Dad met and fell in love. Crazy! We no longer spend holidays together as a whole due to the size of everyone's family but we break up into smaller groups. Our individual islands continue to flourish. As big as the family has become, we still try our best to be there for each other in times of need.

We lost Mom to a brain tumor on October 11, 1994, and Dad had a major heart attack and died instantly on May 3, 2007. Life is hard without them, but life goes on, and we demonstrate our gratitude to two amazing people by being good to each other. I know my parents are proud from wherever they are watching, and that one day we will all be together again; that is the gift of faith.

The boy behind the china cabinet, who protected his crayons, phonograph records, and hid from the world, has come out from behind the china cabinet. I occasionally hold him in my arms and remind him that it is over. He is safe. I am safe. We survived, and together, with the grace of God, we can accomplish anything.

Acknowledgments

Since childhood, I have hungered for the opportunity to talk about Charlie. In adulthood, I have longed to share the truth about Hollywood, as well as share about my time with Mother Teresa and the Missionaries of Charity. I could not have accomplished this task of many years without acknowledging the following people.

A most sincere thank you to author Debby Caruso for journeying with me through the entire publication process; her suggestions, counsels, and introductions to amazing people helped shape my book and story.

To editors, Jennie Rosenblum, and Kim Kristiansen for painstakingly reviewing every chapter, paragraph and sentence of this book. Your attention to detail was needed and appreciated.

Thanks to Lindsay Miserandino and Rachel Driscoll for proofreading the manuscript and providing content-changing suggestions. And to Michelle Menzies for her insightful comments and great grammatical catches.

Thank you to my big sister, Jacqueline, who read the very first draft with great care, provided me with the feedback of a scholar, and encouraged me every step of the way.

I thank the beta readers: Reverend Charles Urnick, Christopher

Shaw, Denise Shaw, Thomas LaGreca, Jess LaGreca, Reverend Scott Pontes, Andrew Brown, and again, Debby Caruso. Your honest feedback helped shape and mold the manuscript.

A special thanks to my favorite Designer, Jess LaGreca, who patiently listened to my neurotic ramblings about the book and the cover over multiple dinners in Manhattan and Hoboken. She crafted my ideas precisely into what I was hoping for. Simon and Schuster is lucky to have you.

Special thanks to Stephanie Anderson at Alt19Creative for beautifully formatting the electronic files for the book at record speed. You rock!

Heartfelt love to each and every person who consistently asked me about my progress and encouraged me to continue to write: my siblings, in-laws, nephews and nieces, and friends. Their simple comments such as, "When will the damn book be ready?" or "I am so excited," incited me to completion.

Warmest thanks to the Missionaries of Charity who still have the capacity to touch my heart and bring me closer to God. Thank you especially to my spiritual mother, the now Saint Teresa of Calcutta.

Lastly, I thank God—that power greater than myself—who has called me, carried me and given me angels that have assisted me in writing, publishing, and most importantly, life. I love you.

About the Author

Paul LaGreca is an artist who has appeared in major motion pictures, television series, and on stage. He currently resides in Bergen County, New Jersey and works in New York City.

Follow him on Twitter: @paullagreca

Like him on Facebook: PaulLaGrecaAuthor

Follow him on Instagram: @pauldlagreca

Find out more at: paullagreca.net

CPSIA information can be obtained
at www.ICGtesting.com
Printed in the USA
LVHW041000030720
659656LV00018B/1277